A PARTISAN GUIDE TO THE JEWISH PROBLEM

A
PARTISAN GUIDE
TO THE
Jewish Problem

By

MILTON STEINBERG

THE BOBBS-MERRILL COMPANY
INDIANAPOLIS   *Publishers*   NEW YORK

THE CORNWALL PRESS, INC., CORNWALL, N. Y.

IN TRIBUTE
TO
EDITH

CONTENTS

A PARTISAN GUIDE TO THE JEWISH PROBLEM

INTRODUCTION

O F MAKING BOOKS on the Jewish problem there has been in recent years almost no end. The issue may not be the most momentous at present before either the world or America. But it is there, surcharged with bitterness and urgency. It is much in the public eye and heavy on the hearts of men of good will, whether Jews or Gentiles. Its implications and consequences make it far larger, so to speak, than its own size. Naturally, inevitably, an extensive literature has grown up about it.

Yet, there are room and need even now, I believe, for a fresh presentation of the theme. Not alone because the position of the Jews, like all social realities, is forever assuming new shapes so that what was said of it yesterday, no matter how true then, is likely to be partly false today. Not alone either because the whole matter has taken on increased gravity with time until it has become all but impossible to attend to it too closely. The fact is that though the subject has been much discussed, it is still little understood.

For example, to many people anti-Semitism is the Jewish problem. That hostility toward the Jews constitutes *a* problem of the first magnitude goes without saying. But to take it for the entire Jewish problem is to oversimplify grossly. For Jews face not only outward toward the world but inward to their own souls, round about toward one another, backward to their heritage, and forward toward the aspirations they share. From any of these directions, not from the first alone, difficulties may arise to beset them.

It must be conceded that the cliché "the Jewish problem" does not suggest too vigorously the complexity and variety of the matters for which it stands. Terse, couched almost always in the singular, it seems to imply some one issue. Hence it lends itself readily to being equated with anti-Semitism, the most spectacular of all Jewish concerns. Worst of all, the phrase has no specific meaning. It is a weasel idiom, loose and complaisant, capable of being emptied almost at will of one content and filled with another.

Perhaps we would be wise to discard it altogether. But it does have a certain standing in human affairs; it is part of the furniture of our intellects; it is a habit of speech to many of us; it is compact and convenient. Let us rather invest it with exact and carefully defined significance, and it can serve us well enough.

Let us understand by it all those interests of mind, hand and heart with which Jews are compelled to deal by virtue of the fact that they are Jews, from which non-Jews are exempt. Death and taxation, in other words, of which Jews feel the incidence no more and no less than others, are not Jewish problems. But anything that touches Jews exclusively or in extraordinary degree is *a* Jewish problem, and the sum total and collectivity of these make up *the* Jewish problem.

When we put the matter so, we discover at once that our field of inquiry divides itself into four distinct sections. The first contains all the issues arising from the fact that the Jew is a member of a larger society with which perforce he maintains constant, ever-changing relationships. If his position at any time and in any respect is unfavorable, this by definition constitutes an occasion for anxiety and effort on his part. If favorable, it may be overshadowed by the threat of adverse developments. *Social Status,* therefore, is one area of the Jewish problem. The Jew, moreover, is implicated not only in the larger human scene, he stands willy-nilly in some relationship also to himself and his fellows. His attitude toward his identity and group may be one of joyous affirmation, or alternatively of misery and repudiation. But a person must in the end approve of what he is if he is to be healthy in spirit. Alongside, therefore, the first field of Jewish problem, we must stake out a second, that of *Self-Acceptance.* Then there is the Jewish heritage, that body of religious doctrine, ritual, ethic, culture and institution created by the past and handed down by it. On all this the Jew must, whether consciously or unawares, carefully or casually, pronounce some judgment. He may reject it *in toto,* embrace it in its completeness, or make some selection from it. He may endeavor to preserve intact and unchanged whatever he takes to himself, or to modify and remake it. *The Tradition* is therefore a third domain of the Jewish problem. Last of all, there is one Jewish interest which has in it something of all the other three; which is from one angle a question of social status, from another of self-acceptance, and from still another of the tradition, and yet which is also a *Ding an sich.* What is more, it is right now the focus of sharp attention and passionate controversy. On all these scores, it had best be presented as an item in itself. I refer of course to the

Zionist enterprise, to the *Jewish Homeland* which so comes to constitute the fourth province of Jewish problem.

Each of these categories contains within itself a number of more specific and concrete issues. These, since they constitute the agenda of this book, will now be listed, each in its appropriate class. By surveying them at this point, the reader will form some notion of the individual elements that make up the Jewish problem, of their aggregate weight and of the order in which they are to be presented. At the same time he will be enabled, if so disposed, to play the eclectic. For, with Jewish problems as with other themes, what concerns one man keenly may bore another to distraction. Given this catalogue of topics, the selective reader will be helped to exercise that ancient, respectable privilege which belongs to him as a reader—the right to skip whatever does not interest him.

PROBLEMS OF STATUS

The rehabilitation of European Jewry and how it is to be effected (Chapter 1, *Out of the Straits*).

The causes and recent history of anti-Semitism (Chapter 2, *Anti-Semitism—Root and Flower*).

What can be done about anti-Semitism and what cannot (Chapter 3, *Anti-Semitism—Nostrums and Remedies*).

How prejudice against Jews endangers the welfare of non-Jews and of society as a whole (Chapter 4, *Anti-Semitism—A Warning to Gentiles*).

The temper and point of view with which Jews ought to meet hostility toward themselves (Chapter 5, *Anti-Semitism—An Exhortation to Jews*).

The facts of the occupational concentration of Jews within the American economy, and what measures must be taken to correct the condition (Chapter 6, *Jews and Their Livelihoods*).

PROBLEMS OF SELF-ACCEPTANCE

The psychic perils that attend the Jewish identity (Chapter 7, *The Sick Soul*).

The choice confronting the individual Jew and the Jewish group between assimilation and survival (Chapter 8, *The Ultimate Decision*).

PROBLEMS OF THE TRADITION

The nature of Judaism and Jewishness, what it is in which the Jewish identity consists (Chapter 9, *A Matter of Definitions*).

The various philosophies of Jewish life now current (Chapter 10, *A Gallery of Jewish Portraits*).

A critique of these philosophies, and the presentation of a more adequate rationale (Chapter 11, *A Tenable Theory*).

What needs to be done, in the light of that rationale, with historic Judaism, its religious doctrines, ethical values, rituals and culture, if it is to prove adequately meaningful to modern Jews and the world (Chapter 12, *A Creative Program*).

How the American Jewish community ought to be organized (Chapter 13, *An Orderly Household*).

PROBLEMS OF THE HOMELAND

The logic behind the Zionist enterprise (Chapter 14, *Zionist Theory*).

The actualities of that enterprise, both the achievements to date and the problems that lie ahead (Chapter 15, *Jewish Palestine*).

The significance of the Jewish Homeland for Jewries of the Diaspora, such as the American (Chapter 16, *The Larger Meaning*).

And finally, an epilogue on the haunting riddle—whether Jewish life is worth the sacrifice and effort it entails. (*The Game and the Candle*).

It was Ahad HaAm, the philosopher of modern cultural Zionism, who once observed sagely that most of the persistent problems of mankind are never solved, that they merely grow old; that once they have achieved a certain degree of venerability, men no longer feel under obligation either to understand them or to attempt their solution. Let mention be made of them and they are likely to be dismissed out of hand as "old questions."

"The Jewish problem," it must be admitted, is such an old question, as is every one of the components to which we have reduced it. Some of them are as old as the dispersion of the Jews, others were born with their emancipation from the Ghetto. Only a few appear to be novel, and even these are likely to be historic headaches under new names. Despite all this, and the pessimistic judgment of Ahad HaAm, we would do well to seek to comprehend the Jewish problem and to wrestle with it. At the least we may win through to clarity of insight, always a worth-while end in human affairs.

Nor ought we despair of exerting some influence of a practical character. Most impasses of the human spirit and of social life are never completely broken. They are at best made partially viable. If then the chances be slight of achieving a final solution for all or any of the difficulties in Jewish living, it may still be possible to render them less burdensome—provided always that the matter in hand is first broadly and clearly understood. To these ends—the comprehension of the Jewish problem, and, if not its solution, at least its mitigation, all that follows in this book is dedicated.

I

PROBLEMS OF STATUS

1

Out of the Straits

IN ALL THE LONG CAREER of Israel, marked by many bloodlettings and persecutions, there has never been a bloodletting half so brutal, a quarter so
vast, a fraction so ruthless as that now being ended in Europe. Indeed,
the annals of human history may well be searched without disclosing a single
parallel and analogous episode. Not that Jews are alone in the pit. All the
peoples of Europe are with them there. All have suffered, bled and been
broken on the rack. But if there be, as Dante suggests, degrees of damna-
tion, then to the Jews belongs the melancholy distinction of having been assigned to Hell's lowest depths. They alone of all peoples and communions
have been marked for total extermination. Their noncombatant dead even
absolutely are more numerous than those of any other people except the Russians. Relatively—that is, in comparison with total populations—their losses
are staggering. In the course of six years, almost one-third of the Jews of the
world have been killed off.

Here are the naked, elemental facts, so far as they can be determined in
the first months of 1945.

At the outbreak of the Second World War there were approximately
16,000,000 Jews on earth, 8,250,000 of them in Axis lands or in countries
which Germany subsequently came to control. Of these, the most reliable
estimates have it, about 5,000,000 have perished.

Now a dead Jew is a dead Jew. Who he was and how he came to die is
apparently not a matter of burning concern to anyone—not to the Nazis
who butchered him; not even, it sometimes seems, to the enlightened citizens of the democratic nations. And yet, the statistical item we have just
adduced is in itself so cold, so impersonal and so abstruse that it must be
concretized if it is genuinely to be comprehended. Let me then add merely
that the mathematical abstraction "about 5,000,000" embraces individual

men, women and children, educated and untutored, devout and profane, good sometimes to saintliness, bad occasionally to villainy, but, in any case, all human, all thirsty for life, all shrinking from destruction; that each of them went to his doom in his own fashion, some burdened by memories, driven by fears, or wild unrealizable hopes, others blank, stunned, and uncomprehending; that the harsh taste of death was for them made more bitter by untimeliness and injustice. Let me say further that there was no sullen brutality, no ingenious savagery, which was not employed to hasten their demise or to intensify its pain. They were machine-gunned, and, bound by ropes, run over by tanks and trucks. They were asphyxiated in death chambers, or in freight cars jammed to capacity and paved with chemicals that exuded poison gasses. Their veins were drained of blood to furnish plasma for wounded Aryan heroes, or were injected with air bubbles. They starved to death slowly because food was allotted to them in quantities too small to sustain life. They dropped from the exhaustion of forced labor, or succumbed to diseases their enfeebled bodies could not resist. And to their honor be it recorded that by the tens of thousands they died in heroic but futile resistance. Without arms except those the underground could smuggle to them or such as they could contrive themselves, they rose in mass rebellions—holding out in the Ghetto of Warsaw for forty days, in Bialystok for a month, in Tarnów, Częstochowa, Vilna, Bedzin, in the death camps at Treblinka and Sobibor for days or hours, but in any case selling their lives as dearly as they could. And now cities, counties, indeed whole countries which knew Jews and their communities, in some instances for two millenniums, are *Judenrein*. The Nazi policy, adopted in cool calculation, of extirpating this people to its last member has at least in some areas attained its objective fully.

These are the dead. As such they need vex us, except in conscience, no further. It is the living who constitute a Jewish problem, who by their very mute existence continue to challenge us to action. Of the survivors there are in turn three distinct bodies: those who have been liberated by the advance of Allied arms, those who have saved themselves by flight or evacuation, those who remain alive but are still trapped in Nazi-held Europe.

In the first category are some 800,000 Jews in France, Belgium, Holland, Poland, Italy, Hungary and the Balkans.

The size of the second group cannot at present be accurately determined. Rough estimates have it that during the war years approximately 150,000 persons succeeded in reaching Palestine, the United States and other lands beyond Nazi reach. A much larger number, approximately 1,600,000, were evacuated by the Soviet government from Poland, the Baltic States and its own territories as they were invaded. Over and beyond these is another body of older refugees, the 432,000 Jews who fled Germany and the lands it engulfed in the period between 1933 and 1939. Of these, many are by now thoroughly adjusted to their new scenes. Many, however, are less fortunately situated. They may find themselves in countries which offer them only temporary hospitality, or else, though confronted by opportunties for permanent settlement, they are for one reason or another incapable of making it good. It is safe then to put at somewhat under 2,000,000 the total number of those Jews who were lucky enough to get beyond Hitler's reach but are still so unfortunate as to be without homes.

Little is known with certainty concerning the third classification—those still alive in what remains of Nazi Europe at the time these lines are being written (April 1945). Of such Jews, the soundest opinion has it, there will be very few. The three categories, therefore, when added together are not likely to exceed a total of three million souls.

Just as all mankind has some share in the guilt of the Second World War, infinitely less than that of the Third Reich, and yet some share nonetheless, so no one's hands are altogether clean of the blood of the Jewish dead. Certainly the record of the civilized governments of the world, by way of compassion and solicitude for the persecuted, leaves much to be desired. In contravention of the injunction of Scripture, they stood idly by the blood of their neighbor, insisting that what Hitler did to Jews was the private business of the German people. From time to time they issued protests; they still continued to do business with the Nazi regime. On them rest the disgrace of an Evian Conference * which could find no asylum—not even in internment camps—for cultivated, honorable and useful human beings innocent of all offense except that of being Jews, and the ignominy of a Bermuda Conference ** equally futile but infinitely more shameful because

---

* The Evian Conference took place on July 6th, 1938. It was a meeting of the Intergovernmental Committee on Refugees which met at Evian.

** The Bermuda Conference was called by the American and British governments for "the relief of a substantial number of refugees of all races and nationalities." The date was April 19, 1943.

the volume and desperation of Jewish homelessness had mounted so mightily. On them lies the sin of ships wandering the seven seas, unable to discharge the most unwanted of cargoes—Jewish human beings. There is Great Britain's transgression: the *Struma* going down with all hands in the Black Sea; coffinships beached and sweltering on the shores of Palestine; the *Patria* blown up by its passengers in the harbor of Haifa; doors to the Holy Land shut tight and in flagrant violation of a pledged word. There is the offense of Russia which, setting up a Jewish republic in the emptiness of Eastern Siberia, could find no room in it for the homeless Jews of Central Europe. There are the iniquities of our own State Department in its administration of immigration procedures and in its contending at each stage that everything possible was being done by way of rescue and relief, only to belie itself in each instance, or be belied by events or by its own subsequent actions. It is not a joyful business, this of disinterring the rotten performances of the civilized governments of the world. If we engage in it, it is in part to recall that the occasion for atonement is not Germany's alone, but in greater part to set up the past as a warning for the present and future.

Of this we may be certain: What remains of European Jewry will be afflicted, thanks to its ordeal, with every conceivable disease of body and mind. Those who are not actually ill will in all probability never be robust again. Their communities will have been left without leaders, institutions or synagogues; their synagogues without Scrolls of the Torah, prayer books, pews and arks, rabbis, cantors and beadles. Their schools will have ceased to exist or, if they survive, will have neither teachers nor texts. Their children will be schooled only in the disciplines of terror. As though all this were not enough, they will be beset, these poor wretches, with a host of complex, stubborn, often insoluble problems. To their complexity and stubbornness let the following random questions testify.

What shall be the prerogatives of domicile of a Jew who, having fled Germany to France, and having been stripped of his German citizenship by denaturalization, without acquiring French citizenship in its stead, and having subsequently made his way into Cuba, now lives in Havana on the strength of a visitors' visa, and on funds supplied by the American Jewish Joint Distribution Committee? Will he have the right to return to Germany? to France? to remain where he is? or to go elsewhere? Where and how shall it be guaranteed that anti-Semitism, governmental or popular, does not interfere with his going wherever it is decided he has a right to go?

What will belong to whom in Nazi Europe once it is liberated? Who will own the house in Vienna which the Germans confiscated from a Jewish owner without the least pretense of due process but which has since passed hands in a dozen bonafide sales? Or the shop in Prague which a Jew sold under Nazi duress, but in a transaction in which every nicety of legal correctness was preserved? What of the wares that once filled its shelves and that are long since gone with the wind? What of stocks, bonds and shares that were extorted from Jews or which they sold at a fraction of their value in order to save their necks? What of property which clearly belongs to Jews, except that the Jews and their heirs have ceased to exist? What of less tangible possessions—the claim of a Jewish physician to a hospital post, of a professor to his chair? And what, to pile Ossa on Pelion, of Jewish communal properties where, of the community, no living creature remains to reconstitute it, or, if there be survivors, they elect not to return to their native scenes?

And how, most perplexing of all, shall it be guaranteed to the Jews that they shall this time be secure in their lives and liberties, secure against governments, individuals and political parties, secure against all encroachment whether within or outside the law?

Riddles as tangled and deep as these—and ten thousand others, no easier and equally pressing—are quite obviously not to be solved offhand. A Solomon, a Daniel, might well be appalled before them. Let us then be realistic and admit that perfect justice will not be done, that blunders will be committed. The most to be hoped is that equity, mercy and wisdom will enter into and fashion the reconstitution of European Jews.

But if our efforts are to exhibit these virtues, then one basic premise, a particularization of the general objectives of the United Nations, must be predicated. At all times, while hostilities continue, in the period of transition from war to peace, and in whatever final settlement may be achieved, the Jews of Europe must be accorded a measure of freedom, security and opportunity, individual and collective, equal to that conferred on non-Jews and on non-Jewish groups round about them.

Given this morally elemental and pragmatically inescapable mandate, given too the Jewish situation as we have described it, a program virtually unfolds itself in twelve cardinal propositions as follows:

I. *The United Nations must expect to continue for a long time and on a vast scale the work which UNRRA inaugurated in 1943.*

It is difficult to think of any move on the part of our government and its allies more glorious for humaneness and foresight than the establishment of the United Nations Relief and Rehabilitation Administration, and the inauguration of its labors on behalf of the destitute of all nations. Equally gratifying have been the approval voiced by America and the world, and the readiness of our Congress to back the project with a vast appropriation equal, in accordance with an international agreement, to one percent of our gross national income. American decency and altruism at their best shine through every step in this development. And UNRRA, though it has encountered obstacles of all sorts, has kept clearly in view the goals to which it is directed.

But we Americans must steel ourselves to a harsh reality which heretofore we may not have faced. This is no ephemeral enterprise to which we have set our hands, nor one to be disposed of with a single appropriation no matter how munificent. The volume of human misery in Europe is incalculable; both resources and the strength for self-help are slight. We may as well prepare ourselves now for a long pull, one which in all likelihood will run on for years.

The job at hand, moreover, involves more than the raising of funds and the distribution of goods. The dictates of equity must be observed as well; that is to say, there must be no denial to anyone of his fair share of relief. None of the prejudices of the Old World, or for that matter of the New, must be permitted to enter into and pervert our good intentions.

Yet no matter how delicately UNRRA steers its course, no matter how adequate its resources, how carefully conceived and executed its plans, a void will still exist to be filled by supplementary enterprises. Certainly there will be place for private philanthropy. First, because the needs of Europe will overflow all vessels available for their containment, and second because individual peoples will disclose deficiencies and requirements peculiar and private to themselves, and hence beyond the scope of public agencies. This will be true especially and in extraordinary degree of the Jews.

For they, though they are only one of many groups which have been victimized by the Nazis, have been persecuted with such ruthless thoroughness that, as a problem in relief, they are a class by themselves. In a continent which is one welter of wretchedness, no misery equals theirs, nor is any extremity so wild. They will be, among the millions of hungry, sick and unclothed, the most horribly starved, most seriously diseased and most universally naked and shelterless. Barely a vestige will be left to them of all the appurtenances of their religious, cultural and communal lives. From these considerations follows a second proposition.

II. *American Jewry ought to prepare now for a program of relief and rehabilitation supplementary to those programs devised by governmental and intergovernmental agencies.*

The Jews of America may as well begin at once to anticipate the future and its requirements. Not that they are novices at raising funds for the sake of European Jews. This has been perhaps their single most meritorious achievement. A community of less than 5,000,000 souls, they have since 1914 through the American Jewish Joint Distribution Committee alone collected at home and disbursed abroad a sum close to $150,000,000. This time, however, the task at hand will be incomparably larger. For while there will be frighteningly fewer Jews to help, the volume of their distress and the depths of their resourcelessness will be beyond all conception.

No matter, then, how much governmental money may be assigned to Jews, there will be need for immeasurably more, more for elemental relief in terms of food, clothing, shelter and medical care; more in terms of the demands of the individual spirit and communal life. Europe's Jews will lack, America's Jews will wish to supply them with thousands of Scrolls of the Torah, hundreds of thousands of prayer books, Bibles and the others paraphernalia of public worship, and the basic equipment of schools and libraries from benches to textbooks. It may very likely prove necessary to send abroad volunteer rabbis, teachers, physicians and social workers to replace those who have perished. Like the ancient tyrant of Syracuse, the Nazis have made a special point of lopping off the heads of the leaders of the peoples they have despoiled. All in all, it would be well were American Jews to busy themselves now with finding the wherewithal for these purposes. And as for the objection that no one knows accurately how much will be required, one conjecture can be safely hazarded in response: no matter how much money is raised, it will not be enough.

III. *All discriminatory racial legislation, whether directed against Jews or others, must be abrogated by the United Nations as soon as they occupy*

*enemy-held territory, and must be kept abrogated by any permanent govern-
ment which may follow in the wake of the armies of occupation.*

It is all too easy to forget that the last established civil law in large parts
of Europe is that instituted by the Nazis, that such legislation, no matter
what its sphere of application, is in the spirit of the Nuremberg decrees of
1935. Under that code Jews are excluded from communal life, denaturalized,
exposed to insecurity in life and property, and in general subjected to ten
thousand bits of discriminatory prescription, all intended to degrade and
humiliate them. The Nazis, needless to say, have long since improved on
their original instruction. They have not only vastly extended and patiently
refined their first ordinances, they have learned in dealing with the Jews to
dispense with law altogether.

With all such devices of the devil the United Nations must have no traffic
whatsoever. The expungement of every racialist ordinance, no matter by
whom issued or where, must be a fixed point of policy, to be carried out
instantly, automatically and without compromise or temporization on the
reconquest of enemy-held territory. Otherwise the democracies will be
guilty of moral self-betrayal, will set evil precedents which most assuredly
will arise to plague them, will dishearten libertarians everywhere, and may
in the end impose on themselves the necessity of reconquering an area of
freedom they should never have surrendered in the first place.

Do I seem to be belaboring my point? Then let me recall the shameful
fumbling on the part of the United Nations with the Crémieux decree. In
that instance it was argued—let me be more explicit and pronounce the
incredibility—the State Department of our country argued that for fear of
objection on the part of Arabs, the Jews of North Africa could not be restored to the citizenship of which the Vichy regime and the Nazis had deprived them. In consequence, the democratic nations sanctioned for some
months a flagrantly undemocratic situation—all for reasons which turned
out to be quite fictitious. For when citizenship was restored to the Jews of
Algiers, not a ripple or breath of Arab protest stirred.

While there is reason to hope that nothing akin to this unfortunate incident may ever occur again, it is always well, in matters of importance, to
be on the alert. Caution is the more necessary because of other episodes
which are, as it were, straws in the wind. The London Polish government
in exile notoriously includes within itself anti-Semitic elements. Again, on

June 25, 1944, Michel Le Troquer, son of the de Gaullist Commissioner of Liberated Territories, was quoted as having declared in an Algiers newspaper that, though the French population had been shocked by the treatment accorded Jews, it would be much "irritated" should Jews attempt to return after the war to their industrial, commercial and political positions. It is not beyond all imagining, therefore, that someday some United Nations administrator or some representative of a restored government may question the expediency of scrapping a piece of discriminatory legislation. With that temptation there must be no toying. For the racialist iniquities of the Nazis and of their helots there can be but one rule—overboard with them, instantly and irretrievably!

IV. *The rights of domicile of Jews in Europe should be broadly envisioned and must be carefully assured.*

As we have already had occasion to observe, no issue concerning European Jewry is more nearly a conundrum than that of residence and repatriation. The problem is tough; a latitudinarian approach to it therefore is the more urgent. The simplest solution, and the most humane, would be to allow to each Jew a free choice among all those countries on which, either *de jure* or *de facto,* he has some claim; to give him, in other words, an option among his native land, the land in which he may have acquired citizenship, the land in which he was living at the outbreak of hostilities or where he may find himself at the end, or, should he prefer, Palestine as the internationally recognized home of his people. Such a course would afford at least some solace to persons who, having been kicked from pillar to post, need the assurance of having homes and of being welcome in them.

Unfortunately there is ground for fear lest the disposition of the matter fall short not only of this optimum but even of the minimal requirements of decency. It is altogether possible that the right of Jews to return even to those lands to which they are native or of which they are citizens may in certain instances be challenged. On May 9, 1944, for example, the American press carried what purported to be the text of a confidential memorandum on the Jewish problem as submitted by the Polish Underground to its government in exile. Among other things this document pointed out that the Jews of Poland had not been altogether eliminated by the Nazis, and that the non-Jewish population would (justifiably, it is implied) "consider the mass reimmigration of the Jews not as a return to their previous position but as an invasion against which it would defend itself even in a physical manner."

Among other peoples, too, there are no doubt individuals and groups who, now that their native lands have been made almost *Judenrein* by the Germans, would prefer to keep them so. At no time nor under any circumstance must the United Nations so much as listen to those who would deny or delay the repatriation of any Jew to his native land. The final settlement ought to provide for more than this; it cannot conceivably be fair or humane if it settles for less.

V. *Whatever arrangements are made for the recapture of property, private and communal, must be equitable.*

The problem of what belongs to whom will be, as we have predicted, one of the toughest tangles through which the peacemakers will have to cut their way. Across this maze there can be no high and easy road, no single, automatic formula which will guarantee justice.

But if the crooked cannot be made straight by any magical spell, there is nevertheless a basic rule, a moral threshold as it were, below which the handling of the problem dare not fall: There must be one law for Jew and non-Jew alike in the return of expropriated possessions, in the restoration of status, in the civil services and private employment, in the restitution to communities of their group assets such as places of worship, cemeteries and public funds. Similarly with the redress and reparations which the United Nations may exact from a defeated Germany—in this respect, as in all others, nothing less than justice must be done, a justice too realistic to be taken in by the legal chicaneries at which the Nazis have been such masters, too stern to yield to anti-Semitism, and too open-eyed to lose sight of the special Jewish tree for the forest.

VI. *Jews must enjoy civic equality on a plane with all others.*

It will not be enough, if democratic ends are to be served, merely to repeal the anti-Jewish legislation of the Nazis. Long before Hitler came to power there were broad areas in Europe in which anti-Semitism was a policy of government or an effective motif in popular opinion. Sometimes such sentiment against the Jews externalized itself in formal law. More often it worked itself out in administrative procedure, still more often in the actualities of social practice. But whatever the medium of its expression, anti-

Semitic pressure has even under the best of circumstances borne steadily upon the Jews of Central Europe. In Romania, Poland, Latvia, Lithuania, Esthonia at all times, aş in Germany most recently, the civic rights of Jews were a sour jest, the equality of economic and cultural opportunity which theoretically belonged to them a wry myth. At no time did they enjoy the individual freedom, civil liberty or political influence which was their due, nor access on a par with others to a livelihood, nor security in their occupations, nor ease of entrance into schools and universities, nor unhampered acceptance in the cultural life of their respective countries.

They must not be reduced after this war, as they were before it, to the status of second-rate citizens. Never again, if the United Nations can prevent it, should Jews, just because they are Jews, be subjected to assault, deprived of the ballot, denied public office, debarred from universities and their faculties. Never again should they be exposed to mass boycotts, or be victimized by that trick in which some prewar governments became so expert, the stunt of driving Jews out of an occupation in which they were heavily concentrated by converting it into a government monopoly and then denying employment in it to Jews. This time the emancipation of the Jews must be real. In law and in fact they must become free men, equal in their freedom to everyone else. They have suffered too bitterly, fought too hard and sacrificed too much for freedom's sake to be put off with less.

What must be made true concerning Jews must be made true equally for Judaism, which, as religion, as culture and in its institutions has also been persecuted. Thus, in some situations, statutes have been enacted to make difficult the observance of the seventh-day Sabbath and the Jewish dietary laws. Jewish schools and educational agencies have been denied their share of public subsidy to which they were in law entitled. The Hebrew and Yiddish languages and their literatures have at times been hedged in with every imaginable restraint. If then emancipation is to come to Jews, it must come as well to the tradition, the values and practices they hold dear.

VII. *In multicultural, multireligious and multinational states, the status of Jews and Judaism must be parallel to that accorded to other religious, cultural or historic bodies.*

We of the western world are habituated to a particular pattern of social organization. The U.S.A., to be specific, is a uninational and unicultural land. That is to say, all of us, regardless of our differences, are members of one and the same nation and share in its civilization. Over and beyond these commitments, we as individuals may assume additional loyalties. We may confess a particular creed and adhere to a special church—whether it be Roman Catholic, Jewish or Bahai. We may further, and in addition to our shared culture, interest ourselves in secondary and supplementary traditions—in ancient classical literature, or Scandinavian or Jewish, depending on our taste and our origins. But any such pursuits are, in the first place, addenda to our common Americanism and, in the second, the manifestation of that individual freedom in which our fundamental law assures us. That is to say, if there is in our land a Roman Catholic Church, or a Seventh Day Adventist, or a Jewish, it is because a number of individuals of Roman Catholic or Adventist or Jewish persuasion have exercised their rights as private citizens and have organized institutions to express their religious convictions. And if there be in this land minority and secondary cultural interests, these too conform to the same design. This is the American pattern; it is good, it works beautifully; I give it my wholehearted support.

But it is not the only pattern for national organization. There were before the war in Europe—and there will be again after it—states of a radically different character, states which are multinational and multicultural. The Polish state was one such. Millions who lived under its aegis and owed it political allegiance, who were indeed Polish nationals, were not of Polish nationality, or of Polish culture, but rather in these respects White Russians, Ukrainians, Jews or Germans. In such a situation—and it is duplicated in the Soviet Union and elsewhere—there exists within one nation a multiplicity of legally recognized nationalities, cultures and religions. In any such multinational and multicultural state, Jews and Judaism, if the Jews so elect, ought to enjoy the status of other elements.

A large body of experience supports this proposition. The Soviet Union, a conspicuous instance of a pluralism of nationalities, races and cultures, has enjoyed extraordinary success in its policy of encouraging the variety of civilizations contained in itself. In the other direction, every attempt to suppress group individuality, from the days of Czarist Russia and the Austro-Hungarian Empire to the present, has led, at the best, to constant social irritation and, at the worst, to the disruption of the overarching political edifice.

For Jews in particular it is most unfortunate when, in a setting of national pluralism, their distinctive group entity is not recognized. For then they must willy-nilly affix themselves to one of the other nationalities and cultures. No matter which they elect, their option will be resented. Under the Habsburg regime Hungarians turned bitter against the Jews, who, as German-speaking, were popularly identified with Germanic elements. A similar turn of events marked the early days of the Czech republic. Indeed it is a singular irony of history that, until Hitler, anti-Semitism in Central Europe found one of its pretexts in the Germanophilia of the Jews.

If then in any given nation everyone is to be of one texture as to nationality and culture, then let the Jews be like their fellows. Let their distinctiveness consist, as in America, only in religion and a secondary culture. But if everyone must be something in particular over and beyond general citizenship, let the Jew be what he in fact is, a Jew; let Jewry be a minority nationality and Judaism a minority culture on a par with those round about it.

VIII. *The rights of Jews and of Judaism must be made explicit in law and treaty, and secured by adequate sanctions.*

The recent sorry history of the Jews in Europe is only in part a story of rightlessness. Except for Germany it is much more a matter of rights held in theory but violated in practice. The tale goes back far into the past, as far at least as the Congress of Vienna which in 1815 extended guarantees to Jews, only to slip into the text of the treaty a "joker" which in effect made these guarantees worthless. A second inning of the same game was played by the Romanians who on winning their independence at the Berlin Congress of 1878 promised to grant full freedom to Jews, and then straightway proceeded to deny them even the form of citizenship.

It must be conceded to the framers of the Treaty of Versailles that they remembered history, both that of the Jews and the analogous experiences of other groups. For they went to extraordinary lengths to assure protection to minorities. Almost all the "succession" states, those created or radically modified by the peace, were compelled to subscribe to minority treaties. These understandings took a variety of forms, ranging from special covenants to declarations made before the Council of the League of Nations. Whatever their shape, they all added up to the same sum. Each contracting state recognized the rights of its minorities as part of its fundamental law and agreed that such rights were to stand under the protection of the League of Nations.

Of the thirteen states subscribing to these pacts, some attempted earnestly to discharge their obligations. Others, it would seem, had never been in earnest about their commitments. At the first opportunity they set about persecuting Jews, limiting their freedom and hampering the expression of their religion and culture. To make matters worse, it proved extraordinarily difficult to bring offending individuals or governments to book. First of all, the injured were compelled to make appeals to the League over the heads of their own governments, with all the risks implicit in such moves. Again the machinery set up by the League for such contingencies was incredibly slow and cumbersome.

In the main, therefore, injured minorities elected to endure present evils rather than expose themselves to unknown and possibly greater perils.

"Once burned, twice wary." This time, there must be no repetition of past blunders. This time the rights of any group, once accorded, must be preserved intact. To this end the following measures are indicated:

A. *Into the constitution of each of the succession states** must be written the principles of equality of all individuals and groups, ethnic, religious or cultural, before the law.*

Thus far we have gone once before. It would be shameful and calamitous if, after a war fought for democratic and humanitarian ends, we were to be content with less.

B. *Into the constitution of each of the succession states the outlawry of anti-Semitism must be inscribed.*

We shall discuss subsequently (Chapter 3) the proposal that western democracies, no less than succession states, legislate against the propagation of group prejudice in their midst. But what Great Britain and the United States do or leave undone does not alter what they may rightfully exact from succession states, the nations they conquer and those they liberate. As it chances, all of the former and many of the latter have been arch offenders against minorities. In such instances, certainly the United Nations may with propriety insist that their constitutions outlaw as a crime all instigation of group prejudice on grounds of race, creed or historical derivation.

C. *The protection of minorities in the succession states ought to be a*

---

* By "succession states" is meant those nations which will have been vanquished in the present war, and those which will have been either created or reconstituted by the United Nations.

major function of whatever world instrument will be devised for the enforcement of peace in the postwar era. These minorities ought to have full, free right of appeal to international authority, ought to be shielded by it against reprisal or intimidation. This international agency in turn ought to be equipped with machinery capable of prompt and firm action for the investigation of complaints and the enforcement of justice.

The principle I have just formulated applies, it should be noted, only to succession states. For the present, nothing on the political horizon lends support to the notion that any of the major powers is ready to submit its internal problems to international review. By every indication neither the United States nor any of its allies—at least none that is in full control of its own destiny—will tolerate appeal by its nationals to any authority beyond itself.

The story runs altogether otherwise with the succession states. For these, if they are vanquished nations, will perforce accept whatever terms may be imposed on them; and, if our allies, they will owe their reconstitution to the United Nations. Let it therefore be required of them that in return for their deliverance they consent to a legally secured status for their minorities.

All this involves a grave and patent unfairness. The great powers will be exacting from their defeated enemies and from some of their allies obligations they themselves are not prepared to assume. It would be better were all nations to be committed to the same terms. But there is no sense in reaching for the moon. By the scheme here proposed, at least a beginning in the right direction shall have been made. Subsequently, when and if the world organization gains in prestige and power, it may extend its custodianship to minorities everywhere.

IX. *Responsible Jewish leaders and organizations ought to be consulted as a matter of course by the individual governments and the United Nations in all approaches to the problems of Jews in Central Europe.*

Such a policy would seem to be the part of intelligence and humanity alike. The Jews of the world are in the first place better informed than anyone else on the actualities of the position of their fellows. Having been engaged for many decades in vast enterprises of relief, rehabilitation and emigration, they know these fields expertly. They understand, as no one else can, the internalities of Jewish life—the sanctities which Jews cherish, the matters of faith, ritual and collective purpose over which they agree and quarrel. What is more, they feel the tragedy of European Jewry with extraordinary acuteness. Every humanitarian, Jew or Gentile, will respond with sympathy to the plight of European Jews. But, as Scripture puts it, "the heart knoweth its own bitterness." Jews can be counted on for an extra touch of sensitivity and solicitude. Witness, by way of confirmation, the whole record of the past decade.

There were—to the glory of Christendom be this recorded—not a few Christians who felt the ordeal of European Jews as their own. But in the main it was the Jews of America who raised funds for relief, organized schemes for rescue, conceived of ingenious projects for resettlement, besieged reluctant or indifferent governmental officials, prodding them to more vigorous efforts.

Regrettably the United Nations have not been inclined to exploit these resources of accumulated experience and fervor. On the contrary, they have with fair consistency, in dealing with Jewish problems, ignored Jews in general and Jewish experts in particular. So, though the Bermuda Conference was convoked for the purpose of providing shelter and sustenance mainly for Jewish refugees, representatives neither of the American Jewish Joint Distribution Committee nor of any other Jewish agency were invited to participate in it. Among all international organizations only UNRRA has so far made any move to avail itself systematically of the aid and skills of nongovernmental bodies, having established the American Council of Voluntary Agencies for Foreign Service.

Certainly, official representation in the United Nations organization is due the Jewry of Palestine. That community is in law and fact a people residing on its own soil and in its own National Home. Throughout the Second World War it has stood valiantly for the Allied cause. To accord recognition in international councils to countries which entered the war at the latest possible moment, and to deny it to this community is to be guilty of the rankest injustice.

Perhaps at this point a disclaimer is due. I am not motivated in writing these lines by jealousy over the prestige of any Jewish organization. In the words of an ancient Jewish sage, I can swear with good conscience: "not to my glory nor to the glory of my father's house!" My sole concern is with the rehabilitation of European Jews. For their sake I would have responsible Jewish agencies and Jewish experts brought into the picture in the future. If this can be effected, we shall be certain that into the midst of the Olympian dispassion, so far and so generally characteristic of the official handling of the Jewish problem, something of hot anxiety and insatiable compassion will be injected.

From everything which has gone before, it should be crystal clear that the reconstitution of European Jewry is virtually a dogma in any argument concerning the Jewish future. I, for one, have neither sympathy nor patience with the contention, recklessly advanced in certain Jewish and non-Jewish circles alike, that the Jewish problem in Europe is hopeless and to be solved only by total evacuation. Such a proposal appears to me to be profoundly immoral, and to make a mockery of all the values for which the world is fighting. It is, in addition, a counsel of despair, since it surrenders all hope of a friendly rapport between Jews and other peoples. It sets a dangerous precedent. It would, still further, constitute an aggression against Jews, this time, however, on the part of humanitarians. For, what of the Jew who does not want to leave Europe? Shall he be coerced, and by his friends? And it is an affront to every Jew who loves the Jewish tradition. Judaism has its shrines in Europe as surely as have Catholicism and Protestantism. The cities of the Rhineland where in the eleventh century the great exegete Rabbi Solomon ben Isaac wrote his masterful commentaries, Vilna where the saintly Rabbi Elijah pursued his researches into rabbinic literature, and ten thousand other places are sacred to religious Jews, who pray that the Jewish faith may again flourish where once it blossomed so gloriously.

There must be no evacuation of Jews, no migration that is either total or in any fashion coerced, from any area on the European continent. This is the rock on which all policy vis-à-vis the Jews must be built. And yet, though no Jew ought to be compelled to move from Europe, many will freely and of their own choice elect such a course.

X. *Among the survivors of European Jewry a powerful urge toward emigration will manifest itself.*

Long before the outbreak of the Second World War, indeed long before 1933 when Hitler came to power, the restlessness of Jews seeking to escape Europe had reached the boiling point. All through the latter half of the nineteenth century pressures against the Jews mounted steadily. Many elected to stand and fight, to work out where they were the issues of their political, economic, social and religious status. Others, and in vast numbers, chose the course of emigration. But since the First World War, countries once hospitable to immigrants lost either the readiness or the ability to receive them. Barriers were set against the free flow of populations, to be rebuilt each decade higher and thicker. Behind the Jews of Europe churned broad flowing and powerful currents, propelling them into motion; before them, about them, stood insurmountable and impenetrable walls. Hitlerite anti-Semitism aggravated the crisis, adding momentum to the irresistible force, and solidity to the immovable object.

Prophecy is always hazardous. But it is scarcely a bold prediction to assert that the Second World War will intensify the long-existent impulse of European Jews toward emigration.

In the first place, the anti-Semite will be with them still. No one knows whether there will be more or less anti-Semitism in Europe when the war is over. But only the most befuddled Utopian can suggest that there will be none. Already there are ominous signs that the European man has not been altogether purified and transfigured. The old antipathies give every evidence of not having been altogether uprooted, not even among the victorious peoples, let alone among the defeated. Besides, be it not forgotten, Europe has for ten years been drenched with the poisonous rains of Nazi propaganda. Only time can reveal how deeply these have soaked into the mass consciousness. Last of all, postwar Europe will for a long time be sick, poverty-ridden, restless and miserable—in sum, an ideal seed bed for group antagonisms.

None of this means more than it says. I am not trying to hint that the war has been fought to no purpose, or that democracy is a failure in Europe, or that life will be impossible for Jews there. I am trying to say only that, even in the postwar era, there will be, in all likelihood, a fair amount of anti-Semitism abroad in the Old World. Despite that fact, Jews, I believe, can count on living reasonably free, useful and happy lives. And, if I have my way, they will be protected in their rights by guarantees in national and international law. But let no one marvel if very many Jews, seared once and justifiably apprehensive, prefer to pick up stakes.

They will be the readier for such a course because little or nothing will remain to detain them. Of the shopkeeper's shop not a trace will be left, of the physician's practice not a patient. Reparations may put sums of money into their hands—a boon by no means to be scorned—but, even so, life for most European Jews will have to be rebuilt from the ground up. Nothing then will retard, and much will urge, that, since a new departure must be undertaken in any event, it be launched in a fresh and more hospitable setting.

Very many of them will want, further, to keep from places associated in their minds with tragedy. For millions of Europeans, Jews and Gentiles alike, terrible psychic hazards stand against the resumption of life in old scenes. The streets they once walked, the homes they lived in are haunted by intolerable memories. This is the sad lot of much of Europe, a subtle, oblique, little-calculated consequence of the Nazi terror. But for the Jew, this torment may be marked by an especial anguish. He may be hagridden by recollections that cluster not only about things and sites, but about persons as well—about his next-door neighbor who in his calamity joined perhaps with his enemies or stood idle pretending blindness and deafness. It will not be easy, if this has been his fate, to go home to such people. Man does not live by bread alone, he needs also confidence in the good will of his fellows.

The Dutch Jew, in other words, will most likely desire to return to Holland. Unless some other circumstance prevents, he will come back to Amsterdam or The Hague with the same sense of joy and release as will be felt by other Netherlanders. For his neighbors, in the hour of his trial, were his friends also. When he was compelled to wear a Jew badge, they, Christians, donned badges also. When he was to be deported they hid him. And the dominie in the church at the corner preached himself into a concentration camp because he insisted on protesting against the maltreatment of Jews and the desecration of their synagogues. Except for blood and creed, these Christians were kin to the Dutch Jew, measuring up to and surpassing the Scriptural observation that a brother is known in time of trouble. But what of other Jews whose experiences may have been less heartening— German Jews, Austrian Jews, Polish Jews, Romanian Jews, Hungarian Jews —all the multitudes who were assailed, pillaged, and murdered if not by their neighbors, then often to their neighbors' satisfaction?

A new Exodus is in the making—an exodus of the blind, halt, lamed, diseased and desperate—an exodus of Jews who have had enough of endemic and persistent anti-Semitism, of Jews who have no reason to return to their former homes or who simply have not the heart to do so.

Quite apart from considerations of justice or compassion, it would be good policy for the United Nations to favor this movement. To inhibit it would be to pen up in the Old World people who do not wish to remain there. It would be in effect an invitation to trouble. On the other hand, to permit and encourage it by providing channels and outlets would be a multiple wisdom. It would give the Jews who are eager for a new scene what they want. It would improve the situation of those who stay put. For if part of Europe's Jews be drained away, the pressures against those who remain behind will be proportionately eased; the chances of a rapport between Jews and Gentiles become at once so much the brighter.

XI. *Any mass movement on the part of European Jews, if it is to be equal to their requirements, indeed if it is to be possible at all, must be predicated on three cardinal realities: (a) that the countries which did not want Jewish immigrants before the war are unlikely to want them after it; (b) that cognizance ought to be taken of the preferences of Jews in selecting lands to be opened to them, and (c) that Jewish migration if it is to be sizable enough to matter must be systematic and en masse, not sporadic and diffused.*

(a) As we have already observed, there was by 1939 scarcely a land in all the world open to Jewish refugees. The arguments advanced for excluding them varied from place to place. In economically advanced countries, such as the United States, it took the form of the contention that mass immigration would aggravate existent and already acute unemployment. In underpopulated and industrially young territories, Australia for example, a dual fear was voiced, lest the established population be engulfed by a tidal wave of new settlers, and lest into a heretofore homogeneous and peaceful community racial problems be injected. Whatever the claim, the effect was the same—Jewish newcomers were unwelcome.

Yesterday's temper will prevail tomorrow. There will be no sudden and miraculous changes of heart. On the contrary the doors that were closed in 1939 will be closed even more tightly in 1946. For in every land there will be new vast problems. Armies will have to be demobilized, and jobs found for officers and soldiers in the millions; industries geared to war will have to be switched over to peace. Everywhere the dark shadow of unemployment impends. Already immigration policies are turning more stringent. In the United States, for example, strong sentiment exists for the total stoppage of all admissions, every proposal of a more liberal policy evoking the severest opposition. All in all, it is wiser not to expect an easy solution of the question and certainly not to count on Canada, Australia, South Africa, the Latin-American republics or the United States for it. These countries may, as humanitarian gestures, agree to accept token groups of refugees, which is, no doubt, something to the good. They can be relied on for no more. The land of promise, if there be one, must be sought for elsewhere.

(b) Jews, even destitute European Jews, are human beings, not cattle to be put onto runways and led away without regard to their preferences. It has become quite the mode for statesmen and editors to dispose of the problems of Jewish migration by considering everything except the desires of the Jews. The globe is scrutinized, some area is selected, and a pontifical judgment is pronounced to the effect that here the Jews ought to be settled. The possibility that the Jews may not like the spot or may prefer some other site is rarely taken under advisement, and if suggested, is dismissed out of hand. Statesmanship and compassion alike indicate another and more considerate attitude.

(c) There is no point in trying to solve the problem of homeless Jews by the method of diffusion, by spreading them as far apart and as sparsely as possible. It has been assumed in the past that an especial virtue inhered in keeping Jewish migration from concentrating itself onto any given area. In part this attitude has represented a concession to realities, since no country offered to take Jews en masse. In part it reflected an apprehension entertained in the main by Jews of wealth and station, who feared that if Jews were settled compactly, their existence would be the more conspicuous and would therefore constitute a stronger provocation to anti-Semitism. On both scores, the policy heretofore has been to direct a handful of Jews to one place, a little coterie to another, a colony to a third—in effect, to bail the ocean with a spoon.

The effects of such piddling were twofold—to leave the problem as large in volume and fierceness as ever, and, curiously enough, to spread anti-Semitism. For wherever Jews settled, and no matter in what minute numbers, their presence tended to precipitate some reaction, some fever of xenophobia, usually short-lived but in some instances quite persistent. So the tragedy of European Jewry was left unabated and a rash of anti-Semitism swept the Latin-American republics and other lands to which the Jews were spreading. The matter must be dealt with more boldly in the future. As much diffused migration may go on as will be possible. Whatever it achieves is so much to the good. But it is mass, systematic and concentrated settlement which alone offers promise of substantial results.

XII. *From the above it follows that the United Nations must designate promptly one or several centers for mass Jewish colonization. These areas must be more than speculatively suitable, nor can they be such as to require decades of preliminary preparation before being opened to settlement. They must be habitable places, immediately available and equal in capacity to the volume of Jewish need. By these requirements, Palestine stands forth as the most eligible, though not necessarily the sole focus of Jewish migration.*

On no score has there been such flagrant irresponsibility as in finding a place for Jewish settlement. The normal, private citizen of good will has been offhanded and careless concerning it; governments have been, to give them the benefit of the doubt, incredibly stupid and dilatory.

The well-intentioned but uninformed individual, confronted by the question, has been inclined to blurt forth benevolently, if not wisely, "There must be some place to which these people can go." Such a judgment seems to be logical. The earth is large and possessed of vast uncultivated areas. Certainly one of these ought to be available for homeless human beings. But for all its seeming reasonableness, the assumption is ultimately naïve. The unsettled areas of the world are less numerous than has been imagined. Uganda, for example, has often been suggested on the ground that it is largely unpopulated. It has approximately 4,000,000 inhabitants. Other places which are blithely taken to be available and desirable are in actuality uninhabitable. So with Madagascar. The world had to be reminded by M. Leon Caiyla, its Governor General: "The only suitable region with regard to climate where European families could be settled would be the upper plateau, but free land is no longer available there." Still other sites which might or might not be fit for Jewish colonization are ruled out by political factors such as governmental policy or public temper. So, at the Evian Conference, when the vast and empty expanses of Australia came under discussion, the representative of that Dominion put a quick quietus on the notion by stating with regret but bluntly that Australia had no intention of importing a racial problem. Indeed there is almost no end to the kindly but altogether lightheaded proposals that have emanated from supposedly intelligent people, as witness the following which at various times have appeared in the public press:

East Prussia, after the evacuation of both Germans and Poles.

Morocco and Algiers, as though these were totally uninhabited and as though their populations would have no opinions on the matter.

The eastern slopes of the Andes, despite the anti-Semitism latent and overt throughout South America, and the closed-door policy of almost all the Latin-American republics.

All that remains is that somebody solemnly propose the moon!

So much for individuals of whom too much perhaps cannot be expected. Unfortunately the record of the humane, civilized and democratic governments of the world is little better. Out of the mountainous international conferences convoked to alleviate Jewish homelessness, two tiny mice have been born. The British government at one time offered to set aside a tract of land in British Guiana for Jewish colonization—a most generous gesture except that no one is certain whether Europeans can adapt themselves to the climatic conditions of the area, except further that it would take at least a decade of preliminary road building, hygienic preparations and agricultural experimentation before the country would begin to be ready for mass immigration. And where are the Jews of Europe to lay their heads in the interim? Little wonder that the entire proposal died a-borning.

The only other concrete proposal emanating from any government came from Generalissimo Trujillo, President of the Dominican Republic, who in 1939 offered to receive 100,000 selected refugees on a tract of land set aside for that purpose. The difficulty of founding new settlements from the ground up is nowhere more clearly revealed than in this instance. Four years after the offer was made there were only 500 persons in the colony. And most recently an investigation conducted by the Brookings Institution has disclosed that the colony is capable of accommodating not 100,000 souls as had been suggested in the first flush of enthusiasm, but a maximum of 5,000.

To such trivialities do all the efforts of all the governments of all the democratic nations reduce themselves. Yet, while ministers, secretaries and undersecretaries groped in darkness, fumbled, started off in diverse directions at the same time, collided with one another and with themselves, and frantically grasped at straws, shadows and delusions, the one immediately available, demonstrably practicable, breath-takingly successful site for the settlement of homeless Jews was stubbornly ignored. I refer, of course, to Palestine. A preposterous blindness had afflicted democratic officialdom. It could see all things except the largest and most obvious. Or if it saw, it was involved in a conspiracy of silence.

The opening of the doors of Palestine to Jewish immigration is the first, the most self-evident and the most clearly indicated measure in any approach to the problem of Jewish mass movement. I would not be misunderstood. In putting Palestine forward I have no intention of rejecting other sites. Such are the dimensions of Jewish need that our choice is not between Palestine and other places. It is Palestine *plus* as many additional centers as may be made available. On the other hand, one must not set loose the bird in the hand for those that may conceivably be perched in the bush. Palestine is in the hand. It is assigned by international covenant to large-scale Jewish settlement. Jews have demonstrated that they can live there, and that most creatively. The spadework necessary in any other land has here long since been done. To ignore Palestine is by every count a stupidity which in its cruelty becomes a sin.

In the legends of East European Jewry, tales are told about the sages of Chelm who were pretty much the Hebrew analogues of the wise men of Gotham. It was characteristic of their "sagacity" that they always saw everything except what was most patent. Amusing, no doubt, and just the sort of blindness that the world has quite consistently exhibited with reference to the Jews and the haven they need. But in this case the obtuseness is scarcely funny. It has caused the death and torture of innocent human beings; it may involve the unhappiness and frustration of millions of others in the future. A joke is a joke; and the Jew, it is to be hoped, has as good a sense of humor as anyone else. But it is understandable that he no longer laughs when the British Colonial Office and the American State Department fail to notice Palestine whenever they look upon those wretched Jews who lack all things, but a decent home first of all.

The catastrophe that has overtaken mankind recently is perhaps the gravest in all human history. No one knows its cost in material things, let alone in the more precious things of the heart and spirit. But one potential good has come with it. The same fires which consumed lives, cities, libraries, landscapes, hopes and dreams have melted down the old, hard patterns of social living as well. The world is moldable today as rarely before in man's career. It is not so pliable, nor are we so skillful as to fashion it straightaway into the Kingdom of God on earth. But it can be formed, now as never before, the least bit after that high design.

Is it too much to ask that in the remedying of so many ancient evils, the evils the Jews have experienced be mitigated also? It is not too much to hope. It is indeed something which men of honor and compassion must demand. For though the Jewish problem is not the only or largest issue on the European continent, it is a challenge in itself; it is furthermore part of the problem of Europe. And any solution of the universal issue must in the end be vitiated by failure to dispose of its constituent particulars.

When then the general task of the reconstruction of Europe goes forward, it must be accompanied by the rehabilitation of European Jewry. For as mankind will do with this people, so long abused as the least of the peoples of Europe, so ultimately it will do to all Europe and in the end to itself also.

2

Anti-Semitism—Root and Flower

THE HORROR WE have just contemplated is from one point of view without precedent and parallel in human history. From another angle, it is only the latest, though climactic, manifestation of an ancient and stubborn evil, the curse of anti-Semitism which has dogged the Jew for the past two thousand years, which has wrought incalculable harm on him, and which, nevertheless and by a surpassing paradox, has contributed in so slight measure to his survival.

Where does it come from, this inveterate and consuming hatred? What are its roots? On what does it feed that it should have outlived the vicissitudes of the centuries, that it should flourish equally among cultured and retarded peoples, in days of prosperity and adversity alike?

These questions are, needless to say, not being asked now for the first time. Anti-Semitism has had a lengthy career, and attempts to explain it have been legion. Still another will be undertaken here. For the hypothesis which is to follow, I make no claims of originality. It is frankly derivative. But it is, I believe, balanced and sane. Riding no hobbies, it represents an attempt to acknowledge truth whatever its nature and source. Its very limitations may therefore be a virtue of sorts. For if I succeed in carrying it off, I shall present to the reader a distillation of all the notions which have been advanced on an old enigma, the lunacies and obsessions purged away, the valid and living insights preserved and neatly ordered.

This then is to be our objective in the present chapter—a theory of explanation for anti-Semitism. But before we move toward it, several general propositions ought first to be noted. In the first place a prejudice that has lasted so long and under such diverse circumstances is likely to spring from more than one cause. The tendency is strong in men to seize upon some single circumstance as the clue to anything they desire to interpret. It is safer to be less economical, to assume that behind any tangled situation a tangle of influences is at work.

Again the odds are heavy that anti-Semitism, since it has outlived so many generations of Jews and anti-Semites alike, derives from forces deeper than the idiosyncrasies of individuals, Jew or Gentile. This is not to say that personal behavior is of no consequence in its making or abatement. The fact that one Jew is conspicuously successful, another flamboyantly self-assertive, still a third offensively ill-mannered cannot be without effect. Yet anti-Semitism has been very powerful in Poland where Jews were conspicuous only for their poverty, and in Germany where the bulk of Jews were painstakingly well bred. And one of the cruelest blows ever dealt to Jews was their expulsion from Spain—a measure directed against a group notably courtly and gracious. Clearly, anti-Semitism is motivated by elemental social drives compared to which eccentricities of personal conduct are at most secondary.

Most important is the recognition that, despite its uniquenesses, anti-Semitism is not without analogue, that it is in the main a specialized and unusually vehement instance of prejudice in general. Roughly speaking, the same drives which precipitate all hostilities, racial, cultural and religious, are at work here. To understand anti-Semitism is to understand group antipathy, and to understand group antipathy as a universal phenomenon is to comprehend that particular instance which is anti-Semitism.

Like other mass prejudices, anti-Semitism is first of all a product of *indoctrination*. Out of the past there comes to every individual the culture of his group. Most of that heritage is useful and morally acceptable, consisting in the language a man learns to speak, the institutions within which he comes to live, values toward which he strives, and insights with which he illumines experience. Yet, like a glacier composed mainly of ice but containing within itself debris also, every tradition is streaked and stained with undesirable materials. Among these will be superstitions, aesthetic blind spots, group prejudices. And these will be transmitted through the very channels in which wholesome elements also move—through the home, the school, literature and the church.

The home, the great conduit for the flow of all virtues, may very easily communicate vices as well. Every household, as Pearl Buck points out, has its own "family culture," its peculiar combination of attitudes and values. Differences in this family culture very often account for differences among human beings, determining whether they will be free from particular prejudices or ridden by them. The atmosphere of one home may make of it an island of tolerance and kindliness amid a sea of bigotry. Against that, another domestic milieu may inculcate racial and religious hatreds.

The process of indoctrination is generally simplicity itself. A mother who early in life was conditioned against Jews may say to her child offhandedly and without reflection: "Do not play with so-and-so, he's a Jew." At that instant a lease on life for another generation may be conferred on a century-old antagonism.

On a larger scale, social institutions often operate to the same result. Anti-Semitism, dispersed through the thought life of the Western world, reflects itself in literature. It crops up in Mother Goose rhymes, in Shakespeare and Dickens; it is not missing from the writings of some of our best contemporary novelists and essayists. The extent of its diffusion should not be exaggerated. But it is not so thinly spread that one must weary himself to find it. And many an innocent reader has picked up the disease by chance exposure to these random focal points of infection.

But of all institutions contributing to the inculcation of hostility toward Jews, organized Christianity has been in the past and regrettably still is the most consistent and potent offender. For centuries it has presented the Jew to the world as the deicide, the man who slew God and must be cursed for his sin. In the Middle Ages the church was, if not the sole author, certainly the principal author of that bizarre and hair-raising misconception of Jews which Dr. Joshua Trachtenberg has recaptured in his volume *The Devil and the Jews,* that caricature whereby the Jew was assumed to be Satan incarnate, desecrator of Christian sanctities, drinker of Christian blood, poisoner of wells, fomenter of plagues, sorcerer, hater of mankind and what not. Who knows how much of the cruel vagary still lurks in the minds not only of untutored European peasants, but in the subliminal consciousness of urbane non-Jews? May not the frenzy of anti-Semitism, its "demonological" fury, to use the term of Mr. Maurice Samuel, have its origin here, in a wild notion concerning Jews which the medieval Christian church created and preached?

To this day, some elements in organized Christianity continue in the same role, occasionally with malice aforethought, most often innocently. The tale of the crucifixion is still a central theme of worship and religious education. And when it is carelessly presented, its influence on group relations can be as unhappy today as a half millennium ago. The seven-year-old child is no biblical critic and no historian. His ability to distinguish the contemporary from what may have occurred two thousand years ago is feeble at best. Confusing the ancient Jews of whom he hears ugly reports with those he knows, he may in his earliest years be made an anti-Semite.

The institutions of Christianity are packed with social dynamite that may explode in directions altogether different from those intended. Dedicated to the saving efficacy of love, they have often served to inculcate hatred. Not that this is a rule. In the darkest days of medieval Christendom, there were not wanting prelates, priests and laymen to resist, often at great personal jeopardy, this perversion of their spiritual purpose. In our time most ministers and teachers of religion are keenly aware of the danger and eager to avert it. Indeed, in recent years a number of Christian denominations have undertaken to survey the pedagogical materials employed in their schools for the very purpose of spotting and eliminating texts and passages which might serve to induce anti-Semitic attitudes. Yet, it is still the fact that though it be inadvertent in the main, some followers of Jesus who preached a gospel of love are perverting with hatred the souls they mean to save.

Once the damage has been done, it may be irreparable. A mind-set may have been created which numberless sermons on human brotherhood cannot eradicate. The child grows into an adult, is exposed to all sorts of educational experiences. Perhaps he turns skeptic or agnostic, breaking with the church of his youth. His prejudices, however, are quite likely to survive all changes. Thanks to early conditioning, to experiences he may long have forgotten, he remains disposed to dislike Jews.

Hatreds, like weeds, propagate themselves. This same adult speaks slurringly about Jews in the presence of his own children and the disease is transmitted to another generation.

The person who has been turned against Jews, no matter how or where, tends to form a conception of them, a mental stereotype. Whenever he encounters real Jews who do not conform to his expectations, he does not surrender the picture to which he is accustomed. Rather he insists that these individuals are exceptions. More than one Gentile has met literally hundreds of Jews who neither speak Yiddish nor gesticulate nor wear beards. Yet he will somehow confidently expect the next Jew to exhibit all these traits.

Individual Jews may be lovable; the stereotype never is. This accounts for the paradox whereby a Gentile may genuinely like some Jews and yet with equal earnestness dislike Jews in general. For he is actually liking and disliking different things—in one case human beings of flesh and blood, in the other a figment of the imagination.

He who has been conditioned against Jews will never be done with his bias; he must forever justify it. Be it remembered that he has picked up his antipathy early in life, that he is unlikely as an adult to be able to recall how he came by it. He finds himself then with an attitude for which he can indicate no cause. But if he is true to human nature, he will be reluctant to concede that he is being unreasonable. It must have taken extraordinary hardihood for the person who did not like Dr. Fell to admit that he did not know how or why. Most people, made of softer stuff, are much less candid. Let them hate something or somebody, no matter how arbitrarily, and they will find an excuse for themselves. So the anti-Semite by indoctrination will search out some rationalization of his prejudices. Is he a conservative? Does he espy a Jewish radical? He will proclaim, "This is why I am against Jews. They are all radicals." Is he a radical and has he spotted a Jewish banker? He will cry, "This is the reason I cannot abide Jews. They are all capitalists." If he is a member of a social set into which Jews are trying to make their way, he will contend, "No wonder Jews are unpopular. They are always pushing themselves where they are not wanted." And if he is himself trying to penetrate into an exclusive group from which Jews among others are debarring him, he will object to Jews because they are clannish. The very fact that the arguments advanced for anti-Jewish prejudice are mutually so contradictory exposes them for what they are: rationalizations rather than reasons, "good" reasons rather than "real" ones. The former are, of course, a part of the story. Only the latter make it intelligible.

Anti-Semitism is, in the second place, a consequence of *economics*. In a competitive society there is a sense in which the hand of each man is against his brother, in which every one advances at the expense of others. The Gentile, struggling for a livelihood, takes the greater success of a fellow-Gentile with such grace as he can muster. He knows the rules of the game, and while he may feel that the game is all wrong, he does not often protest against anyone playing it skillfully. But when his competition comes from Jews he is likely to turn sullen. He feels that this is a hazard to which he should not be subjected; that in a Gentile world only Gentiles ought to be permitted to engage in the desperate gamble for bread.

The presence of outsiders at the common social table is never welcome. It will be resented with especial bitterness when there is not enough to go around. Hence, anti-Semitism—indeed all intolerance toward minority groups—takes on intensity during economic depressions. For then the job held by the Jew, Negro or Catholic is wanted by members of the majority group. Then the bread eaten by tolerated "outsiders" seems to be taken out of the mouths of those who "belong" but go hungry.

This truth is put forcibly in an anecdote, in a tale told of a missionary who, taking up residence with a savage tribe, was accorded a most hospitable reception. His hosts were generous particularly with their staple food, a fruit indigenous to the country. Pleased and startled by the openhandedness of the barbarians, the stranger inquired whether this was their normal practice. The answer he received is most illuminating:

"When the fruitage is abundant," he was told, "we eat and give to strangers as much as they desire. When it is only adequate to our needs, we eat and give none to strangers. And when it fails, we eat the strangers."

The record of persecutions of Jews affords large-scale confirmation of this thesis. All through the Middle Ages assaults against them very commonly either coincided with economic recessions or were transparently shot through with and impelled by financial interest. Religion, quite generally the front and the ostensible occasion for pogroms, was often no more than a façade for less honorable motives. This truth is borne out equally by the history of anti-Semitism in the modern world. In Poland and Romania, for example, anti-Semitism has long been endemic, but so too has poverty. In Germany a latent anti-Jewish bias broke loose only in the wake of an economic collapse. And it cannot be merely a coincidence that sentiment against Jews in America has twice grown fierce in recent years, and on both occasions in the midst of depressions.

Economic adversity is then a prime breeding ground for anti-Semitism. But it serves to encourage it in another more devious fashion. Every society contains individuals who in one respect or another are the recipients of extraordinary benefits at its hands. These people have an especial stake in their world. But when the order which has treated them so generously falls upon evil days, they are threatened as to their privileges. It then becomes to their interest to divert the attention of the hungry and naked who at any moment may decide to strike out at the social structure. To this end, nothing is more convenient than the presence of a minority such as the Jews. For when people have once been induced to blame Jews for their wretchedness, they are less likely to discover its true causes. And when they are breaking Jewish heads, they are not expropriating feudal barons or capitalists.

This is not to say that financiers, industrialists and magnates resort to these devices deliberately and with diabolical cunning. Nor do we mean to suggest that they assemble in solemn conclave and, as in the old dime thrillers, vote to sacrifice the Jews to their own imperiled interests. As a rule things go much more innocently. They simply come to the conclusion that it is to their advantage to spur on some demagogue agitating against the Jews—and behave accordingly. In any case, so it worked in Russia where the Czarist regime aided and abetted organized anti-Semitism; and in Germany when the Krupps and Thyssens formed an alliance with the Nazis as a counter-measure to mounting radicalism. So, there is reason to believe, it has on occasion operated in America. Always the spirit has been the same, something akin to the prudence which impels a householder to take out insurance against burglary.

Any prejudice, no matter how stimulated and fed, has its site in human nature. The thought-life and mood-flow of man, however, are not inert. They are active agents. Subject to external influences, they yet constitute positive forces in their own right. So with anti-Semitism. It is among other things the expression of *psychological factors,* of traits inherent in human nature.

The first of these is a strong tendency, present apparently in almost all individuals and societies, toward the "dislike of the unlike." This impulse would seem to be in part a survival from the remote human past. To the savage every strange phenomenon represented potential danger. Primitive men did well to suspect each novelty and to try to destroy it. And we, to this day, are still possessed of vestiges of this characteristic. We too are uneasy over what we cannot comprehend, and quick to suppress it. Now the Jew is in a degree an unknown quantity to Gentiles. His background is unusual; his modes of life are different from theirs or are suspected of being so even when they are not. He evokes xenophobia, the eternal protest of human nature against the strange and the stranger.

Behind "dislike of the unlike" still another psychic force is operative: man's resentment against that which is extraordinary. Habit, as we all can testify, is comfortable. That is why we are so fervently attached to the normal and familiar. In dealing with them, we do not have to think. We simply repeat well-worn, time-honored, automatic responses. Exceptional situations on the other hand cannot be disposed of so conveniently. They require a reflective pause, a period for the contrivance of unique modes of action. They make us think, and thought is painful.

As a result, we are all impatient with the extraordinary. We are quickly annoyed, if we are conventionalists, by the ways of Bohemians; if Bohemians, by the conduct of conventionalists. The reading of editorials with which we do not agree is likely to infuriate us. The most desirable house guest outlives his welcome if only he stays long enough.

So with larger social adjustments. The members of any group are usually at ease among themselves. They can afford to deal with one another on the plane of habit. But let an outsider appear among them and they become wary. They watch themselves, they calculate their behavior; in sum, they are "self-conscious." They keep asking themselves whether they can properly say this before the stranger, or do that. Sooner or later the necessity for self-scrutiny and deliberation becomes a nuisance. They end by wishing that the intruder would get himself off. But suppose he does not oblige them by doing so? An active resentment may be endangered. Hence it comes to pass that Gentiles would often prefer to do without the company of a quite unexceptionable Jew. He puts them too painfully on the *qui vive*. The process, needless to say, works in reverse also. Jews who are altogether comfortable with one another may turn awkward as soon as a Gentile pops up in their midst, and may sigh with relief once he is gone.

Still another wellspring of group hatred, deep and ever-flowing, is the process of transference and projection, the "scapegoat" mechanism. It is this motivation which Mr. Ben Hecht describes so brilliantly in his *A Guide for the Bedevilled,** a book whose heart is very much in the right place, even if its head is befuddled at times. "I write," he says, speaking of Jew-baiters, "of fools, pipsqueaks, social impostors, spiritual harelips, tormented homosexuals, lonely sadists, intellectual bankrupts; of unctuous gossip-mongers for whom speech is a form of masturbation; of bile-peddlers, and invalids whose teeth ache, whose bladders drip and whose hearts are a sackful of worms; of religious zanies who woo God by spitting in his eye, and anti-religious zanies who fill the dark of their heads with ugly screams; of

---

* Quoted by permission of the publishers, Charles Scribner's Sons.

cunning rabble-rousers lusting for a nickel's worth of power, and of the dough-headed rabble ever ready with its fake coin and its sickly cheers; I write of all that mincing and bepimpled, clapper-tongued and swivel-brained tribe of lame ducks who make up the ranks of the anti-Semites."

Mr. Hecht in this passage may be afire with indignation, his rhetoric may be explosive, but he makes a valid point. The anti-Semite is very likely to be an embittered soul, eaten up by a sense of insignificance, consumed by frustrations, seething in consequence with blood lust and violence. Like all persons in pain, he wants to strike out, to claw, to destroy. But even in frenzy, he is unlikely to go berserk. He will avoid assailing anyone stronger than he and capable of retaliating in kind. He will pick on someone big enough to make bullying a satisfactory experience, but not big enough to strike back.

Closely interwoven with this pain-driven impulse toward violence goes a yearning for self-extenuation. We are dealing with a wretched individual. Life has disappointed him. It has brought him few good things—love, fame, health, comfort and wealth. It has been generous only with evils—obscurity, poverty, a sodden marriage, or galling, irritating physical ailments. Now man is ever reluctant to assume responsibility for the ills which befall him. For to do so is to endure not only those ills but self-reproach also. Wherefore he will go to any lengths to assign the blame for his misfortunes elsewhere. Jews are admirably suited to such purposes. They are widely diffused so that one need not look too far for them. They are, at least some of them are, prominent. The charge that they are the cause of any particular evil presents therefore at least a show of plausibility. At the same time they are a small group and hence can be assailed with relative impunity.

Like the frustrated person, the frustrated society is likely to turn upon Jews. A people no less than an individual often achieves a *stimmung*, a general tone characteristic of itself. This may be one of joy and self-approbation. It may also be one of disillusionment and resentment. Show me a society in the latter case, and I will show you in it tendencies toward violence, either against other nations or else against a minority element in its own midst.

In speaking of the temper of a community, I am making no mystical assumptions. Dr. Richard Brickner in his *Is Germany Incurable?* posits the notion of a whole people afflicted, *qua* people, with psychic or mental disorders. I make no such suppositions. What I have in mind is much more simple. Let a nation undergo economic adversity, and many of its citizens will suffer unemployment and poverty. Let it meet military defeat, and much of its population will feel keenly their country's humiliation. If then the political reverse, or the economic catastrophe or the hardship, whatever its character, be sufficiently severe, enough individuals *as individuals* will be made sufficiently unhappy to create a general temper of public and collective misery.

. What happens next is a matter of record. The Church Father, Tertullian, protested that no matter what went wrong in the pagan Rome of his time, whether the Tiber overflowed or the price of corn went up, the Christians were blamed, and one remedy only urged: *Christianos ad leones.* Witness, further, the fate of the Jews, particularly those of Germany. To explain it one need not argue that the German soul is inherently different in quality from any other, or that the Germans are a paranoid people. One need assume only that enough Germans as individuals were sufficiently inflamed by their militaristic tradition and sufficiently hurt by the First World War, by the inflation and the depression, to make popular the cry: *Judaios ad leones.*

Our account of the psychic motivation behind anti-Semitism, to be complete, must take cognizance of still another hypothesis. In a variety of forms, the theory has been propounded that hatred of the Jew, while it may be strengthened by all the forces we have listed, derives ultimately from an altogether different source, from a compulsive protest of the subconscious mind of the Christian against the authority of the Christ personality. Such, to take the clearest instance of this school of thought, is the argument of Mr. Maurice Samuel in his brilliant essay, *The Great Hatred.*

Mr. Samuel begins by denying what we have steadfastly assumed, namely that anti-Semitism is one more instance of group prejudice in general. Antipathy toward Jews is marked, he contends, by a fury and irrationality such as no other social bias exhibits. No other group, he points out, has ever been so widely and persistently detested; no other people has been subjected to such cruelties; about no other body of human beings have such bizarre, demonological tales been told.

Indoctrination, economic conflict, the dislike of the unlike, and the scapegoat mechanism may explain other mass antagonisms; they may even account in part for anti-Semitism, but only in lesser part. For behind anti-Semitism another force is at work, infusing it with its extraordinary fervor and passion.

Christians, Mr. Samuel maintains, have always shown ambivalence toward the Christ. On the one hand they have admired and sought to emulate him. On the other hand, they have resented him for inhibiting the spontaneous expression of their impulses, for marring their illicit pleasures with intrusions of conscience. The Christ personality, in other words, is that of a censor not only to professing Christians but even to many secularists, anticlericals, atheists. Like any censor, like anything or anybody that stands between men and their desires, he is hated.

Loving and resenting him at the same time, men are furthermore precluded from giving vent to their rebellion. Even in the privacy of their souls they dare not speak their blasphemy, let alone in public, in the face of widespread and powerful Christian sentiment. Hence they do as people have always done with a suppressed emotion. They divert it onto an associated object.

The son who cannot admit that he detests his father strikes out not at him but at some interest identified with him: his religion, his occupation or his political views. To the Christian mind, Jesus is inextricably bound up with the Jews. Among them he was born and lived; their teachings served as the basis for his doctrines, on their Scripture he stands. Rebelling against the Christ, Christians transfer their antagonism from him onto his people.

Jews, by Mr. Samuel's construction, are hated not, as has so long been imagined, because they are Christ-killers but for the exactly opposite reason, because they are Christ-givers, because they have imposed on the world a moral system and so have fettered men with ethical inhibitions.

This entire line of argument is quite plausible. The process Mr. Samuel describes may well have a share, perhaps a large share, in the making of prejudices against Jews. But attractive as the hypothesis is, too much must not be claimed for it. In the first place, if the theory cannot be refuted, neither can it be established. And it is always wise to be chary about propositions of this type. More pertinently, Mr. Samuel, having asserted the uniqueness of anti-Semitism, argues that its causation must be different from those behind other group prejudices. But is it so certain that hatred of the Jews is an unparalleled phenomenon? Does not a mob burning a Negro exhibit its analogue? And as for demonological tales, is there not a demonology about the Negro as a rapist, as possessed of a distinctive body odor, as an insurrectionist biding his time to strike out at white people?

This then must be our final appraisal of Mr. Samuel's hypothesis—that it points to a cause of anti-Semitism, likely not certain, in any case one among several.

Anti-Semitism, last of all, is a product of *manipulation and design;* it can be, as recent history has amply demonstrated, the result of a tactic calculatingly adopted and executed.

The emotions of men in the mass are of terrific power. He who can rouse, saddle, mount and control them can travel far and fast. This then is the great trial of ambitious men, the temptation to awaken and exploit dormant social passions to their own ends.

To such purposes anti-Semitism lends itself readily. It is always present in the Western world and therefore always available. Moreover it is likely of and by itself to grow intense in periods of distress. The demagogue's task is made easy. He need only make manifest and self-conscious that which is latent; he need only channelize in the direction of his own goals forces which are already powerfully but aimlessly astir. Let the appropriate charms be pronounced often and loud, and the evil spirits will respond. Onto the Jews will explode the accumulated force of generations of indoctrination, the anger of jealousy and economic misery, the irritations arising from the dislike of the unlike, the violence of men visiting onto others the anguish of their own errors and frustrations. And such will be the power of the blast that it will sweep those who have set it off to their private objectives.

It is a pliable and potent tool, resentment of the Jews, capable of being adapted to many ends either simultaneously or in succession. As Hitler, Mussolini and their imitators at home and abroad have demonstrated, it can be used to win political power, to secure it once it is won, to disrupt the internal unity of enemy countries, to persuade men and nations to policies to which otherwise they would never give their assent. Little wonder that so many have been tempted to try their hands at it. Of the anti-Semitism in the world, no slight part is made by men whose business it is to create it.

The proof of a pudding notoriously is in its eating; of a hypothesis, by the same token, in the facts. So with the theory we have just propounded. No matter how reasonable and likely it appears, it must pass yet one more crucial test. It must demonstrate its ability to account for all manifestations of anti-Semitism, including the most baffling.

Prejudice against Jews has taken some strange turns in modern times. It has gone through amazing transformations, has reversed and contradicted itself amazingly. Consider, by way of illustration, two classic anti-Semites, Torquemada and Hitler, and the startling differences between them. The Grand Inquisitor complained against Jews that they refused to become Christians like the majority of men but clung rather to their differential identity. Hitler's contention runs in diametrically the opposite direction: that Jews are assimilating themselves to the society round about them, that they are surrendering their uniqueness and becoming indistinguishable from non-Jews.

Again, it might be expected of two men who share a consuming hatred against a particular people that they would now and then talk a common language, that they would advance, at least occasionally, the same arguments. Actually they inhabit different universes. The medieval Spaniard always conceived the Jewish problem as a religious issue, to be solved by conversion; the modern Nazi sees it in racial terms, and insoluble except through extermination.

There is a third and deeper contrast between our specimen anti-Semites. The Grand Inquisitor worked with medieval men, bigoted, illiterate, diseased and poverty-stricken. But modern anti-Semitism, coming to the fore in the final quarter of the last century, has no such antecedents. It emerged from a scene as bright and as well illumined as mankind has ever known, from a soil and atmosphere of culture, science and general literacy. The democratic state and the physical well-being characteristic of the nineteenth and early twentieth centuries provide its habitat. A staggering question arises: why should anti-Semitism have been reborn at a time and in a climate which by every rule of logic should have proved uncongenial to it?

Within modern anti-Semitism lurk deep and haunting riddles. Against these we shall now proceed to test our theory of causes.

These are the supreme paradoxes in the recent history of anti-Semitism:

The paradox of a prejudice which has reversed its purposes without changing its nature;

The paradox of a prejudice which has abandoned one rationale for another, and still somehow remains what it has always been;

The paradox of a prejudice which, supposedly the result of obscurantism and poverty, has come to heightened life in an age of enlightenment and plenty.

The first paradox of modern anti-Semitism, its reversal of purposes, has quite generally escaped notice. Yet it is a fact, and one of no slight significance. Prior to the nineteenth century the anti-Semite objected to Jewish individuality. He protested against the refusal of Jews to become Christian in religion and European in culture. Implicit in his recriminations was the promise that he would open his arms to them as soon as they put away their peculiarities and became like himself.

Then, with the coming of the Emancipation, large numbers of Jews began to take the anti-Semite at his word. For one reason or another, they did a fairly thorough job of sloughing everything recognizably Jewish from themselves. They were not only ready to accede to what had been demanded of them, they were eager to do so. They crowded into the bosom of their erstwhile critic and waited to be embraced.

The anti-Semite was embarrassed. He had all along assumed his own sincerity. But now that Jews were meeting his terms, he found himself no better disposed toward them than formerly. He felt no overpowering urge to take them to his heart. All in all, his antipathy, he discovered, was just as strong against Europeanized Jews of the latest model as it had ever been against those of the Ghetto. He shifted his ground. His anti-Semitism perforce took on a new guise. He now began to object to Jews because one could not spot them, because they were in fact ceasing to be Jews and becoming instead exactly what he was.

Is it not apparent that both arguments are equally rationalizations? Under the influence of the causes we have enumerated, the anti-Semite found himself obsessed by an irrational attitude. So long as Jews insisted on remaining different from others, he seized on that as his justification. Once they began to conform and the conventional pretext no longer worked, he invented a new one which, true to the reversal of circumstances, was the very antithesis of the old.

At this point the first paradox, the reversal of goal, merges with the second, the shift of rationale. The anti-Semite, as we have already pointed out, is forever under the necessity of advancing some excuse for his prejudice. And it must be a good one—good enough to enable him to indulge with a clear conscience in a mean and nasty sport. Little wonder then that many an anti-Semite has in one lifetime outlived a whole succession of rationalizations, and that, over the centuries, mankind has done likewise.

Indeed, all through the past hundred years or so, anti-Semitism has been pretty much a prejudice in search of a pretext. Before that time, religion had supplied the classic excuse. The Jew was persecuted, it was supposed, because of his stubborn rejection of the Christ. But the day came when this device stopped working. In the wake of scientific discoveries and industrial inventions a new phenomenon appeared—the non-Jew who was himself not a Christian, who also refused to acknowledge the Christ as Saviour. As soon as such secularized Christians became numerous, as they were by the time of the French Revolution, it was no longer possible to condemn in Jews an attitude shared by non-Jews also. Besides, in small but increasing numbers some Jews were ready to become Christians, or at the least to undergo baptism. Quite obviously a fresh indictment, containing novel charges, had to be drawn in lieu of the classic bill of complaints. A new reason had to be improvised for disliking Jews, and that quickly, or the dislike would be exposed in all its senselessness.

The first attempt to satisfy this so urgent need was the theory of Christian Nationalism, propounded by Friedrich Ruhs, professor at the University of Berlin, protagonist during post-Napoleonic days of a return to the *ancien régime* and enthusiastic advocate of the re-establishment of the Ghetto. Professor Ruhs took cognizance of the de-Christianization of many Gentiles. He deprecated that development but declared it irrelevant so far as Jews went. For, no matter what the individual might do, the state, he contended, remained a Christian institution, based on Christian sanctions, allied officially with the Church, dedicated to the preservation and embodiment of Christian ideals. And if that were so, Jews had no portion in it. It was an inspiration, this idea of Ruhs and others like him. It sought ingeniously to retain Christianity as a sanction for anti-Semitism if for nothing else.

Clever, it was not clever enough. For, as the nineteenth century wore on, the process of secularization went on apace. An increasing proportion of the people of Europe ceased to be Christian in any significant sense. It became ever more artificial to claim for the state a character which so many of its citizens did not exhibit. What is more, the movement toward the disestablishment of national churches was gaining momentum. The state was divesting itself of Christian associations. Most disturbing of all, many passionate anti-Semites were irreligious, even antireligious. With what grace or logic could they employ Christianity as a club against Jews? Some new scheme, transparently, was required.

So toward the middle of the century still another doctrine came into vogue, not Christian nationalism now, but nationalism unqualified and unhyphenated. Under this theory man lived to serve his country. But the various nations were uneasy neighbors. They threatened one another's borders, possessions, colonies and markets. At any moment war might break out among them. The state, then, contended the nationalists within each country, must be strong. It must be characterized by a monolithical unity of thought, feeling, culture and ethnic origin. Otherwise it would be able neither to win for itself a place in the sun, nor to defend such positions as it already held. And that, of course, ruled the Jews out of the picture. For the Jews were of foreign racial stock and of alien culture. They were therefore incapable of true patriotism, of complete and unreserved attachment to the national community.

This in essence was the case of Heinrich von Treitschke, of Adolf Stöcker, of those who railroaded Dreyfus into a penal colony and of a host of lesser lights. But it also was not good enough. It was, in the first instance, too complex and intellectualistic, too hard to understand, to serve as a ground for a mass mood. And it was equally too vulnerable. The European Jews were, as Jews have been pretty generally when permitted, staunch patriots. That fact they could establish without difficulty. There were records of enlistments in the Franco-German War to be cited, casualty lists to be quoted, medals for valor to be exhibited. And as for Jews being harmful to the state, not even Stöcker, though he was court chaplain to the German Emperor, could make that seem plausible at a time when one Jew, Albert Ballin, was building the German merchant marine, and so many others were unmistakably strengthening the German state and enhancing its glory.

The plight of anti-Semitism just before the turn of the present century was truly sad. By that time it had, for reasons soon to be presented, long been in the ascendency. And yet at the very moment of impending triumph it found itself without an ideological leg to stand on. Human passions, however, are not easily frustrated. Thrice defeated in its efforts to achieve a rationale, anti-Semitism was soon off on another, and this time more successful, attempt. It found and adapted to its own use the concept of race.

The theory which emerged has been so widely publicized and is so generally known that it scarcely requires restatement here. Succinctly put, it holds that as there are breeds of dogs, so there are races of men; that of these races the Aryan Nordic peoples are by natural endowment physically the strongest, ethically the noblest and intellectually the brightest; the Jews on the other hand are a low ethnic type, being inferior in body, devious in mind and perverse in spirit; that both the excellences of the former and the corruptions of the latter are biological traits, inborn and indelible; that the Jews are a constant threat to the health, corporeal, psychic and social, of the groups among whom they live; that to this impasse there can be only one solution, the removal of the Jewish menace either by quarantine or extermination.

This entire argument, as has been demonstrated times beyond number, is so much nonsense. There are no pure-blooded races, history having done a pretty thorough job of mixing up the various biological strains. No people is uniformly possessed of any particular physical characteristic, be it size or shape of skull, color or texture of hair. If any one people did reveal some bodily trait peculiar to itself, it would still have to be demonstrated that that trait was somehow correlated with a particular quality of the mind or spirit. Last of all, individuals of all backgrounds when subjected to the same environmental influences and stimuli exhibit on the whole pretty much the same capacity for any given intellectual or emotional interest, whether it be science, music or ethical idealism.

The new line taken by anti-Semitism in recent years is therefore a sequence of errors and frauds, bound together by shoddy logic. Yet it is perfectly suited to the purposes for which it was designed. It converts an irrational prejudice into a kind of social hygiene. It transforms the anti-Semite from a hoodlum into a physician fighting a dread disease. It possesses the added virtue of offering no loopholes for individual Jews. Under every antecedent rationale, some Jews had to be accepted. When anti-Semitism stood on religious grounds, the Jewish convert to Christianity could not be rejected. When national interest served as the justification, room had to be accorded the indisputably patriotic Jew. But this latest doctrine blocks out from society every Jew no matter what his character, career or attainments. For it operates on the premise that the fault lies not in will, thought or action but in the very fact of Jewishness.

It is impressive too, with all its paraphernalia of statistical tables, skull measurements and historical research. Yet at the same time it is easily comprehensible. The illiterate person need not understand its subtleties. What it says in effect is what he has always insisted on: namely, that there is something inherently wrong with Jews, no matter how decent they appear. It is moreover a contention that stirs passion, with its hair-raising suggestions of contagious disease and corruption of the bloodstream. And, most important of all, it justifies every cruelty. It makes the Jews out as lepers whose foul touch must be averted no matter by what means. It is in sum, in everything except truthfulness and tenability, the perfect apologia for anti-Semitism, that ideal rationalization after which the hate-driven have been groping for a century and more.

But why a new excuse just at this juncture? After all, the period from the beginning of the last century to the outbreak of the First World War was one of increasing physical comfort, of advancing science and letters, of mounting prosperity, of ever higher literacy among all the peoples of the West. The impulse toward group antagonisms should have ebbed, and with it the need for rationalizations. How then shall we account for a development the reverse of all reasonable expectations? At this point we come to grips with the third of our paradoxes—the recrudescence of a primitive passion in an era of enlightenment.

It is by now a matter of common knowledge that all was not gold in that glittering world before 1914; underneath its glow of health, fevers raged. Diseases were abroad among men, no less dangerous because they went unnoticed at the time. Of these, three in particular served to aggravate anti-Semitism.

For the past hundred years, Western Europe has been on the downgrade economically. Prior to that time it had served as both the workshop and counting house of the world. Increasingly, as the century went on, lands that had been markets to European factories established their own industries, and debtor nations drifted toward self-reliance. The foundations supporting Europe's standard of living grew ever narrower. At the same time, opportunities and outlets for emigration dwindled. The old territories of settlement, the former dumping grounds of surplus populations, were now well settled. A contracting economy, and no escape for the dispossessed and underprivileged—can one conceive of a situation more likely to call ancient hatreds into new life?

To confound this already unhappy confusion, the process of urbanization, so long productive of blessings, went awry. Ever since the Industrial Revolution there had been a drift from the countryside to the cities. Most of the new inhabitants of industrial centers turned to factories and workshops for a livelihood. But a fair portion of them entered middle-class occupations, becoming clerks, shopkeepers, accountants, jobbers and civil servants. These, however, were just the areas of economic enterprise in which Jews had long been concentrated. Out of the ensuing clash of interests came almost inevitably an accentuation of anti-Semitism.

This process, common to all European lands, is to be observed with unusual clarity in Poland. In that country Jews had constituted for over five hundred years a large part of the *bourgeoisie*. To this end the kings of medieval Poland had solicited their immigration. But in the latter half of the nineteenth century Polish young people began to desert farms for the cities. The countryside could no longer sustain them; America was closing its doors. And if the urban pursuits they were entering had long been pre-empted by Jews, so much the worse for Jews. From their peasant background they derived a predisposition toward anti-Semitism; in fierce competition on the streets of Warsaw and Lodz their inclinations were confirmed.

Parallel with these economic mechanisms, and in no slight measure an expression of them, ran a second influence adverse to the position of Jews. For all the triumphs of democracy during the nineteenth century, the forces of reaction were still not done for. Quietly, imperceptibly they were busy mustering their strength for a counterattack. The advocates of the *ancien régime*, in some instances out of selfish interest, in others out of idealism, had steadfastly refused to make peace with the French Revolution and what it represented.

About these focuses new groups clustered—capitalist and middle-class elements, afraid of discontented masses, and therefore eager to deprive them of the weapons which democracy had put into their hands; *petits bourgeois* trapped in obscurity and genteel poverty, and hence, to use the old Ciceronian phrase, *cupidi rerum novarum;* laboring men disillusioned with political parties and parliaments as instruments for social reform. The powers of reaction gained in strength.

At the same time enthusiasm for the democratic process ebbed steadily. The bloom was off this fruit which had been plucked two generations earlier with such high expectations. Men forgot how terrible absolutism had been. They knew only the present evils of a free political order—that it was slow and cumbersome, that it operated with such a din of debate and controversy, that it seemed so feeble and dilatory before the vast economic problems of the modern world.

Over and beyond this, there must be recorded, at least as a possibility, a revolution in the general human temper. No one knows but that there is among men in the mass an oscillation of mood akin to that in individuals. Such a notion becomes at least plausible when one considers fluctuations of fashion, the alternation throughout history between moral indulgence and asceticism, between convention and revolt; the rhythmical swing of literature from classicism to romanticism and back again. If there be such a pendulum movement to the collective human spirit, then it may well be that the latter nineteenth century was a time when the balance wheel, having moved far toward libertarian values, began to swing toward the opposite pole.

In any case, the period after the revolution of '48 reveals in retrospect a large-scale reaction against democracy. And with the repudiation of democracy went also the abandonment of all its works—including, among others, the emancipation of the Jew. It is then no accident that social reaction is so closely associated with anti-Semitism. For to rebel against the democratic spirit is to rebel against the freedom and equality it brought to all minority groups, the Jews not least among them.

The economic miseries of our industrial civilization and its political disillusionments would by themselves have been sufficient to superinduce in thousands of men a sense of frustration. Those who hungered amid plenty and saw no hope of a better condition, those who had believed in democracy but could envisage no prospect of its triumph over social problems would most naturally turn bitter. But another development also contributed to the distillation of a widespread distemper. The historic religions had lost their meaning for millions of modern men. Yet when the old gods went, no new gods came to supplant them. The individual was left ravaged by confusion and futility. He became, along with tens of millions of his fellows, the typical modern man—the man who does not know what he shall believe or do, who is uncertain as to what is true and false, good or evil, and what the whole business of living is about.

But bewilderment and frustration are great vexations. They are torment of the soul as difficult to endure as those of the body, and as strongly evoca tive of irritability and resentments. Happy men are likely not to hate Frustrated men almost always do and, if they hate hard enough, they wil find release somehow. At which point the Jew conveniently enters the pictur once more, this time as the butt of a general malaise of the human spirit

The great eruption of anti-Semitism in our time is therefore altogethe intelligible. All through the centuries, it has been building up steadily: ir an unbroken flow of indoctrination against the Jews; in economic conflic and adversity; in psychological mechanisms of dislike for the unlike, o scapegoatism and perhaps of rebellion against the Christ personality; anc in deliberate manipulations of which scarcely a single generation failed to produce some instance.

Even in the enlightened and humanitarian decades just past, this proces of storing up the dynamites of antipathy continued, less overtly but more dangerously. For among the materials deposited in the subterranean maga zines below the level of decency were some of extraordinary inflammability —the inordinately acute economic impasse of modern Europe, its ideologica reaction, and the psychical embitterments of contemporary man.

The Nazis are of course not free from personal guilt for the cataclysm they engineered. But in a sense they were for Germany, as Germany was for the world, no more than a percussion cap, a flash of fire setting off explosives accumulated among all peoples and throughout the ages.

3

Anti-Semitism—Nostrums and Remedies

WHAT CAN JEWS DO to defend themselves against anti-Semitism?
For those of Germany and of Central Europe, this question is
meaningless. In their case it is too late to avert the catastrophe.
All that is possible is to mitigate its consequences. But the Jews who live in
America and in other democratic lands are in an infinitely more fortunate
position. They have freedom of action; they can still influence events and
incline the course of destiny. Facing a present not altogether favorable,
raced against a future over which they have some reason to be apprehensive, what policy are they pursuing, what tactic have they adopted in their
efforts to preserve themselves?

The answer to this query is simple: American Jewry has no program for
repelling the danger that impends. In fact, strictly speaking, there is no
American Jewry, if by that phrase is meant an integrated community possessed of organs for the determination of its will. There are only individual
American Jews, 5,000,000 of them, without rabbinical hierarchy, recognized
leadership or high command to direct them. Each Jew then enjoys the
questionable privilege of acting on his own. Or, what is little better, he
may affiliate himself with one of the several loosely organized and mutually
competitive associations seeking to deal with the problem.

Yet in the face of a peril, potentially so grave, American Jews have almost
to the last man given some attention to it and arrived at some conclusion
concerning it. Current among them is the widest variety of opinions as to
how anti-Semitism is best to be understood and dealt with. These theories
and proposals, as might be expected, are of unequal merit. Some are the
products of hasty and superficial thinking. Others reflect careful observation and analysis.

Unfortunately, it is the former, the formulas of frenzy as they may well be

65

denominated, which enjoy the widest vogue, constituting for anti-Semitis
what nostrums represent in hygiene. For like all human beings who fin
themselves pressed by an urgent issue, Jews are prone to cast about for ea
explanations and most obvious remedies. Their tendency to think hurried
and grasp at straws is the more understandable because so much is at sta
for them, because further, the time at their disposal may be short.

Common to all the folk strategies are a premise and an inference: t
premise that Jews are themselves responsible for the ills they endure, ar
the inference that their position can be improved only by modifying the
behavior. Such a conclusion has a kind of logic to justify it: the world cor
plains against a group of people, *ergo* there must be something wrong wi
them. Regardless of the tenability of this reasoning there are Jews ar
Gentiles in numbers who are convinced of its validity. The only moot poir
as they see it, is the specific trait or deficiency in Jews that occasions t
difficulty. On this score they divide into three schools of thought. Son
blame the conspicuousness of Jews, especially in public affairs; others the
alleged bad manners and social gracelessness; and still others the fact th
thanks to their religion and group cohesion, they stand out as different fro
those among whom they live.

Naturally enough, the home remedies reflect the folk diagnoses. If Jewi
conspicuousness be assumed as the cause of the disease, then inconspicuou
ness must be the cure; if bad manners, then a heightened concern with t
amenities; and if difference, then its elimination. Each tactic is then
the first instance a deduction from a premise.

It is dictated also by a certain commonsensical realism, quite independe
of all theoretical interpretations. For the Jews are a small group surround
by a mass of Gentiles, potentially hostile to them and too numerous to
resisted in pitched battle. What courses are open to them? Let us imagi
an individual in similar circumstances. Such a person, it would seem, c
run to cover; can try to avoid irritating those he fears, to behave in
exemplary a manner that they shall find no pretext to set themselves up
him; or can attempt to imitate them so faithfully that they shall mista
him for one of their number.

In other words, both folk diagnoses and what appears to be comm
sense unite in suggesting three procedures—self-suppression, self-correcti
and, so to speak, self-Gentilization. Let us examine these in turn.

There are in America prominent Jewish bankers, manufacturers, authors, physicians, dramatists, lawyers and what not. There was a time when Jews were pleased with the success of their fellows, when they felt that it reflected creditably on their group. Then they hailed with joy the literary achievement of their authors, the discoveries of their scientists, and the fame of their famous men generally. More recently they have become uneasy about all, feeling that conspicuous attainments serve nowadays to rouse resentment. As they see it, the greater the number of Jews who climb high and the higher they climb, the more noticeable they become, the more inviting target they present. It has, in fact, become almost a Jewish folk dogma that anti-Semitism is largely an expression of Christian jealousy.

The truth of the matter is that Jews have been by no means so uniformly successful as is commonly supposed. The most that can be said accurately is that some Jews have done very well in some fields, and moderately well in others. There are many areas of great economic and social importance into which Jews have not penetrated at all. Moreover, the great masses of Jews, as a visit to any Ghetto will demonstrate, are no better off than the run of mankind. The advocates of the policy of inconspicuousness are well aware of all this. They disregard it on the ground that what matters is not the facts, but the Gentile's idea of the facts.

Let us also and for a moment disregard actualities. Let us grant further the dubious contention that "Jewish success," real or supposed, makes anti-Semitism. What, when all this is conceded, can be done about it? The answer is: nothing. Even if the Jewish community were efficiently organized and well disciplined, as it is not, it could not prevent a Jewish high-school student from capturing honors, a scientist from executing a piece of research, a musician from playing well, an author from writing a good book, or a merchant from conducting his business efficiently. And if it could inhibit any of these developments, it ought not, on moral grounds alone, to attempt it.

On one score the advocates of Jewish inconspicuousness are most zealous. They insist, beyond all else, that Jews must not hold public office. No one, they argue, presents so easy a target for invidious attack, no one invites jealousy so largely as the person in political life. Every Jew in office, they believe, jeopardizes all his fellows. And it is an open secret that in this spirit some of America's most "substantial" Jews opposed the appointment of Mr. Morgenthau to the Cabinet, and of Mr. Frankfurter to the Supreme

Court. This Jewish fear of the Jew in politics is, moreover, not entirely unfounded. The honest mistakes of a Jewish officeholder are more likely to be misinterpreted than those of a Gentile. And should he slip morally, the anti-Semite is certain to make capital of his lapse.

Once again, there is nothing that Jews collectively can do to keep Jews individually out of politics. And once again, even if the Jewish group possessed such control over its members, it ought not to exercise it. In fact, the policy of self-suppression is in this specific area, as in others, totally devoid of merit. It is, in the first place, a tactic of suicide. For, if it be once granted that out of caution Jews ought to withdraw from public life, then by the same logic they ought to retreat from just about everything else. The Jewish governor of some state is doubtless in a conspicuous position, but so too is the Jewish banker, clothing manufacturer, physician or motion-picture magnate. A Gentile walking down the main street of some American city may be little mindful of the Jewishness of a member of the Supreme Court of the United States. He cannot help reading the names over the doors of department stores. In brief, the policy of inconspicuousness would, if followed to its logical consequences, imply the renunciation of every desirable activity. It would amount to the Jew cutting his own throat in order to forestall the remote possibility of somebody else someday cutting it for him.

And this strategy is, finally, irreconcilable with American idealism. If Americanism means anything at all, it means that all individuals shall have equal opportunity to find self-fulfillment. This dream has not yet achieved perfect realization. It remains nonetheless the very soul of our democracy. For the Jew to try to save himself by self-suppression is in effect an admission that Americanism no longer functions. It is a betrayal therefore of our national spirit, an act of treason the more shameful because it is neither necessary nor efficacious.

In the over-all policy of inconspicuousness, one special variant merits a moment's attention. There is another kind of prominence over which some Jews are uneasy and which many would like to obviate—the unwelcome attention that comes to them as a result of the radicalism of some of their fellows. The argument runs that, whenever a Jew is a Communist, or a social dissenter of whatever brand, he causes Gentiles to become conscious of Jews as disturbing elements in communal life. Anti-Semitism, supposedly, is the result. Hence many Jews hold that neither they nor their fellows have the right to unconventional attitudes. In the main, in taking this position they have Communism, Socialism or New Dealism in mind. But they may include any bold stand on any heated controversy. So, just before Pearl Harbor some Jews were very busy urging on Jewish isolationists and interventionists alike the wisdom of holding their tongues.

Now in truth, Jews are not especially predisposed toward advanced opinions. On the contrary, they are as a whole quite conventional. I state this fact not to applaud it. To me it is an occasion for some disappointment. From the heirs of the prophets, better is to be expected than complacency. Approval or deprecation aside, Jews are pretty much a middle-class, urban group, exhibiting attitudes, interests and ambitions typical to their station.

But even if it were to be demonstrated that a disproportionate number of Jews are radicals, what, it may well be asked, can the Jewish group be expected to do about it? It lacks the power to coerce social heretics into orthodoxy. And if it possessed the power, the ethical propriety of its use would be, to say the least, profoundly questionable. In this application as in all others, the strategy of inconspicuousness turns out worthless. It rests on doubtful assumptions of fact, leads nowhere in practice, and is throughout under a cloud of moral suspicion.

Just a little can be said for the second popular alternative—the correction of the manners of Jews. Jews, the advocates of this course assert, are often crude, noisy, vulgar and unrefined. They argue with headwaiters and ushers, they overdress, they raise their voices in public. The Gentile observes with distaste and becomes an anti-Semite. Let Jews become impeccably polite; the Gentile, no longer annoyed by exhibitions of vulgarity, soothed rather by the courtliness of refashioned Jews, will decide that they are decent human beings after all, and treat them accordingly.

This, then, is the doctrine of Jewish salvation according to the revelation of Emily Post—and unspeakably ingenuous it is. It proceeds, in the first instance, from a silly premise—that the conduct of Jews is, as a whole, worse than that of others. For this assumption there is no evidence whatever. To be sure, the first generation of Jewish immigrants to this country, like all other newcomers, may be unfamiliar with its amenities. But that means only that their manners, derived from another code, are different, not that they are bad. In any case, their children and even more their children's children, molded by a new world, turn out quite indistinguishable in both their graces and gaucheries from other Americans.

Nor does this theory take cognizance of the fact that the most violen
explosion of anti-Semitism in history was directed against the urbane an
polished Jewry of Germany, or the further fact that in America the cult
vated Jew is as much victimized by prejudice as the boor. Finally the entir
notion of a reform of manners as a cure for the Jewish problem would seer
to imply only one program—the setting up of schools of etiquette amon
Jews. So far as I know, no one has earnestly made this proposal. Perhap
the restraining factor is that while many Jews profess this doctrine, no Je
is ready to admit that his are the bad manners. Where then will pupils b
found?

The last of the folk programs is that of deliberate disguise. It asks for
change of labels and uniforms, a sort of mass turncoating. It demands tha
Jews become so much like Gentiles that the latter will come to regard ther
as members of their own group. Like its two fellow programs, this on
springs from a philosophy of anti-Semitism. It finds the causes of hostilit
to Jews in the fact that their names are unusual, and so too are their mode
of worship. They maintain philanthropies of their own. They associat
largely with one another and marry among themselves. In brief, they ar
a group apart.

This is the analysis. The inference is that Jews must cease to be disturb
ingly different. They must strip from themselves all distinctively Jewis
characteristics. On how far the Jew must go in remaking himself there i
little agreement. Some feel that he need eliminate only external and flagran
differences; others demand that he recast his very soul. The program ther
ranges in scope from changing names and minor habits, all the way t
complete self-de-Judaization. With assimilation as an approach to the entir
Jewish problem we shall deal elsewhere. For the moment we are concerne
with it only as a tactic for dealing with anti-Semitism.

How efficacious is this strategy likely to be—the chameleon's strategy, a
it may fairly be called? It should be observed before we go farther tha
Jews like other Americans have tended spontaneously and naturally to tak
on the American coloration. Within the very first generation of migratio
to the New World, they have almost without exception adopted the Englis
tongue, the governmental ideals and behavior patterns of American life
And there is no Jew who is anything but sympathetic to this development
The issue is not, and never has been, whether the Jew should be Ameri

nized. The question is not Americanization but de-Judaization, and its
power to neutralize anti-Semitism.

To this end, I am convinced, de-Judaization is ineffective. In the first
place, the great masses of Jews, ready though they be to surrender the
trivia of Judaism, will not give up its central values—its religious outlook,
ethical aspirations, important ritual forms and major cultural motifs. Of
this, thanks to their loyalty to the tradition of their fathers, they are incapable. Nor is it required by the democratic process.

But even if the proponents of this procedure were working with more
tractable materials than the Jews, they would still have set themselves to a
futile enterprise. For if they seek salvation in the elimination of lesser Jewish traits, the perseverance of anti-Semitism in America, where such differ-
entials have already largely been eliminated, frustrates their hopes. If they
have pinned their faith on total assimilation, then the precedent of Germany
confounds them. There Jewry had achieved a measure of assimilation unequaled in any other land. So far as anti-Semitism went, to no avail.
Obviously the advocates of de-Judaization have drastically misread the
problem of group tensions. They assume that anti-Semitism is occasioned
by the Jew's loyalty to Judaism, that it springs from his refusal to go over
to the majority, lock, stock and barrel. That circumstance may furnish an
excuse for a bias; it is not its cause.

All the folk programs alike share in one defect: a staggering naïveté as to
the true causes of anti-Semitism. These, we have seen, are broad, deep, and
lodged near the very heart of modern man and his society. The believers in
samples and nostrums take a more cheerful view of the situation. Assuming
that the disease is only skin-deep, they are confident that it can be cured
with salves. Misinformed as to who is sick and in what member, they apply
their remedies not merely to the wrong parts but to the wrong bodies. Which
means that in the end all these popular therapies are a waste of time, a misdirection of energy, and, gravest of all, a diversion of attention from the
true causes of the malady.

Least pardonable in them is that they are destructive of the self-respect of
Jews. To tell the members of a group that they must move always on tip-
toe, and then only through the bypaths of life; that they are by nature
unpleasant human beings, and must therefore never cease remaking themselves; that they must slough an ancient and honorable tradition is to ask
innocent people to behave like criminals. Let the advocates of such programs

once have their way with the Jews, and it will be a sorry day. For the resul
will be not to affect the course of anti-Semitism, but to strip Jews of th
sense of their own worth.

Rejecting the folk remedies, we turn to consider afresh our original ques
tion: what can Jewry do to protect itself against anti-Semitism?

Education is the first of the more constructive procedures. Anti-Semitism
be it remembered, is in part the consequence of an educational process, o
oblique indoctrination and deliberate propaganda. A process of counter
education is therefore clearly indicated. This should follow a number o
converging lines. By every available means and at every propitious momen
the attempt must be made, first, to dispel misconceptions of the Jews by
disseminating the truth concerning them; second, to refute the canards circu
lated by professional anti-Semites; third, to inhibit the inculcation of anti
Semitic attitudes at their sources, by sifting out of Sunday-school textbook
passages that implant hostility to Jews, by putting parents and clergymen or
guard against those random utterances through which social antagonism
are so often transmitted, and by purging literature of attitudes conduciv
to group prejudice; fourth, to uncover the nature and the ulterior purpose
of anti-Semitic propaganda and propagandists, to reveal, for example, tha
anti-Semitism has served as a cover for Nazi activities in this country
that it is the front for native fascism in almost all its forms, to estab
lish in the popular mind the awareness that racialism is un-American an
antidemocratic.

Concerned with just these enterprises are various agencies. Some of these—
the American Jewish Committee, the American Jewish Congress, the anti
Defamation League of the B'nai B'rith, the Jewish Labor Committee—ar
entirely Jewish in composition. Others, such as the National Conference o
Christians and Jews, are interdenominational. Still others are under exclu
sively Christian auspices. Unfortunately, there is much less co-ordinatio
among these organizations than is to be desired. In the case of the variou
Jewish agencies, which naturally carry the major part of the burden, thi
condition has been a virtual calamity.

We shall consider this unhappy situation at some length when we discus
the structure of the American Jewish community. For the present, let m
say only that the disunity of American Jewry is not as near total as it onc
was. In the National Community Relations Advisory Council, for example

promising experiment in interorganizational co-operation is under way. Nevertheless, and despite recent gains, integration of effort is still a hope rather than an effective reality. Against every prospectus for countereducation against anti-Semitism, no matter how glowing, must be pitted the truth that the best program is worthless unless it rests in hands large, skillful and strong enough for it.

Other difficulties, too, stand in the way of neutralizing anti-Semitism through an appeal to reason. Group prejudices are often deeply ingrained and stubbornly held. No lone meeting, no isolated lecture, no single piece of literature can affect them. They are, moreover, widely diffused. It will not be sufficient therefore to work on small groups or limited segments of our population. Only mass education broad, sustained and intense, can leave discernible imprint.

What is more, the best education has its limitations. It is scarcely likely to budge an emotionally convinced anti-Semite, whose antagonism lies below consciousness, at levels where reason cannot penetrate. One can no more argue with obsessive anti-Semitism than with claustrophobia or paranoia. Jews, in other words, ought to recognize realistically and in advance that some of anti-Semitism is beyond the reach of normal educational processes, and will respond, if at all, only to psychiatry.

All this means only that no panacea for the ailment exists, that too much must not be expected from any single course of treatment. To balance the score be it noted that if prejudices are occasionally too deep for easy correction, very often there are either no prejudices or only the faintest suggestion of them. In such instances cures and immunizations are possible. Granted then that countereducation is far from a cure-all, it remains an important ameliorative nevertheless.

There is still another device whereby Jews may exert some influence on anti-Semitism. Group tension, it will be recalled, has among its sources the dislike of the unlike. Now the Jews are in some respects different from Gentiles. To the unique aspects of their group life and tradition they are entitled without apology. Besides, not difference is the irritant, but difference that is not understood, the disquiet which arises from mystification. The closer Jews and Gentiles are knit, intellectually and socially, the less the malaise between them. Whence it follows that every healthy, normal association between the two groups is so much to the good.

Mutual relationships, however, must be natural to be beneficial. There i
not the least point in dragging masses of Jews and Gentiles together witl
the instruction, tacit or expressed, that they are to achieve mutual under
standing. An artificial situation can be productive only of awkwardness an
estrangement. Yet once again the fact that this tactic is not all-conquerin;
does not neutralize its efficacy when wisely applied. With every sponta
neous friendship across group lines, every free meeting, every unforce
exchange of opinions and attitudes, some suspicion is dispelled. When sucl
encounters are multiplied by millions, their total influence is far fron
negligible.

Jews and Gentiles come together most auspiciously when they meet fc
shared purposes. The two groups have many interests in common. Botl
taken as units, are concerned equally with maintaining their respectiv
religious traditions against secularism, with the problems of good goverr
ment, with the survival of democracy, with the achievement of a human
and equitable economy, with the attainment of a just and durable peac
among nations, with, in brief, man's struggle to remake reality after th
ideal. It is when Jews and Gentiles labor together for the ends both group
cherish that mutual insight is most likely to be fostered. Here is no art
ficiality, but the naturalness of men striving shoulder to shoulder for th
same purposes.

No matter what the absorption in education, in the breaching of barrier
between groups, one elementary yet cardinal truth must never be obscurec
Anti-Semitism is an evil thing to be fought. Alongside the courses we hav
already outlined, a third must be charted. Jews should resist anti-Semitisr
with every tool, skill and energy at their disposal.

The law is their ally. They ought to avail themselves of it to the ful
Where anti-Semitism takes the form of hoodlumism, Jews must not hes
tate to call on the police and the courts. There will be cases where th
Jew-baiters are hardened ruffians. Let them be tried and sent to jail. Mor
often the offenders will be misled adults or youngsters on the loose. Her
it is the duty of municipality and state to provide corrective education an
to see to it that it is brought home to those who need it. Under no circum
stance should anyone be allowed to assail or insult Jews with impunit
Nor should Jews hesitate in the slightest to apply political pressure o
mayors, chiefs of police or superintendents of education who prove lack.

daisical about enforcing order or fostering it. It is the business of government to keep public peace and to protect law-abiding persons.

By the same token, no Jew ought to allow himself to be libeled or slandered *as a Jew*. As an individual he may swallow in silence any insults he can stomach; as a member of a group, stringency rather than leniency is his course. For now more than his own honor may be involved. At balance may be nothing less than the dignity of all Jews. Every serious misrepresentation of Jews ought therefore to be nailed as soon as issued. Should it express inadvertence or ignorance, its author should be carefully and considerately set to rights. When it is the work of malice, the law against slander and libel ought resolutely to be invoked.

Public opinion too is, on the whole, opposed to racial discrimination both in principle and as a matter of public welfare. This means that new legislation, federal and state, to protect Americans in their rights can be secured. It is possible, for example, and I am convinced most necessary, to establish codes of fair-employment practice and agencies for their enforcement. It is possible and necessary to outlaw the dissemination of group prejudice from all public mediums. Newspapers, for example, should be enjoined against accepting advertisements of a discriminatory character; hotels and restaurants from debarring persons because of race, creed or color; common carriers, railroads, ships, busses and planes, from practicing Jim-Crowism in any form.

One further proposal designed to shield minorities is so far-reaching and moot that I must pause over it. I have in mind the recommendation often put forth that propagation of group prejudice be declared a crime, that all incitement to hatred because of race, creed or color be made punishable in law. Over this a powerful case can be made in either direction. The weight of the argument, however, seems to me to lie—not by much and yet by enough to be decisive—with the affirmative.

As we have learned recently and to our grief, there is nothing innocent or trivial about mass antagonisms. They are not what they have so often been mistaken for—private, innocuous vagaries. To the contrary, they are consuming fires, veritable pests. We who have just suffered one outbreak of the plague can ill afford to view with indifference the possibility of its recurrence.

Against a danger so real and imminent every nation must be on guard.

Somehow it must contrive to keep the peril within bounds. Now legislation cannot control ideas and emotions. There is, for example, no known device by which society can prevent men from thinking homicidal thoughts. But the community can and does forbid the execution of murderous deeds or their incitement.

By the same token, the state cannot enact affection between Gentiles and Jews. What non-Jews think about their Jewish fellows is legally their own business. But how non-Jews behave in this respect is another matter, and one of more than private concern. Not only the welfare of the Jews, the tranquillity of the community and perhaps ultimately the peace of the world may be involved. In the teeth of these considerations it is arrant nonsense to contend that the state has no interest in restraining agitation against racial, cultural or religious groupings in its midst.

But what of civil liberties, of the right of any free man to criticize anything or anybody? Would not legislation against the inculcation of anti-Semitism spell the end of this most precious of privileges? That this would be the effect has been the contention of many best spirits and most devoted lovers of freedom in our time. They regard the remedy as worse than the disease, holding that any legislation designed to inhibit racialist agitation will in the end endanger the classic democratic freedoms.

I too believe in civil rights and in the ability of the truth to vindicate itself in the long run against all perversion and misrepresentation. I am furthermore aware of the risks inhering in any measure that limits expression. Yet I know that even now freedom of speech is not absolute, that the state will silence me if what I say is libelous, salacious and indecent, or if it moves others to riot or revolution. Nor do I feel my freedom to be seriously challenged by such restraints. In borderline cases I trust judges and the people to whom they are responsible to distinguish between legitimate speech and its abuse, a method that has worked fairly well, most of us, I think, will agree. If our liberty is already qualified, and without disastrous consequences, for the sake of social well-being, why can it not be hedged also to prevent an explosion of racialism? In sum, I would like to see every government, including our own, promulgate legislation carefully drafted to protect freedom of expression yet designed to make assault upon minority groups an offense against the state. Here too is a job to which Jews together with others may well put their hands.

Perhaps I ought to add that in urging Jews to resist anti-Semitism determinedly I do not intend that they shall put chips on their shoulders and turn truculent, or encourage hypersensitivity in themselves. Excesses and degenerations of self-respect are to be avoided like the plague.

Nor could the course of resistance here recommended be of much avail against a tidal upsurge of anti-Semitism. The Jews are not only a minority, they are in Western lands a small minority. Their strength and social influence are therefore limited. But a virulent anti-Semitism, too, has weak beginnings. There is a period in its growth when it has not yet attained its full diffusion and bitterness. At this stage, it may be relatively easy to nip it in the bud. And for that purpose, the resources of the Jews, especially when reinforced by those of Gentiles of good will, may well be adequate.

Even when the disease has become epidemic, even when there is no wisdom, counsel or power left to the Jews by which they may withstand it, they ought still to put up a game fight. For when all else is lost, honor and self-respect may still be saved. And it is the part of human dignity not to acquiesce in an injustice. The gesture of protest may be futile. It should be made nonetheless, if not for its effect on the situation, then for its own inherent rightfulness.

The Jews should be further emboldened in that they do not defend themselves alone. Anti-Semitism, as we shall see, threatens the ultimate decencies of civilized man. To oppose it is therefore to enlist in a high cause. Over such an assignment there should be no hesitation; from such a position there can be, no matter how grim and hopeless the prospect, no withdrawal.

The attainment of a greater measure of economic security for all is still another method whereby Jews can assure their safety. Anti-Semitism, it will be remembered, is in considerable measure the consequence of the normal competition for a livelihood, especially of the embittered struggle for survival that goes with general social distress. Where the roots of a disease lie, there the remedies must be applied. The economic system being a cause, its improvement is a clearly indicated corrective.

If the insecurities that plague men can be eliminated, if freer access to good things can be won for them, if the poverty and frustration that cripple them can be mitigated if, on the economist's graph, the alternation of high curves of prosperity and deep valleys of want can be flattened into a straight line pitched high in the scale of satisfactions and opportunities—then not only shall a great contribution have been made to human welfare but the motive power behind antagonisms, racial, religious, cultural and national, shall have been abated.

The implications of this analysis are obvious. The Jews must put themselves behind every well-considered program that seeks, within the framework of the democratic process, to humanize the economic order. Save through the breaching of the great impasses of economics, they have no hope for the continuance of their present freedom or for a brighter future. To be sure, the achievement of a juster society is the obligation of all men. Yet it devolves upon the Jews with especial directness. For theirs is most immediately the heritage of the prophets and sages who centuries ago first cried out against communal iniquity and earliest saw the vision of a Kingdom of God on earth. The tradition of the Jews unites with their self-interest in making the good society very intimately their concern.

Here then is another remedy for anti-Semitism, but, be it observed, only one among several, and then a remedy not a cure. It is at this point that Marxists in general and Communists in particular misconstrue the problem. Regarding economics as the primary determinant of all social processes, they naturally see it as the cause of anti-Semitism as well. Not as *a* cause, but as *the* cause, all other influences being secondary and derivative. Created by an economic order, anti-Semitism, they hold, will vanish only with the liquidation of that order and the attainment of a classless, noncompetitive society. In support of their case, Communists point with pride to Russia.

The pride is justified. In a land where anti-Semitism was almost pandemic the Soviet leaders undertook the Herculean labor of its extirpation. They declared anti-Jewish utterances and acts to be crimes against the state. They launched extensive and vigorous programs of education against the evil. They have stood firm in their insistence on equality of opportunity, political, economic, cultural and social, for all. Far-visioned, resourceful and determined, they have achieved a high measure of success. There is not only far less open anti-Semitism in Russia today than in any other advanced society, but, unless the evidences are misleading, much less that is covert and concealed. Not that it has been altogether eliminated. From time to time prior to Russia's entrance into the Second World War legal prosecutions of Jew-baiting were reported—a clear indication that the old Adam has not been rooted out. Yet great progress has most certainly been made.

The question remains: to this end result how much was contributed by Soviet economy? That it has been a factor of weight in the defeat of anti-Semitism in the U.S.S.R. seems undeniable. Russian Socialism, however, is as yet far from total. There is still competition among the people of the Soviet Union, competition for higher pay, better jobs and positions of power and prestige. It may be less fierce than elsewhere. But it is there, and its presence beclouds the argument that the Socialist economy alone pulled off the amazing feat.

What is more, the very procedures followed in Russia deny Marxist assumptions concerning anti-Semitism. Soviet Communism, had it been consistent with its premises, should not have bothered with the problem at all. Since economics, under its theory, was the basic cause of the evil, the remaking of the economic order should have been enough by itself. The leaders of Russia and of the Communist party have proved shrewder than their preachments. They were not content to await that automatic deliverance on which their doctrine bade them count. They went out and worked for it. They attacked anti-Semitism frontally by punishing its expression, and from the flanks by preaching and educating against it. Their very use of legislation and indoctrination constitutes an admission on their part that group prejudice, having causes other than the economic, requires more than economic reconstruction for its correction.

How much of Russia's advance on the front of group relations is to be assigned to economic factors as opposed to others? No one can say. Influences like education and fear of the policeman on one side, a co-operative social order on the other can be neither weighed nor measured.

How shall it be asserted of one: this is greater or heavier than the other? Perhaps, if we Americans went at anti-Semitism with the fervor and resolution exhibited by the Russians, we might, without remaking our social system, succeed as well as they. But then it is not my purpose to indulge in speculation on hypothetical possibilities. I am concerned right now with making a particular point: that the example of the U.S.S.R. does not confirm the Communist dogma of the single source of group prejudice.

Perhaps a word of caution and moderation is in place at this juncture. The record of Russia on anti-Semitism, as on so many other scores, is admirable. And yet, I for one—and I hope I shall not be held ungenerous for it—am waiting to see whether time will not tell. Communism in the Soviet Union is in its initial stages. It is still a new, burning vision, and its fire right now kindles the more brightly because of the terrible war in which the Russian people are acquitting themselves so heroically. But I cannot help remembering that it was so before.

The Christian in the days of the primitive church was once as fired by his Christianity, as was the democrat, during the eighteenth and nineteenth centuries, by his democratic dream. There is a time early in the evolution of an ideal when men are ready to sacrifice anything for it, even their prejudices. The test of a vision comes not when it is first conceived, nor when it is first applied, but when, having met with some success, it becomes a matter of humdrum workaday routines. Then old attitudes tend to reassert themselves. At least, so it was with Christianity and democracy—both ideologically incompatible with anti-Semitism and yet somehow acquiescent in it. Will it be so someday with Communism? I do not predict that it will. I say only that the climactic test is not yet. As the Soviet Union emerges from war conditions, as it solves its internal problems—as, in brief, it ceases to be a missionary cause and becomes instead a commonplace—only then will it be possible to judge whether it has escaped the normal waning of ardor and compromise of commitment.

Be that as it may, the Communist is mistaken about the causes of anti-Semitism. His blunder, however, is only partial; it consists in exaggerating a truth. Despite it, his position is solid at core. Economics, if not, as he holds, the sole source of group antagonisms, is nonetheless a very powerful contributant. Whence it follows that the reform of society to eliminate poverty and insecurity must stand high on the agenda of unfinished Jewish business.

There remains a final tactic for the campaign against anti-Semitism, larger and broader than any other, less indeed a tactic than a life principle for Jews. I refer to the interlinking between their destiny and the democratic process and spirit. History, at first glance, would seem to argue otherwise. It is of record that both Jewry and its tradition have lived successfully under systems other than the democratic, under the Roman Empire with its slave capitalism, under medieval feudalism, under the monarchical state, under the early and still not democratic modern industrialism. What is more, Jews, as we have just seen, appear to be thoroughly at home in the Soviet Union. A people that has managed to get along under such a variety of social forms would not seem to be tied to any one in particular.

The Jews of our day must accommodate themselves to real, not to historical or speculative possibilities. These are strictly limited in number, being in fact confined to two—the democratic and the totalitarian. The second of these means almost certainly the end of the Jewish enterprise. That is its import, even if it should disavow Nazi extremism. It is of the nature of totalitarianism that it shall allow of no other gods beside the state, ascribe to the individual no inherent rights, and assign to the minority group no status except the unhappy one of marring the national unity of blood, soil and aspiration. Under these circumstances a very hardy minority group might conceivably continue to exist; it could scarcely prosper or find its career pleasurable.

Only the democratic order, repudiating the Baal of *Gleichschaltung* and setting up in its place the ideal of self-fulfillment for all, is favorable to the welfare of minorities and to their special and differential interests. Indeed, only in a democratic order are Jews free to act in their own defense and to resist anti-Semitism. The Jewish wagon, in sum, is tightly hitched to the democratic star. It ought to be hitched there because the historic ethic of Judaism is so heavily and richly libertarian. Where idealism may falter, necessity compels. Jews must follow that star because on any other path the chances are high that they will be stripped of their spiritual baggage, if, indeed, they do not have their throats slit in the bargain.

Nor does the precedent of the Soviet Union argue to the contrary. For no matter what judgment is pronounced on Russian politics and economics, whether they are condemned as irremediably totalitarian or appraised more hopefully as potentially democratic, there can be no hesitation over Russia's treatment of its minorities. Here Russia has been unmistakably democratic, in the sense that it has recognized both *de jure* and *de facto* the right of minorities of race, nationality and culture to exist, has protected the individual in attaching himself to his group, and has, to an unprecedented degree, encouraged self-expression by its various ethnic and cultural elements.

To be sure, the ointment is not without flies. Religion in the Soviet Union has had tough sledding, the Jewish religion along with others. And the Jewish culture that the Russian authorities have chosen to encourage is, by a quirk of the doctrinaire mentality, not the historic Jewish culture but a recent and mutilated fragment of it. Judaism, as contrasted with Jews, has not fared too well in the Soviet Union up to now.

Matters however have recently taken a more favorable turn. The Soviet government is revising its policy with regard to all religion, Judaism included. If a parallel revision takes place with reference to Jewish culture, the entire position of Judaism will improve immeasurably. In any case, the status of Jews leaves nothing to be desired, a circumstance corroborating the point I am trying to make—of a tight relation between the fate of Jews and the democratic system. For, once again, it is in just the areas where Russia is most thoroughly democratic that its Jews move with maximal freedom and security.

This then is the last and most basic Jewish strategy vis-à-vis anti-Semitism, that the American Jew shall be militant on behalf of human freedom. No encroachment upon it can be alien to him. Every effort to extend it is his business. Both as Jew and as American he must regard the cause of democracy as his own. His situation allows of no alternative. Either the democratic way survives or he perishes.

Along these lines then Jews can with wisdom and propriety proceed: they can educate against anti-Semitism; they can seek to dispel the clouds of estrangement that separate Jews from Gentiles and to encourage mutual friendliness between the two groups; they can stand firm in defense of their persons and their liberties; they can join with others in resisting social reaction and in draining those economic quagmires where fascism, chauvinism and racialism breed; they can and must be stalwart in defense of democracy everywhere.

They are, quite obviously, not impotent before the danger that threatens them. At their disposal is a variety of devices, techniques and programs, all promising, all hope-inspiring. Yet in elemental realism they must recognize that they are not masters of their future.

In the first place, they constitute no more than a sliver of the population of any Western land. This is a point of extraordinary importance. It means that no matter how thoughtfully Jews analyze their situation, how courageously and skillfully they handle it, their influence will rarely be decisive. It implies furthermore that their best resistance will be unavailing against a convulsive, mass anti-Semitism.

Again, every project we have scrutinized is slow-acting. Not one is likely to yield quick returns. All are predicated on long perspectives sustained through wide sweeps of time. But since a crisis may arise at any moment, there is always the chance that they may become productive too late.

Last of all, our program involves Gentile participation all the way through.

There is not a single item in it that Jews can tackle by themselves. They can appeal to the reason of non-Jews only if the latter will listen to them. Understanding between the two groups obviously requires the co-operation of both. Certainly the Jews cannot unaided reform the world's economy or save its democracy. Nor can they hope to put up a defense of themselves in any spirit better than that of a last desperate stand, unless mankind in general preserves its sense of fair play, unless it gives them at least a fighting chance.

From all these considerations, two conclusions follow. The first is that the destiny of Jews is largely not of their making and may well be beyond their control. As we have seen, they are not powerless before it; at the worst their exertions will have some effect on the course of events. And, all else being equal, their weight may be enough to swing the scales. Like the astrologer's stars, they may incline but not compel.

When then they have put forth every effort onto the world external to themselves, they still have one task to perform. They must put their spirits in order, so that come weal, come woe, they shall comport themselves well. It was Socrates who once defined philosophy as a *peisithanatos,* "a persuader of death," meaning thereby not that wisdom acquiesces in evil—on the contrary, it resists it tooth and nail—but that having led in the good fight, it must prepare the heart for whatever outcome. What the astute old Athenian prescribed for men in general is very sage counsel for Jews today. First, the fight, vigorous and hopeful, but also a spirit steeled to intrepidity.

A second inference follows from the fact that Jews must depend in their struggle against anti-Semitism on Gentile support. That war, if it is to be waged at all well, must be waged by Gentiles primarily. Jews can and should give their maximum assistance. The greater part of the burden will have to be carried by the larger and stronger group. To count on anything else is to expect the tail to wag the dog.

What started out as a program for Jews turns out on closer scrutiny to be a program for Gentiles, or to put it more accurately for Jews and Gentiles alike, that is to say for society as a whole. Startling as is this development, it is by no means illogical. On the contrary, it points to the crucial truth that anti-Semitism is not a Jewish but a social problem. It is not the Jews who create anti-Semitism and it is not the Jews, no matter how they conduct themselves, who can eliminate it.

It follows therefore that the entire prospectus we have worked out for the Jewish group devolves in the end on mankind as a whole. It is mankind that must assume the initiative and responsibility for enterprises of education and co-operation, for the defense of all minority groups, for the regeneration of the economic system and for the preservation within itself of the democratic spirit. For the evil has its origins in society as a whole; there it must be cured.

4

Anti-Semitism—A Warning to Gentiles

THAT ANTI-SEMITISM is abroad among us is no secret. Some of it is of course the consequence of Nazi precedents and propaganda, something implanted in our midst by Hitler's agents and imitators. But much of it is thoroughly native, the product of our own heritage of prejudice, of our economic tensions, of our domestic frustrations, individual and collective, and of a pretty thorough working over which all of us have had at the hands of home-grown Jew-baiters, both professional and amateur.

Like everything else, anti-Semitism in America has had its ups and downs in recent years. In the wake of the First World War, prejudice against Jews seems to have reached what was then a record high. With the unmasking of the Ku Klux Klan, the return of prosperity in the mid-twenties, and most of all in response to a general revulsion on the part of the American people, it receded. But at no time did it altogether disappear. After 1929 it was again in the ascendancy. The collapse of the prosperity of the Coolidge era, the bold experiments inaugurated by the New Deal, a general mood of social restlessness and uncertainty, the persistence of mass unemployment—all these reawakened smoldering antagonisms. The winds of German propaganda, too, began to blow, fanning the fire. And the violent debate which raged from 1936 on over American foreign policy poured oil upon it.

During the three years before Pearl Harbor, the attack on the Jews took on formidable dimensions. Thus in 1940 there were in the United States, as Donald S. Strong informs us in *Organized Anti-Semitism in America,* as many as 121 organizations which had anti-Semitism as their prime purpose. Most of these were fly-by-night enterprises, petty rackets of trivial significance. But some possessed considerable strength in human material and finances, derived from both German and native sources. Nor did the movement lack "respectable" advocates. Clergymen, men of letters and members of Congress gave it aid and comfort. And elements in the isolationist bloc began in 1940 and 1941 to echo anti-Jewish slogans, obviously in the hope that these might prove effective in winning popular support for their cause.

With Pearl Harbor, anti-Semitism once more entered upon a recession. Americans, almost universally, rallied to the defense of their country, bent their energies to prosecuting the war, and partly because they were too busy to listen to it, partly because they saw in it a threat to national unity, closed their ears pretty generally to anti-Semitic propaganda.

How serious anti-Semitism was at its climax, just before America's involvement in the war, cannot be determined even in retrospect. That anti-Jewish organizations were numerous, widespread and vocal, that men of weight in public and intellectual affairs were beginning to express anti-Semitic attitudes boldly, that an attempt was afoot in isolationist circles to make political capital of the Jews—these are adverse indications. Against them, however, must be numbered a variety of favorable circumstances: the strength of the democratic tradition, the historic sanity of the American people, the open condemnation of anti-Semitism by almost all the important persons in the nation, the indignant repudiation from so many quarters which has met every public utterance against the Jews from Lindbergh's at Des Moines in 1941 to Hamilton Fish's in 1944.

But not only are the signs confusing in that they point in opposite directions, the weight to be ascribed to them cannot be accurately fixed. How large, for example, was the influence of the Christian Front? How earnest and courageous were the elements opposing it? Indeed, had a survey been conducted in November of 1941 as to the attitude of every American concerning Jews, had it been determined exactly how many were sympathetic and how many hostile toward them, the findings would have been of questionable worth.

Of what avail are statistics as to a sentiment unless they are accompanied by one all-important item, an index to the intensity with which the sentiment is held? Emotions, however, cannot be measured as to their strength. Which means that had a Gallup or Roper poll been taken just before Pearl Harbor, or for that matter at any other time, it would have given us no clear-cut information as to the gravity of anti-Semitism.

But if we cannot be certain about the past, we most assuredly ought to be reserved concerning the future. In other words, anyone who is free with predictions as to the course of anti-Semitism is talking irresponsibly on a matter on which in fact no one knows anything.

This much, however, can be safely asserted: America is yet to undergo its great test on this score as on so many others. For if the war be one crisis, the postwar period will almost surely subject us to other serious trials. Then, without the unity enforced by the enemy, we shall have to come to grips with staggering national problems. The times, there is reason to believe, will be far from tranquil. But it is on social adversity that anti-Semitism feeds. Wherefore we may assume in all sobriety that the American people is destined to meet the demon once more and to wrestle with him in mortal combat.

It is my own hunch, which I present for whatever it may be worth, that most Americans are pretty well armored in spirit against the evil. The number of Jew-baiters among us has always been, and I believe always will be, small. We are, after all, a people fortified by strong religious idealism, by the democratic spirit and the Anglo-Saxon tradition of fair play. At the same time we are, as Whitman put it, a nation of nations, a condition unfavorable to the spread of group antagonisms.

Our peril, as I see it, is not that the majority of Americans will be converted to active anti-Semitism. It consists rather in two other circumstances: in the fact that many Gentiles are totally indifferent to what befalls Jews, all on the naïve and erroneous assumption that it is none of their concern; and in the further fact that there is among very many Gentiles if not the substance of anti-Semitism, at least a trace of it—if not its active and self-conscious body, then its secret and unacknowledged shadow.

I have in mind a widespread ambivalence concerning the Jews, a psychic tension between compassion and scruple on the one side, and antagonism on the other. Or to put it more concretely, I mean the mood of a non-Jew who is horrified by what Hitler has done and yet feels an impulse, of which to be sure he is ashamed, to applaud it; who regards Jew-baiting as disgraceful and yet wonders covertly whether it is not pretty much what "they" deserve; who protests against a pogrom but will neither employ Jews nor allow them into his country club.

This is not anti-Semitism; it is too negative, too torn emotionally, too much conscience-ridden and principle-bound to merit that ugly name. It is, furthermore, passive, a sort of nonfeasance rather than malfeasance. But it is not without weight. It has suffocated many an upsurge of mercy. More than any other factor it paralyzed American hands and hearts when a refugee-laden ship prowled our coast seeking an internment camp, a desert even, onto which to dump its human cargo. This latent bias in some Gentiles and the indifference of others may yet give the working, envenomed anti-Semite his chance in America.

That is why I am writing this chapter. I wish to warn my non-Jewish fellows against the enemy that lurks among them, and in them. This admonition applies not merely to the relations between Gentiles and Jews; it is valid for the attitudes of any population toward any minority. The reader may, if he so chooses, make his own adaptations of what follows to other groups. Our theme however is anti-Semitism and the peril it represents to non-Jews.

Nor do I mean to be disingenuous. My stake as a Jew in the attitude that you as Gentiles take toward anti-Semitism is large and immediate, infinitely larger and more immediate than yours. But your destiny also is involved. Unless you act on this score as befits Christians and democrats you will do yourselves, your children, your society and the values you cherish irreparable harm. What I mean to say is this: you must take a bold stand against anti-Semitism of any type in public affairs, and against any latent traces of it in yourselves. Above all else, you dare not be indifferent to the issue on the ground that it is none of your business. It is your business and you must attend to it. Otherwise you will sow wild oats and ultimately reap a whirlwind.

Remember, if you indulge anti-Semitism or tolerate it or ignore it, you will in the first instance be risking whatever it is which we Jews have to offer to your lives. Needless to say, we have no monopoly on talent. Yet we have our share of it, and a tradition of learning to boot. Had Hitler come fifty years earlier, you might today be without the gifts of Einstein, Ehrlich, Bergson, Buber and a host of others. Who knows of what other intellects and hearts, of what other spiritual and social endowments he has already deprived you, and of what those who come after him and are fashioned in his image may rob you in days to come?

Nor should you forget for an instant that every racial hatred is in part a consequence of social dislocation and a psychic escape from it. Its charm consists in that it diverts attention. Hence it is a trap for the unwary. Toy with anti-Semitism and then, whenever you come face to face with economic adversity or frustration, you will take out your orneriness on the Jews. In a sadistic fashion that may prove pleasurable. But while playing the game, you will be neither searching out the true causes of your misery nor attempting to correct them. What is more, the longer the sport continues, the longer you permit yourselves to be diverted from real issues, the graver your actual evils will become.

Again, those who prod you toward anti-Jewish prejudices have their own purposes in mind. Should you commit yourselves to their clever and unscrupulous hands, you may in effect be surrendering yourselves to purposes alien to your own and contrary to your interests. You shall have entered into the most profitless business known to man, the cat's-paw's. Let the precedent of what has befallen the decent elements in the German people stand as warning against such a course.

Nor can your toleration of anti-Semitism turn out in the long run to be anything else than a prelude to the suppression of your Christianity. In a peculiar fashion synagogues are the first line of defense for churches. First it will be Jews and Judaism. Later it will be Christianity and Christians. So it ran in Germany. So it must run anywhere. Smile then on the active anti-Semitism of others and the lurking anti-Semitism in yourselves, and you can be quite sure that some day, after we Jews have been disposed of, you will find yourselves next in line.

The democratic process to which you are devoted, which protects your freedom, is also involved. Words like liberty, fraternity and equality are universal in reference. Either they embrace all, or they can ultimately embrace none. Let exceptions be made to them and they are done for. It was Lincoln who once insisted that America could not remain part slave and part free and still preserve its heritage of freedom. That insight is as valid today as when it was first uttered.

But anti-Semitism will exact from you still another toll. It will corrupt your character. Hatred is not a mood to be confined neatly. It feeds on itself and grows strong. The longer it lives, the broader its appetite. A man may begin by hating one individual; he will end with a hatred for many. He may start with an antagonism against a particular group; he will finish with an enlarged capacity for cruelty. Easy is the descent into Hell. Had the German people not allowed itself lesser meannesses, it would never have been capable of monumental brutalities. You, American Christians, are decent human beings now. You dare not begin the process of whittling down your decency.

Nor can Christianity survive in your hearts if anti-Semitism is present within them also. For one is a denial of the other. As Christians, you believe in the worth of every human being, in the unity of mankind under God, in principles of peace and compassion. How will these ideals appear to you should you have traffic with racial prejudices? Will they not seem pretty phrases but no more? Will not the whole body of your Christianity, its doctrine, its rituals and its morality, come to reek with fraud and hypocrisy until it will have lost all value in your eyes? Anti-Semitism may destroy Judaism by destroying the Jews. But it destroys Christianity also, more slowly but no less surely, by paganizing the Christian personality.

It is then a high price which the piper of racialism will exact for his tune, should you elect to dance to it. You will lose whatever gifts we Jews may have to bring you; you will be diverted from your real problems and their solution; you will surrender yourselves into the hands of demagogues for exploitation; you will invite on yourselves the fate to which you shall have consigned the Jews; you will endanger your freedom and democratic institutions; you will encourage a brutalization of your own spirits; and you will sacrifice your religious heritage on the altars of Moloch.

I doubt that the whole business is worth your while.

I do not like to put the matter in terms of self-interest, whether on your part or mine. I would much rather that we resisted social evil on grounds of idealism, because most of us are religious people, and because all of us believe in democracy. These motives alone should move us to gird up our loins. But if there be any Gentile who is weak of heart and tempted by the powers of darkness, let him recall what we have just recorded, and let his loyalty to the light be confirmed by concern over his own welfare. For in this instance, as in so many others, honesty and decency are the best policy. By them one saves his neck as well as his soul.

5

Anti-Semitism—An Exhortation to Jews

WE JEWS FACE A FUTURE that is unpredictable, that may very well prove beyond our powers of control. Our destiny cannot be prophesied because anti-Semitism is, as we have observed, too complex a phenomenon and dependent on too many variables for its course to be foretold. And we are not altogether the masters of our fate because, as we have also noted, all our efforts to direct it are predicated on at least a measure of Gentile co-operation and sympathy. Of these, since they lie outside ourselves, we can never be altogether sure.

Against the future and whatever it may contain, there are measures, all the measures listed in Chapter 3, whereby we may hopefully seek to mold it aright. But—and this is a crucial point—it is not enough for us Jews to do the right things with reference to anti-Semitism. We must also think and feel correctly concerning it.

If we reason confusedly we shall most certainly blunder in selecting lines of action for ourselves or, adopting the proper course, shall fail to execute it suitably. More relevant and urgent, we require clear heads and stout hearts for the sake of our own souls. For, should events go against us, we shall need insight that our fate be intelligible, and courage that we may be able to endure it manfully.

Now, it is not only Jews who face unforeseeable and possibly unmasterable tomorrows. This is a condition common, in greater or lesser degree, to all mankind. Men are not therefore consigned to either passivity or despair. They simply do the best they can in the light of their understanding and in accordance with the requirements of self-respect. So with us Jews as we look toward what lies ahead. We may not be able exactly to weigh or measure our present crisis, we may not be capable of prophesying its evolution, and it is quite conceivable that it will grow too big for us to handle. We can still determine how in wisdom and honor we ought to conduct ourselves.

Given a truthful analysis of our situation, given a decent concern for our own dignity, given too a firm commitment to the moral values of the Jewish tradition and of American democracy, certain principles, so to speak, dictate themselves, principles for action, but even more for thought and feeling.

Principle 1. The rights and obligations which Jews enjoy in America are theirs as of right, and not through the sufferance or toleration of anyone. They must not be compromised in even the slightest degree.

We Jews are not second-class citizens. The basic documents of the American commonwealth, its essential character, guarantee to us as to all Americans the privilege of seeking and holding public office, of a free choice of occupation, of unrestricted expression of our political opinions and of access to our country's cultural and spiritual treasures. From these rights, no matter under what compulsion, we must not retreat. We must be unyielding on our freedoms generally, but most particularly on those against which pressure may be exerted. As we gave no ground before the assault of isolationists in 1940 nor the insinuations of Mr. Hamilton Fish in 1944, we ought not to give an inch to any future onslaught. Each of us has a right to his political opinions whether on domestic or international questions. And if many or most Jews happen to think alike, that is nobody's business except their own. Under no circumstances and by no threats must we ever be deterred from the convictions to which our consciences as American citizens may incline us.

Nor should we allow ourselves ever to be bullied out of any legitimate business or profession to which we may feel ourselves called. Much was made a few years ago, by anti-Semites and near anti-Semites, of the large role played by Jews in the motion-picture industry. Much has been made too of the fact that one of America's greatest newspapers is owned and operated by a Jew. This in my judgment is all the more reason for Jews who happen to be engaged in these occupations to persevere in them. Not that these pursuits are better than others. My sole point is that it is the rights which are challenged that must be most forcibly reasserted.

As it happens, I am one of those who are seriously concerned with the economic redistribution of American Jewry. I believe that there ought to be fewer Jews in white-collar occupations and more in industry and agriculture. But an occupational restratification, if and when it is undertaken, must be a voluntary effort on the part of Jews, not a surrender to coercion. It must be motivated by the hope of enhancing their lives and making them more creative, not by the dismal tactic of appeasing the anti-Semite.

The refusal of Jews to compromise their rights and duties as American citizens is dictated by several considerations. These we have already had occasion to enumerate. They are so important and so often neglected in practice that they will well bear repetition.

Intransigence is in part a matter of self-interest. If we agree to a with-drawal from any one of our privileges, we may in the end be left with none. It is furthermore a counsel of wisdom. For any concession will most cer-tainly be made in vain. The non-Jew who is not anti-Semitic does not ask sacrifices of us. The convinced anti-Semite will not be placated by them. It is an issue, too, of dignity and honor. Should we be moved to abandon our full freedom out of fear, we shall necessarily and deservedly appear as cowards in our own eyes. We shall thereby have done serious damage to our self-respect.

Most of all, stubborn insistence on our status ought to be inspired by a sense of obligation to America. Anti-Semitism is the initial skirmish in the totalitarian attack upon democracy. We Jews, as it chances, have been as-signed to the outermost position in freedom's defenses. Should our station fall, the fascist will have easier going thereafter. For us to abandon our post in the hope of cajoling the anti-Semite would be to present the enemies of America with a telling victory. America and mankind deserve better at our hands than spiritual treason.

Principle 2. Since anti-Semitism is not created by the behavior of Jews, Jews would do well to stop blaming themselves and one another for it.

The real sources of anti-Semitism, as we have seen, consist in deep-seated social forces. Against factors of such large moment, the behavior of single persons, whether Jewish or Christian, is of comparatively little import. When a society is balanced and sane, a Jew may misbehave and no notice will be taken of him. When a country is sick and restless, all Jews may conduct themselves unexceptionably; they will not avert the irritability of non-Jews.

This is not to say that the deportment of the individual Jew is of no influ-ence whatsoever. It does provide a peg on which anti-Semites can hang their bias. But if they were not anti-Semitic to begin with, they would not isolate the Jewishness of the person who misbehaves. They would see only an ill-bred human being. If they are sufficiently anti-Semitic, they do not need occasions to justify their attitude. Let us Jews all behave irreproachably and they will still find fault with us. They will even invent myths to rationalize their prejudices, spin stories of international intrigues, cabals and conspiracies, of vast horrendous plots.

In brief, while the actions of individual Jews may have some role in the accentuation or diminution of anti-Semitism, that role is secondary or tertiary. In the whole picture, against deeper, larger influences it is, as a causative factor, virtually negligible.

I would not be misunderstood. I am not denying that some Jews are ill-mannered and others immoral. I believe, however, and I base my belief on careful observation, that Israel has neither monopoly on, nor disproportion of black sheep, that Jews as a whole conduct themselves no worse than do others, and, thanks to the influences of their tradition, considerably better than might be expected in view of the treatment which has always been meted out to them. Beyond all else I am convinced that the occasional black sheep, like the occasional saint or genius, has only the slightest effect on the course of anti-Semitism.

Nor am I pleading in defense of gaucherie or unethical behavior on the part of Jews. As a Jew who feels no small pride in his Jewishness, I want eagerly to see all Jews comport themselves with grace and high-mindedness. But I am concerned with these purposes as ends in themselves, as mandates of Judaism, as expressions of a moral imperative resting on all human beings.

In any case I am repelled by the contention that Jews ought to remake themselves in order to obviate anti-Semitism. The facts of Jewish behavior seem to me not to justify such an approach. The consequences for Jewish morale are certain to be destructive. The whole tactic represents a cheapening, abuse and diversion to unworthy ends of the admirable ideal of self-realization. And it is, as a strategy for combating anti-Semitism, an unadulterated futility, since it addresses itself to remote and virtually irrelevant factors rather than to real causes.

From the principle that anti-Semitism is not a consequence of Jewish behavior, unmistakable implications flow. In the first place, we Jews owe no one the slightest apology for ourselves and one another. Again we ought to be on guard against the tendency, so natural and yet so unjustified, to indulge in mutual scrutiny and recrimination. To a disheartening extent we have yielded to this temptation. East European and German Jews, Zionists and non-Zionists, religionists and secularists, Jewish conservatives and radicals have slipped into the habit of blaming one another for situations for which in actuality no one in particular is responsible.

Nor have we confined our finger-pointing to the privacy of the Jewish community. More than occasionally one Jewish group has attempted to throw others to the wolves, has stood before the Gentile world and, not content with protesting its own innocence, has named other Jews as meriting the anti-Semite's accusations. The psychological mechanism involved in performances of this sort is obvious. The child who has not yet learned not to tattletale will almost unfailingly blame his fellows for any misdeed with which he may be charged. Such conduct is to be expected in children. It is scarcely worthy of mature men.

Last of all, there must be no sense of guilt or inferiority among us. We are not a lower breed of human beings. And if an anti-Semitic storm impends, we must not be stampeded into believing that we have by our own monumental deficiencies invoked it on our heads. We must discern, for our own morale as well as in the interests of objective truth, that it is a consequence of vast impersonal factors, political, economic and psychological.

Principle 3. Whatever can be done by Jews to resist anti-Semitism ought to be done with all the vigor, courage and militancy they can muster. Beyond that, having done their best, they ought to forget about the whole business.

Anti-Semitism is, whether in deeds, words or sentiment, an assault on Jews. Normal human beings defend themselves when they are attacked. What is more, anti-Semitism is an unwarranted and undeserved assault. Morally regarded, it is a piece of effrontery, of unmitigated impudence, perpetrated at the best by mean and stupid persons, and at the worst by the conscienceless and depraved. It should therefore evoke everywhere, and particularly in its victims, a mood of righteous indignation and the determination not to endure insolence at such hands. To ward off unprovoked attack with the utmost vigor, and to resent it are reactions so natural that the underscoring of a temper of militancy in Principle III may seem superfluous.

But we Jews are a peculiar people in more senses than Scripture intended. Responses typical of the rest of mankind are not necessarily ours. We are "sicklied o'er with the pale cast of thought." And when we encounter instances, large or trivial, of anti-Semitism, we do not react spontaneously.

Rather we get ourselves into a Hamletlike pose and enter into a debate with ourselves and one another.

We ask whether it is not wiser in the long run to ignore the unpleasant incident. Have we seen the inward parts and reins of the person who insulted Jews or threatened them? Are we so sure that he is truly an enemy and troubler of Israel? Besides, the whole episode may be unimportant. By taking cognizance of it we may be endowing it with a significance it does not possess. Indeed by giving it publicity, we may be helping to put bees into otherwise beeless bonnets, and so to diffuse the very evil we wish to check.

Or we may tell ourselves that opposition to anti-Semitism comes with better grace and efficacy from Gentiles than from Jews. The latter are to be expected to object to hostility toward themselves. No neutral will be impressed by anything they say since it must be *ex parte* in character. But if non-Jews who have no stake in the matter intercede on behalf of Jews, then, it is argued, every bystander must be persuaded of their innocence.

No proposition could be more mistaken than this, no tactic more misguided and no notion so revealing of inner moral insecurity among Jews. An innocent person waylaid by thugs will expect and welcome the aid of law-abiding citizens. But he does not stand idle until it is forthcoming.

Or we Jews, if we are philosophically minded, may remind ourselves that the anti-Semite, himself the victim of circumstance, is more to be sympathized with than scorned. Indeed he is, so long as we bear in mind and act in conformity with a shrewd comment of Samuel Johnson. "If a madman," Boswell quotes his master as saying, "were to come into this room with a stick in his hand, no doubt we should pity the state of his mind; but our primary consideration would be to take care of ourselves. We should knock him down first and pity him afterwards."

Finally, even when we Jews at long last reach the point where we are ready for action, we are still likely to be deterred from it. Casting about for leadership and support from the Jewish community, we find it so disorganized and divided, so confused and chaotic, that we are once again left to our private devices and vacillations.

This is the sad, summary truth because of which the sounding of a note of militancy becomes imperative: we Jews not only defend ourselves less boldly and effectively than we might, we have so tangled ourselves in our own dialectics that many of us have grown uncertain of the very propriety of self-defense. Most of us take anti-Semitism lying down. All too often we are on our bellies when we ought to be on our feet, fighting hard.

Does this seem an exaggeration? Then let the unseemly tale of Boston Jewry give evidence. For months on end in that city and its environs hoodlums ambushed Jewish children and adults. The Jewish community did not so much as stir in protest. It was too uncertain whether to make an "issue" of the situation; it preferred too much to have Gentiles intercede; it was too disorganized even for effective consultation among Jews. The uncertainty of the adults paralyzed the children as well. The Ghetto guttersnipes of a generation ago, foreign-born "greenhorns" though they were, acquitted themselves better. Attacked by gangs, they did not hesitate to form gangs of their own for self-protection.

What happened in Boston, and elsewhere as well, is that a complicated, almost metaphysical tangle was made of a simple matter. We Jews, like everyone else, ought to defend ourselves directly, instinctively, without the slightest hesitation or misgiving. Our spirit should be that of the old honorable motto: *Nemo me impune lacessit*—No one attacks me and gets away with it.

We must not see provocation where none is intended; we ought to give the person suspected of anti-Semitism the benefit of every reasonable doubt; we should not exaggerate the significance of chance remarks or random incidents; and always we ought to use the methods of persuasion and education first and as long as there is any hope for their success. But where we find that we are dealing with real anti-Semitism, and that it is not amenable to reason, we ought to hit at it as hard and as often as we can, and with everything not explicitly forbidden by the Constitution, the Decalogue, and the rules of the Marquess of Queensberry. Perhaps in this way we may swerve the incipient anti-Semite from his anti-Semitism. Under any circumstance we shall have kept our self-respect.

Then, when once we have exerted ourselves to the utmost and attempted everything within the range of our strength and ingenuity, we ought resolutely to put the whole business out of our minds. Certainly we should try to stop worrying, fretting, almost stewing about it. I know some Jews who these days die in heart, are reborn again, and perish still once more with every sign, favorable or adverse, of public sentiment concerning Jews. This, I protest, is not living at all. It is existing in misery, and that over an evil which, for all anyone knows, may never come into being.

Principle 4. The Jew needs today, as never before in modern times, a vital and significant Judaism.

Since we are faced with the threat of an evil which we did not make and may be unable to control, the state of our morale becomes all-important. How well can we "take" it—the uncertainties of our present status and the even uglier actualities which the future may hold in store for us?

The answer to that question will depend in great measure on our attitude toward Judaism. All of recent Jewish experience validates this assertion. The assimilated Jew in Germany was most completely demoralized by the triumph of Nazism. The Jewish religionist or Zionist came through best in spirit. For the latter, while he endured equally with others, felt that he was enduring for a significant cause, whereas the de-Judaized Jew of necessity regarded himself as paying extreme penalties for the sake of something meaningless to him. And it is not suffering per se which men find intolerable but suffering devoid of point.

Polish Jewry in its last agonies suggested the same conclusion. The *Contemporary Jewish Record* of August 1941 in an article entitled "In the Warsaw Ghetto" described a Jewish newspaper published in that Nazi-contrived hell. Its columns gave grim testimony of vast tragedies, personal and communal. But they also reported discussions of the Jewish religion, Zionism, Hebrew literature and programs for adult education. This picture of starving, maltreated Jews struggling to save their souls is infinitely poignant. It is also heroic with evidence of a will to live that sprang from, and was invigorated by a conviction of purpose.

What, one wonders, of those Jews in that Ghetto who, having no Judaism, no faith, tradition and people, were left with only their own misery?

As for the American scene, it is sufficient to say that here too the degree of demoralization among Jews is roughly proportional to the degree of de-Judaization.

And so it must be. For the ability to endure any evil, no matter of what nature, depends always on three factors: on the self-respect of the person who undergoes it, on his ability to enjoy his existence despite it, and on his conviction as to the general purposefulness of his life. But the self-respect of Jews *as Jews* can be derived only from a knowledge of the Jewish heritage. The enjoyment of Jewishness is possible only to one who participates in Jewish practices and enterprises. And the purposefulness of Jewish life involves an appreciation of and dedication to the ideals of the Jewish tradition.

It may seem a far cry from the anxieties which now plague American Jews to Jewish education, the observance of ancestral rites, participation in Jewish communal purposes, and the effort to establish a rapport between the Jewish individual and the classic themes of Judaism. They are nonetheless bound together inextricably. The serenity of Jews in their present situation, their courage in their future lot are, in actuality, being determined at this moment by the disposition which they are making of their Jewish heritage.

Of our four Principles for thought and feeling, it should be noted last of all that they are valid regardless of any estimate of the present gravity of anti-Semitism, regardless of the future that may unfold for the Jewish group in America. I have already registered my conviction as to the improbability of an acute or violent anti-Semitism emerging in this country. Given the American system and temper, such a turn of events seems to me unlikely. We have every reason to labor for and expect the best. But it is possible to conceive less desirable contingencies. It would therefore be wise to be prepared in spirit for any eventuality.

If, then, the clouds now on the horizon eventually blot out the sun, if a violent storm breaks over us, if, though we resist every inch of the way, we are forced into Ghettos, even so, under these Principles, we shall have comported ourselves with dignity and courage; we shall have defended both our own rights as human beings and the humane tradition of mankind. Come the worst, we shall still possess a doctrine of faith and freedom, of truth, mercy and righteousness by which and for which to live.

But if, as is by far the more plausible expectation, the signs of an impending tempest turn out false omens, the Principles we have enunciated are still relevant. By adhering to them we shall lose nothing and gain much. We shall pass through our crisis bravely and honorably. We shall help in the defense of democracy, and we shall in the meantime draw from the treasuries of the Jewish past to our personal enhancement and to the more abundant service of America.

6

Jews and Their Livelihoods

THE JEWS OF AMERICA are highly concentrated in certain limited fields of economic enterprise. This is a fact, as we shall soon establish. But no less important than the fact are its implications. How, for example, did Jews get that way? Are they so often shopkeepers or lawyers because, as the Nazis argue, such occupations are in their blood, or has biology nothing to do with it? Are they engaged economically as they are because, without being of essentially different stuff from anyone else, they have been molded by special historical forces? The background of the fact is therefore one theme that invites exploration.

Its consequences, its influence on Jews and Gentiles, are another. Is it desirable or undesirable that Jews be disposed economically as they happen to be? Or is our fact "neutral" in character, to be neither approved nor disapproved, but simply to be accepted? On this point informed and responsible opinion is sharply divided. Our second inquiry then will be into the arguments pro and con on the question. Once we have examined these, we shall know better whether there is, or is not, a third item on our agenda, whether the Jewish situation requires remaking or can be allowed to perpetuate itself.

On the first question, as to what molded Jews into their contemporary shape, let me say bluntly that I hold history to be entirely responsible, and heredity not at all. Jews are, I am convinced, by natural endowment pretty much of a piece with mankind as a whole. If they exhibit peculiarities, one need postulate no especial biologically transmitted traits to account for them. Environment—that is to say, their group tradition, their social position or both in concert—is quite adequate to explain their differential characteristics.

In ancient times there was nothing in the least unusual about the pursuits of Jews. Rooted in the soil of Palestine, they were farmers, artisans and merchants like, and in about the same proportions as, the peoples round about them. Nor did they disclose any extraordinary aptitude for finance or trade. As late as the first century, Josephus could say in an obiter dictum that Jews did not engage generally in commerce. Into the last days of the Greco-Roman world this condition persisted. With the diffusion of Jewish urban settlements throughout the Empire more Jews may have gone into trade, but never to a conspicuous degree. To the end, Greeks were the bankers of the classical world, and, together with Syrians and Egyptians, its leading merchants.

For five centuries on end thereafter this pattern maintained itself unbroken, except for one fairly significant change. Sometime during the Dark Ages, Jews began to engage extensively in international commerce. With the disintegration of the Empire, the old system of trade broke down, leaving an economic void. To fill this, Jews were peculiarly fitted. They alone, amid the disorganization and parochialism of early feudal society, possessed an international language, a universal system of courts before which all Jews, no matter what their places of origin, were equal, and a chain of Jewish communities that served Jewish merchants simultaneously as hostelries, asylums, market places and storehouses. Given these advantages, they turned naturally to import, export and barter, coming so to dominate the scene that the words *Judaei* and *mercatores* passed as virtual synonyms. Yet, in the main, the older occupations continued to engage them heavily. And a visitor to the Rhineland of the tenth century, or to Babylonia or Spain, would in all likelihood have found most Jews farmers or artisans.

All this changed in the eleventh century. Stimulated by the Crusades, religious passions ran high. Attacks on Jews became common, and anti-Jewish legislation as well. Edicts were issued forbidding Jews to own land or to hire Christians as domestics or farmhands. The Jewish farmer was slowly but relentlessly forced off the soil. At the same time, the rise of the guilds, which were religious as well as economic corporations, drove the Jews out of the handicrafts, leaving them only the industries that were too petty for Christian notice or that ministered primarily to Jews.

Nor did Jews long continue in international commerce. The Crusades had familiarized Christians with the trade routes. Merchants from the Lombard and Hanseatic cities now traveled and did business along them. Possessed of resources larger than Jews could muster, protected as Jews were not by their governments, they proved more than a match for Jewish competition.

By the twelfth or thirteenth century Jews had been dislodged from that field as earlier they had been expelled from others.

Jews were left in the end with shopkeeping, local trading, handicrafts restricted in scope and market—and moneylending. Nor, as a rule, was it permitted to them to engage in that broader, more lucrative and honorific form of moneylending known as banking. This was pre-empted by the princes and merchants of the great commercial cities. As a financier then the medieval Jew was rarely anything more than a pawnbroker. Even in usury he did not go undisturbed. For the nobles who tolerated and protected him regarded themselves as his silent partners, entitled to the lion's share of his take. Ghettoization, the confinement of Jews to limited and undesirable neighborhoods—this, in a word, is the substance of medieval Jewish history, economic as well as social.

Now group patterns once established are hardy. They have a way of persevering, even after the conditions that created them have disappeared. After the French Revolution many of the old constricting forces ceased to be operative. At least in Western Europe the full gamut of occupations opened itself to the Jews. Once again they could choose to be farmers, or mechanics.

The past, however, had by now developed a momentum of its own. Young Jews casting about for livelihoods tended to elect those of their fathers. Conditions, to be sure, were much more favorable. If they would be merchants, they no longer had to be peddlers. Yet, in substance, if not in form, their pursuits continued to be those of their forebears.

The sole notable new departure of the nineteenth century was the entrance of Jews into the professions. The Jewish lawyer, physician, journalist, dentist, accountant, musician, scientist, teacher and author with whom the modern world is so familiar made their appearance. But even this was only the rechannelization of old interests. For, having always revered learning, Jews flowed naturally, as though by a kind of spiritual gravity, toward bookish occupations. They merely transferred their zeal for knowledge to new objects.

The spontaneous impulse of Jews toward the professions was encouraged by a general rise, during the nineteenth century, in the standard of living—a circumstance that made place for great numbers of professional men. It was abetted further by the individualistic character of most of the professions.

A physician or a lawyer need not ask an employer, who may be an anti-Semite, for a chance to work. He simply hangs out his shingle.

But if Jews took advantage of one opportunity opened up by the modern world, they missed almost altogether the chance offered by the machine. The nineteenth century, the industrial revolution at its peak, created a new mass-class, skilled labor. Jews were not, however, an appreciable part of it, and for readily understandable reasons. In the first place, thanks to their long exclusion from artisanry, they lacked all background for it. Indeed they had even made a virtue of their disability and had come to look down upon manual labor. A psychic obstacle stood then in the way of Jews turning to industrial employment. What is more, since their emancipation was belated, they found the field already pre-empted by non-Jews.

In only one branch of manufacturing did Jews assert themselves—the needle trades. Here they did have a tradition. There had always been Jewish tailors. Not even when the guilds were most powerful had they succeeded in preventing Jews from manufacturing clothing at least for their fellow Jews. When the industrial revolution came, some Jews were equipped with at least this one technical skill. In Czarist Russia in particular the clothing industry was both sponsored and manned by Jews. Indeed, the only modern Jewish proletariat of consequence grew up in cities like Lodz and Warsaw, centers of the needle trade for the east of Europe.

This is the economic background out of which Jews came to America. On their arrival in the New World they were heavily predisposed in favor of business and trade, the professions and shopkeeping. They lacked, except for tailoring, any inclination or aptitude for industry. As fate would have it, American conditions strengthened them in their historical tendencies.

The period of largest Jewish immigration, that from the eighties of the last century to the First World War, was one of great commercial expansion. The professions too were upswinging mightily. Very naturally then the Jews rerooted themselves in just the enterprises they already favored. Even the clothing industry was ripe for them on their coming to America. As it chanced, the technique of mass production was not applied to tailoring until late in the nineteenth century. Jews therefore were for once not too late to get in on the ground floor.

This is not to say that migration brought no significant changes in the economics of Jewry. The son of the Jew who had peddled across the German countryside sometimes became, on the American scene, the owner or manager of a department store, and his son in turn the manufacturer of the goods his father had sold. The East European Talmudical scholar was reincarnated in his descendents as a physician, an attorney, an accountant or a teacher. And the scion of the tailor of Lodz might very well turn out to be a dress manufacturer, a designer, a cutter or a jobber in textiles.

In some respects, the historic pattern was altered radically. Thus large numbers of Jews entered clerical and semiclerical occupations as bookkeepers, stenographers, and salesmen—enterprises that were novelties in Jewish employment. So too with Civil Service to which they were attracted by the intellectualistic overtones of the qualifying examinations, by the white-collar character of the work and, not least of all, by the merit system that so largely neutralizes the adverse influences of anti-Semitism.

The Jewish farmer is another novelty of our time—not, like the white-collar worker or government employee, a spontaneous, self-generating phenomenon, but pretty generally a planned creation. No traditions impelled him to the soil. Nor was agriculture an expanding field, an occupational vacuum into which he was sucked. On the contrary, the drift of American economy for half a century and more has been away from the countryside.

The American Jewish farmer represents in no slight measure an assertion of conscious purpose. He is likely to be a Jew who, convinced that Jews are "abnormally distributed," has set about correcting the unbalance. Quite deliberately he has remade himself.

As might be expected, the number of Jewish farmers, while impressive, is still far below normal proportions. Of the four and three-quarter million Jews in America, approximately 100,000 persons derive their livelihood from agriculture. This must be set against a figure of 17.5 percent for the total American population.

The present economic status of American Jews is therefore the resultant of two forces: the momentum of the Jewish past, the impact of America. The facts of that status have recently become an object of scientific study. What is perhaps the best summary of the findings to date is contained in the article "Economic Trends," by Dr. Nathan Reich, published in the symposium entitled *The American Jew—A Composite Portrait.**

---

* Quoted by the permission of Harper and Brothers.

Dr. Reich confirms in the first place the urban character of American Jewry. Of the 4,770,000 Jews of the United States, over 4,000,000, he estimates, live in cities of 100,000 and over. "While Jews form barely 4 per cent of the total population in the United States, they account for 11 per cent of the population of all cities of over 100,000 inhabitants, but comprise only a minor fraction of one per cent of that of the rural areas."

Our assumption that Jews are highly concentrated occupationally is corroborated also by the best available statistics. By Dr. Reich's analysis, between 35 and 40 percent of the Jews are engaged in commerce and trade, as opposed to 13.8 percent of the general population; between 15 and 20 percent in manufacturing as against 26.3 percent; and 10 to 12 percent in the professions as against 6.8 percent. What is more, within these areas, the Jews are further limited. In trade they are confined heavily to retail trade, and within that to the sale of food, clothing, furniture and drugs; in manufacture, to the light industries producing consumers' goods, and within these, to clothing, headwear, furs, printing and foods; and within the professions, to law, medicine, pharmacy and dentistry.

Scientific studies, it is clear, support the general impression of an intense occupational concentration of Jews; on the other hand, they refute the popular notion that Jews dominate the American economy. In 1936 the editors of *Fortune* Magazine published *Jews in America,* a survey of Jewish ownership and control. This booklet reveals that there are large areas—heavy industries such as steel, coal, chemicals, transportation, electrical goods, oil, rubber and automobiles—in which Jews figure virtually not at all; that their ownership of textile factories ranges from 5 to 16 percent; that if Jews are active in insurance, it is almost exclusively as brokers; that only in the garment industries, distilleries, boots and shoes, motion pictures and retail trade is their role large, though, in the last of these, they represent only 5 percent of chain-store ownership.

As for Jewish influence on finance, it is, the editors of *Fortune* demonstrate, negligible. Jews are a mere 7 percent of the directors of the member banks of the New York Clearing Association, and the banks on which they appear are quite consistently not the largest. And while of the membership of the New York Stock Exchange 18 percent is Jewish, the largest houses are almost uniformly non-Jewish in personnel and control.

There is, of course, nothing fixed or rigid about these facts. Changes are in progress. Dr. Reich affords us a vivid summary of these, the dynamics of Jewish economic activity as they may well be called.

Taking as his standard of measurement the contrast between immigrant Jews and their native-born children, he notes a tapering off of the tendency toward commerce, trade and manufacture, and against it an upswing toward the professions, clerical occupations and Civil Service. This movement, he observes further, runs roughly parallel to the general drift of our economy, the percentage of Americans engaged in white-collar occupations and government employ showing a fairly steady and marked increase in recent decades. Only in commerce does the evolution of the Jewish group reveal an aberration from the norm. Fewer second-generation American Jews are entering that field, whereas in the total population the reverse trend is discernible.

These are, in broad outline, the facts about the economic status of American Jewry. What, if anything, ought to be done about them is a moot point. Among others, Dr. Reich is convinced that the occupational distribution of Jews presents no problem of consequence. In the other direction, many students of Jewish affairs insist that a planned redistribution of the American Jewish group is imperative. In support of their case they advance five contentions.

1) The present concentration of Jews encourages anti-Semitism. It makes the Jews inordinately conspicuous. It places them in just those enterprises which, it is claimed, are unproductive. Jews do not tend the soil, dig coal, build or work machines. The food they eat is produced by others; their livelihoods are derived from traffic in things not of their own making. This, it is held, is both economic parasitism and an avoidable jeopardy, presenting the anti-Semite with the slogan sounded so often in Germany and echoed here: Jews do not create; they exploit.

Western society, furthermore, evaluates occupations according to a scale of its own. It may not confer largest rewards on the farmer or the mechanic but it is incorrigibly sentimental about them. In its eyes, the bronzed tiller of the soil, the brawny artisan in the factory, are romantic figures. These men, it believes, do the world's real work, hard, painful, exacting, but glorious. The absence of the Jew from their company is conspicuous, damaging to his prestige, and dangerous to his security.

2) The occupational concentration of Jews has consigned them to an

economic position that is basically unsound. First of all, young Jews tend to see only a few pursuits as possibilities for themselves, and these are likely to be already overcrowded by other Jews. So, though New York City already has too many lawyers, accountants and physicians, other Jews insist on entering the professions. They continue to turn to shopkeeping at a time when chain stores are making the survival of the independent merchant questionable; they become small scale manufacturers in the shadow of vast nationwide industries. In sum, they persist unwisely in forcing themselves into occupations which, because of overcrowding or basic unsoundness, cannot sustain them.

3) The concentration of Jews in these fields is harmful to their moral character. The young lawyer who cannot make a living at his profession is subjected to a severe strain. Necessity may drive him to the sacrifice of ethical principles. And the merchant who struggles against the fierce competition of other merchants, and even more of mammoth chain stores, may in his efforts to survive be beguiled into cutting a corner here or there.

4) Jewish youth is presented, in its hour of decision, with only a fraction of the possibilities as to careers. Like other human beings, Jews have individual talents and predilections. Ideally each young Jew should have the full range of occupations presented to him so that he may elect the one for which he is best fitted. But since the Jews he knows—and it is mainly with Jews that he associates—conform pretty much to one economic pattern, he must in effect make his choice within its limits.

This is unfair to him. It may lead to the waste of his potentialities, making of him a round peg in a square hole, exposing him to the wretchedness of those whose life work is uncongenial. Were Jews, however, to disperse themselves economically, young Jews would have a broader variety of occupations to choose from, their chances of self-realization and maximal usefulness would be the brighter.

5) The concentration of Jews is said to constitute a source of psychic abnormalities in the Jewish personality. Because of it, Jews suffer from a sense of inadequate integration with American life as a whole. They know that there are large areas of American enterprise, many of prime importance, that are virtually *Judenrein*. In much that is America and sustains it their group has no share. Theirs, in consequence, is a sense of rootlessness, of being on the fringe of things rather than at the core. But were Jews to achieve a more representative distribution, this malaise would disappear.

Even the Jew who is himself not a farmer or a mechanic would enjoy the assurance that through his fellows he has had some part in producing the bread he eats, the building he dwells in and the machines he uses. His integration with America would be total, whereas now it is overshadowed by an apprehension of incompleteness.

At the same time, it is contended, the internal life of the Jewish group would be enriched immeasurably. As matters now stand, Jews are forever meeting other Jews who, like themselves, are business or professional men, and who in consequence have nothing fresh or novel to offer their fellows. The atmosphere of Jewry is stale, its scene poor in variations, and hence in stimulation. With a broader gamut of occupations, this disability would be overcome. Jewry would be made up not only of physicians, lawyers, accountants and clerks but of machinists, welders and wood-turners also. Since much of the time of Jews is spent in Jewish company, their experiences would be broadened. The horizons of Jewish individuals would open up; the Jewish community as a corporate body would be endowed with a full spectrum of colors and tints.

Such is the case of those who favor Jewish occupational "normalization," as they are wont to call it. The elements making up that case are obviously of unequal merit, some, indeed, devoid of merit altogether.

Thus, that anti-Semitism is a by-product of the peculiar economic distribution of the Jewish group is most questionable. Prejudice against Jews springs, as we have already seen, from sources other and deeper than these. Nor is it at all clear that an accountant at his ledgers is more provocative of bias than a machinist at his lathe. To a convinced anti-Semite, both men are Jews and hence equally irritating; by a person of good will both will be assumed to be decent people making an honest living. Is it so certain furthermore that a shift in occupation would serve to mitigate group tensions? Jews have by now long been taken for granted in certain fields. Let them however invade others, and delicate equilibriums may well be disturbed. New resentments may be kindled in those hitherto exempt from, but now exposed to Jewish competition.

Let it not be forgotten, either, that in American history there has been more than one minority group composed almost entirely of farmers and artisans, which was still the object of widespread prejudice—witness the German and Irish migrations in the '40's of the nineteenth century, or the Finnish at the turn of the twentieth, or, as Dr. Reich points out tellingly, the American Negroes at all times.

As for the notion that the normal occupations of Jews are sterile and parasitic—this, on analysis, turns out to be so much economic romanticism. The distinction commonly drawn between creative and uncreative pursuits is pretty much a myth. There are of course unproductive activities. A gambler, for example, can scarcely be said to make a substantial contribution to the common weal. But the proposition that a physician or an accountant is less useful to society than a farmer or ditchdigger is nonsense. A vastly complex system of production and distribution requires a wide variety of services for its smooth operation. Nor is the merchant dispensable. For, in the idiom of classical economics, he creates time and place utilities. All in all, the drawing of lines among occupations as to their relative creativity is at the best an act of naïveté, and, at the worst, as in Nazi propaganda, a demogogic device.

There remains then no reason for assuming that the economic normalization of Jews would appreciably affect anti-Semitism, let alone eliminate it altogether. But to deny that occupational redistribution is a sure cure for one malady is not to dismiss its worth as a remedy for others.

Here the case is much more impressive. It is, for example, manifest folly for young Jews to continue to press into conventional but overcrowded fields. By their perseverance they do in effect court financial failure and moral deterioration. Again, Jewish youth ought to have the full gamut of careers laid before it so that it may make its choice in closer conformity with personal aptitude. Certainly Jews ought to have access to the soil and the machine, not only for purposes of livelihood but equally for the normality of their experiences. And there is little doubt in my mind that being a Jew would be both pleasanter and more exciting were Jews cut less consistently in one occupational pattern.

Not then as an answer to anti-Semitism but as a contribution to the welfare of Jews—on this ground the economic redistribution of Jewry may well be urged.

This proposition must not be misunderstood. I am not suggesting that Jews evacuate old areas of enterprise. Nor do I propose that they aim for an exact correspondence with the occupational distribution of the general populace. There is neither sanctity nor special virtue in the statistics that describe how Americans earn their livelihood. Certainly I envisage no sudden transformation of the economic activities of Jews. The proposal at hand is one to be realized slowly.

And should it be undertaken, it must be with a full awareness of the serious obstacles in its way. Not only the professions of law and medicine, as practiced in metropolitan centers, have been overcrowded. In very recent years farmers and experienced artisans by the millions found the going very hard. A stampede of Jews into agriculture or industry might prove an open invitation to disaster. First, the entire American economy would have to be surveyed carefully for the purpose of discovering and exploring territories capable of absorbing fresh labor supplies. Then, and not until then, would the time be ripe for the second step—the training of young Jews in the best methods of entering upon and maintaining themselves in these fields.

Other obstacles too must be surmounted. The regrouping of Jews will unquestionably be met with resistance from outside the Jewish group. Neither employers nor labor are likely to welcome the change. After all no workingman wants more competition than is unavoidable, and, if he is a bit of an anti-Semite, he certainly will not be cordial to competition from Jews. As for the managers of factories and public utilities—let this circumstance be noted: if heretofore Jews have been found only infrequently in the heavy industries, it is not always because they have desired it so. Very often they have sought employment there only to be kept out.

The Jews of America will have to organize themselves to overcome these disabilities. On this task they can proceed hopefully. Let them establish a centralized agency for the education of offending employers and labor; let them conduct their campaign of enlightment with patience, wisdom and sympathetic insight into the mind-sets of those they wish to persuade; let them address their plea particularly to American fair-mindedness and the tradition of equal opportunity—and they may in the not too remote future open to themselves closed gates.

To this purpose American public opinion must be roused. The Jews are not the only victims of occupational discrimination. On behalf of all who are denied a chance to work because of race, creed or color, codes of fair employment practice must be enacted, and agencies set up for their enforcement.

Serious resistance to our proposal, though in the main by way of inertia rather than opposition, will come also from the Jews themselves. They are, be it remembered, the descendants of fathers who, having been debarred from field and workshop, came to regard their disability as a privilege. From this spell they have as yet not altogether freed themselves. They may grant that Jews ought to turn in new directions for their livelihoods. Yet in planning for their own children, they are likely to forget what they have accepted in principle. They will still want their sons to become doctors or merchants.

What is required is nothing less than a psychological revolution within Jews. The possibility of a radical reorientation is established by what has happened in Palestine. There several hundred thousand Jews, deriving from the same background as those of America, have achieved a transvaluation of values. Having made a veritable religion of labor, they have plunged gladly, indeed passionately, and let it also be said successfully, into farming, the handicrafts, industry, even into sailing and fishing.

What can be done in Palestine should not be impossible in America. A long process of education and reconditioning was necessary in one place; it will be equally necessary in the other.

Nothing in this presentation should be construed as a retreat from the position taken in Chapter 5, that Jews must insist on their freedom to pursue any legitimate calling. As American citizens—and there can be no compromise on the point—this is their privilege. The wisdom and expediency of Jews confining themselves to certain occupations may be a subject of debate; their right to do so is beyond all discussion. This is a point I have made before. If I make it again, it is because I think the repetition necessary and worth while.

Out of the foregoing, a program of action emerges:

1) Access on the part of Jews to all occupations must be guarded zealously.

2) To this end there must be no submission to anti-Semitism in any area of employment, whether public or private.

3) Every effort must be made to open to Jews fields from which hitherto they have been debarred, thus encouraging their wider diffusion in the totality of American life.

4) A systematic survey of the contemporary economic scene should be undertaken for the purpose of spotting new forms of enterprise for Jews.

5) The Jewish community should undertake through education to correct those psychological attitudes that in effect narrow the range of choice for most Jews when they seek a livelihood.

6) American Jewry ought to establish agencies to train young Jews in occupations new to their group, and to help them get started.

A program such as this, I repeat, is no neutralizer or inhibitant of anti-Semitism—a purpose for which it is not intended. It has as its goal rather the improved welfare of Jews as individuals and of Jewry as a corporate body. Let these ends be achieved and a contribution will also have been made to America as well, which after all is neither stronger nor healthier than its component elements.

II

PROBLEMS OF SELF-ACCEPTANCE

7

The Sick Soul

I F ANTI-SEMITISM is the most spectacular Jewish problem and, in a practical
sense, the most urgent, the issue of Jewish morale can fairly be said to be
in its own quiet fashion spiritually the most desperate. For, so long as he
keeps his self-respect, an individual can endure anything no matter how
grievous. But let him lose that and he will be incapable of joy, creativity,
perhaps even of life itself. Wherefore, Goethe observed brilliantly, the greatest evil that can befall a man is "that he should come to think ill of himself."

To this disease of the psyche, some American Jews have fallen victim.
How many, no one knows; but there are at least thousands who "think ill
of themselves," who suffer from shame, who are plagued by a sense of
inferiority—all because they are Jews. And occasionally one meets a Jew in
whom the malady is virulent, a Jew who literally hates Judaism, other Jews
and himself. That this condition is actual and not uncommon is attested
by some of the keenest observers of contemporary Jewish life.

So, writing in *The Menorah Journal* of the summer of 1942, Professor
Salo Baron asserts: "There are in all western Jewish communities innumerable Jews whom I have frequently ventured to style the 'inverted Marranos.'
Those appear and act outwardly as Jews; they are recognized as Jews by
themselves and their environment. But they deeply resent this fact which,
for one reason or another, they cannot alter. Such inverted Marranos, hating
their Jewish heritage and involuntary allegiance, usually become self-haters
of a pathological kind. They not only destroy their own peace of mind; they
are a menace to the equilibrium of the general as well as Jewish society
around them."

To the same effect, Professor Kurt Lewin testifies in *The Contemporary
Jewish Record* of June 1941: "That self-hatred is present among Jews is a
fact that the non-Jew would hardly believe, but which is well known among
the Jews themselves."

Despite Dr. Lewin, one need not be a Jew to spot the phenomenon where it is present. A perceptive Gentile, if he is on the alert, can detect it readily. Mr. Louis Adamic for example not only has had no difficulty in identifying the malady, he has given an expert clinical picture of its nature and course. In his *What's Your Name* he tells the bizarre tale of Miss Julia Drink-water—Anglo-Saxon to the fingertips and New England Brahmin as to the manner born, who turns out in the end to be Cora Rabinovitz of the Bronx and Brooklyn, a Jewess who yearned so to be of *Mayflower* stock that in misrepresenting herself she was fulfilling her life's dream rather than perpetrating a fraud; who, in any case, was so fearfully ashamed of what she was that she preferred to disappear rather than confess the ugly truth about her origins to her impeccably Gentile fiancé.

It should not be supposed that a temper of self-contempt is general among American Jews, let alone universal. And where it does exist, it only rarely reaches the acute and virulent stage of self-repudiation. Nor should it be imagined that only Jews are susceptible to this disease. Malaise over one's identity, and self-rejection because of it are by no means uniquely Jewish manifestations. As Mr. Adamic's writings demonstrate, as is made unmistakably clear in literature on the American Negro, the phenomenon crops up in other groups as well. But these, be it noted, are always minorities, and always disparaged minorities. This fact provides a sure clue to the causes of the phenomenon, both among Jews and others. Quite obviously it is the response of the individual to two circumstances—the strain of a differential identity and the pressure of popular disapproval.

It is now clear why Jews should have so little immunity against this ailment. For they embody to an extraordinary degree its two preconditions. They are, in the first place, not only a minority, but a universal minority. Theirs is a dissenting religion, a distinct cultural heritage. What is more, they are constantly exposed to public criticism. Sometimes, as in recent years, this beats at them like a sledge hammer. At other periods, it is quiescent. Quiescent but never absent. Exclusions, ostracisms, affronts are always part of their existence.

The relatively peaceful prejudice that is the normal lot of Jews is infinitely to be preferred to the wild anti-Semitism of the Hitlerian era. And yet, psychically at least, the former can be more destructive than the latter, just as the prick of a pin, under certain circumstances, can be more dangerous than its stab. For he who is stabbed will be too conscious of pain to abide it.

He will attempt to pull away from, or to resist his antagonist. And if he is so bound that he can do neither, he will grit his teeth and endure, but in any case will not view his condition as normal and hence tolerable. But he who is only scratched, who is at most irritated, may grow accustomed to his discomfort and come to disregard it. In which case and before he is aware of it, the point of friction may have become an ugly, festering wound.

The very recent and very spectacular anti-Semitism of Hitler has no doubt made its contribution to the disintegration of morale and self-esteem among Jews. But in the main where Jewish self-respect has crumbled, it is more often as a consequence of a succession of pinpricks, each unimportant in itself, but all adding up to a general infection of the spirit. Consider for a moment the psychic influences, consequences of a minority status and of group prejudice, that play upon the American Jew.

In the first instance, he tends to feel himself, even under the most favorable circumstances, not altogether wanted by the society of which he is a part. No matter what his theoretical legal rights, he is not socially quite the equal of his Gentile fellows. No matter how cordially he is received it is never without some reservation. Even in liberal lands therefore he is likely to regard himself as something of a stepchild, well treated perhaps, but a stepchild. One need not know much about the workings of the human personality to understand how devastating this can be. Child psychology has made much of the conviction of being unwanted, indicting it as the root cause of all sorts of maladjustments. Such has been for over a century the psychic status of the Jew.

Again, the Jew senses that just because he is a Jew, he is subject to special insecurities. Like all human beings, he must submit to inevitabilities and inexorabilities. Death and taxation are as certain for him as for anyone else. But as a Jew, he is exposed to an additional set of risks and perils. For at no time can he be overly confident as to the stability of his position. The majority group may at any hour undergo a change of heart concerning him. Given extraordinary stresses, it may cease to be fair and law-abiding. Inevitably he worries, as anyone must whose position is dependent on others. Insecurity is therefore a constant in his psychology. Under normal circumstances it diminishes almost to the vanishing point. Fears of any nature after a while begin to appear foolish when the dreaded event has failed to materialize. So, people who live on a volcano that has not erupted for some time attain eventually a fair measure of equanimity. They never lose their apprehensions altogether.

In addition, every Jew at some time or other has reason to conclude that he has been penalized for his Jewishness. If he is seeking employment, if he is a student applying for admission to a medical school, if he is an instructor who wishes to be a professor, or a parent who desires to enroll his daughter in a finishing school, or a suburbanite who would like to be a member of the local golf club—he knows that his identity multiplies the hazards and obstacles in his way. Were he no Jew, he quite naturally tells himself, he would have his desire.

Sometimes these people are quite right in their assumptions. It is their Jewishness that keeps them from achieving their purposes. On the other hand, their identity is as often altogether irrelevant. If they fail it is because of themselves, not their group. Unfortunately Jews, like other human beings, are so constituted as to be reluctant to pass adverse judgment on themselves. Hence, whether with justice or not they will hold their Jewishness at fault for whatever goes wrong with their lives.

In the light of this logic—and it is logic of a sort—Jewishness comes to be regarded as a misfortune, an unchosen but inescapable handicap, like a physical deformity. It is a mean trick played by an unkind fate. Having conceived a resentment, the Jew is very likely to direct it against other Jews. For by a continuation of the same reasoning they are by their very existence responsible for his difficulties. What is most wrong with Jews, it begins to appear, is that there is a number of them. If he were the one Jew in the world he would certainly meet no anti-Semitism. If, failing that ideal condition, the body of Jews were small enough it would never provoke unfriendly attention. There are simply too many Jews. Besides the world offers only a limited amount of social advantage to all Jewry—a sort of ration of jobs, acceptances and opportunities. From his viewpoint each additional Jew means that he has less, that at a table on which there is already not enough, another boarder has seated himself. So our specimen Jew comes to rebel not only against what he is, but against his fellows as well.

The whole story however is still not told. Two other factors, one positive and one negative, contribute powerfully toward the disintegration of self-esteem within Jews. Anti-Semitic propaganda is addressed to Gentiles, not Jews. But Jews listen, and may also be convinced by what they hear. They are persuaded that they deserve their bad repute. Does this seem incredible?

Then reflect on the Jew's position. In books and newspapers, in lectures, in conversations he overhears, it is dinned into his head that he and his kind are pretty bad specimens of humanity. He is told that he is obnoxious socially, unclean physically, degraded morally. Sooner or later he may begin to reason with himself that there may be something to all this ado, that where there is smoke there must be fire.

But once again, should he reach the pass of believing that the anti-Semite has a case, he will refuse to concede that it applies to him. Whatever truth may be in it, he assures himself, must refer to other Jews. Whereupon he gets very busy scrutinizing Jews outside his circle, hoping to detect in them the vices catalogued by the anti-Semite. And, as would be the case with any group of human beings, he manages to find some Jews who are the kind he is looking for.

Now his condition is sad indeed. He has come to believe the worst of all Jews except himself and his coterie. Yet the world somehow refuses to see the distinction among Jews that is so clear to him. If he is a restrained person he will forever entertain, though never voice, the hope that Gentiles will in the end perceive that he is "different." If he is less meticulous, he will be crass enough to proclaim his exceptional nature. In any event, he will hold himself aloof from other Jews. So by a strange turn, anti-Semitism victimizes the Jew in a fashion anti-Semites never conceived. It converts him to its cause.

All this would have been without effect on Jews were it not that something has disappeared from their make-up. The medieval Jew was subjected to a full-blooded anti-Semitism that compares impressively with contemporary Jew-baiting. His exclusion was absolute, his security, even of life, virtually nonexistent. Yet, whatever anti-Semitism might do to his person and possessions, it scarcely touched him psychically. Certainly he was never seduced by it into despising himself or his group. Against that he was protected by his tradition. His religion invested his existence as a Jew with intimations of eternity. Knowing the culture of his people, identified with it, he felt that it enriched and stimulated him. The prophets, saints and sages of the Jewish past were his companions. No matter what the anti-Semite might say or do, he knew that Judaism and Jewishness were honorable and meaningful realities. That knowledge armored his sense of worth.

For many modern Jews these preservative forces are no longer operative. Having abandoned their religious tradition, ignorant of the Jewish past, unedified by its present, uninspired by any aspirations for its future, they have nothing on which to sustain self-esteem. Jewishness to them is simply a disability. They have lost the secret of that spiritual prophylactic which enabled their fathers to preserve their psychic wholesomeness.

A sense of being unwanted, a feeling of insecurity, special penalties, exposure to hostile propaganda, together with the absence of an inner life calculated to regenerate self-respect—these are the forces that have played uninterruptedly upon the Jew for over a century.

Their consequences are many and diverse. In the main, their effect is to engender the mood of "thinking ill of one's self"—or, to put it in current psychological jargon, an inferiority complex. Jews, in other words, come to regard themselves as inherently not as good as Gentiles. This temper will in some individuals be faint, no more than a vague malaise; in others, however, it will be embittered. But whatever its intensity, a sense of inferiority and the unhappiness attendant on it are natural consequences of the adverse circumstances we have described.

That Jews react variously to the same stimuli, some becoming very sick and others emerging unscathed, should occasion no surprise. Diseases of the spirit behave much like those of the body. Each of us, for example, is constantly under physical attack from pathogenic organisms. Most of us possess enough inner resistance to defend ourselves without ever being conscious of the struggle. A smaller number is sufficiently infected as to be taken to bed. Even of these, the majority recovers full health. It is only a handful that is permanently invalided. The very fewest die.

In an exactly analogous fashion, Jews have reacted to the unhealthy psychic influences that surround and infest them. Many Jews, perhaps the vast majority, come through untouched, entirely sane and balanced in their attitudes toward the Jewish identity. They have escaped infection, in some instances because of natural health of the spirit; in others, by virtue of the immunity afforded by a vigorous Judaism; and in many cases doubtless through blind luck, just as one may, by pure fortune, escape the ravages of a plague. A smaller number, having been mildly infected, have psychic scars and disabilities more or less serious to show. Still fewer have been profoundly corrupted. The very fewest have been spiritually destroyed.

The Jewish group then constitutes a sort of inverted cone of psychological responses, tapering downward from a base, at which unhappiness over a

Jewish identity is vague and fugitive, to an apex where it is acute and passionate.

Consider, first of all, the largest section in whom the psychic damage has been slightest. At this level, restlessness over Jewishness is by definition least. But it exists. And it reveals itself in acts, moods and postures not pronounced but not without significance. Thus, it has contributed to the social stratification of American Jewry. Jews, whom the world carelessly assumes to be of one piece, actually are divided into quite distinct classes. Spanish and Portuguese Jews feel themselves superior to German Jews. German Jews look down upon East European Jews. Various brands of East European Jews speak slightingly of one another. Every group of Jews, in other words, condescends to some other, making all of Jewry a vicious cycle of more or less kindly contempt.

Now all social groups are divided into classes. It is apparently an unlovely human necessity that men must have someone to look down upon. The stratification of Jews is then by no means a unique phenomenon. Group snobbery among them is the same old, ugly thing as among others. Yet it is something more. It is an act of dissociation, a subconscious gesture of separation, whereby the individual Jew hopes to ward off from himself the disapproval that beats on his fellows.

Their sense of insecurity accounts, too, for the close scrutiny to which Jews subject one another. However conscious the world may be of undesirable traits in them, that awareness is infinitely more acute in Jews themselves. In an apprehension keen sometimes to the point of anguish, each watches his fellows. The conservative shudders lest he espy a Jewish radical; the radical is sickened that other Jews should be conservative. And both alike live in horror lest they come upon some third Jew who offends morality or etiquette. As within families that do not feel sure of their position, there is among Jews an excess of self-consciousness, of mutual supervision, of accusation and counteraccusation.

The sense of inferiority on the part of Jews asserts itself still further. It is responsible for their tendency to "play down" their Jewishness, to render it inconspicuous and to strip it of all distinctiveness. It accounts for the practice whereunder Jews give their children the most flamboyantly Anglo-Saxon or French names, or names of distinctly Christian association, but in any case not Jewish names—a practice so common that it has become a safe presumption that anyone carrying an Old Testament given name is likely to be a Gentile.

A disintegrated sense of worth breathes in the sentiment, often voiced in Jewish circles, that a particular act, gesture, idea or ideal is too "Jewish"—a criticism infinitely revealing since, obviously, nothing of which one approves can be too true to its character.

None of these manifestations is of large moment. All however are symptomatic of emotional disturbance, suggestive of the fact that Jews are uneasy over their identity and, because of it, uncertain of their own worth.

But the gravest consequence of psychic malaise among Jews, even in this, its mildest form, is to be found in their group life. For quite naturally, Jews who are uneasy over their Jewishness will be reluctant to associate themselves with anything Jewish. They will stand aloof from the Jewish community or will strive sedulously to keep it as inactive as possible. They will resist the Jewish religion and Jewish culture.

When they are exposed to instruction in Judaism, even indeed when they themselves seek such instruction, their mind-set may prevent the educational process from "taking." They may block out or minimize what they learn; they may be incapable of learning at all. As thousands of children have difficulty with arithmetic because they dislike the teachers who present the subject to them or the schools in which it is taught, Jews forever keep repelling Jewish knowledge no matter how it is drummed into them because they are not at peace with the core fact of Jewishness. This circumstance, as rabbis and Jewish educators will testify, constitutes one of the largest single obstacles against imparting to Jews a familiarity with their heritage and the will to live by it.

Everything touched by Judaism suffers in consequence. The insecure Jew may turn antireligious simply because religion comes to him through the Synagogue which is perforce a Jewish institution. Or he may manifest sympathy with every religious communion except the Jewish. Even in the Synagogue itself the process of self-repudiation leaves a trail of destruction. It impels those under its sway to seek to fashion Jewish faith and worship not after its own genius but in conformity with prevailing non-Jewish patterns. Conversely, it induces antagonism toward all distinctively Jewish forms. Many a Jew has difficulty in making peace with the most beautiful and meaningful of ancestral Jewish ceremonials simply because these depart from majority practice and in consequence are unmistakable tokens of Judaism.

Where in Jewish life can the unhappy influences of the sick soul not be discerned? Jewish education, for the child and the adult alike, is its victim. The Jew maladjusted to his Jewishness is not only, as we have already observed, himself loath to learn, he will seek to prevent instruction for others or to limit it to the barest minimum. He will frown on Jewish art, music and literature, either rejecting them out of hand or at the best suppressing whatever spontaneity and exuberance they may exhibit. Himself uncomfortable over his Jewishness, he wants beyond all else that it shall be inconspicuous.

The clearest instance of this temper is to be found in the controversy over Zionism. In favor of the establishment of a Jewish Homeland in Palestine there are, as we shall have occasion to see, many and compelling arguments. Against it on the other hand a case can be made—less cogent to be sure, but a case nonetheless. And much of anti-Zionism is entirely candid and forthright, motivated altogether by the logic of the negative. But much of the opposition derives from totally irrelevant considerations.

To the Jew who desires beyond all else to stifle Jewishness, a Jewish Palestine presents the most painful of prospects. It means the establishment in a particular place of a large self-determining Jewish community, Jewish in identity and in universal recognition. Let that community come into being and everyone looking toward the Near East will inevitably think the word: Jew. But the most ardent dream of the Jewish escapist is that that monosyllable may be forgotten by him and the world.

Now it becomes possible to understand the fury with which some Jews have attacked the Zionist program. Now too we can see why they may concede its virtues and still resist it tooth and nail. An old shrewd folk epigram has it that one does not refer to a rope in a family, one of whose members has died on the gallows. This is Jewish Palestine in the imagination of those Jews to whom Jewishness is of the nature of a secret shame. It is a public reference to their disgrace.

We have been moving steadily, as the reader may have observed, from the trivial to the graver manifestations of a disintegrated Jewish self-respect. We now stand at that level in the cone at which only one course is open to Jews—flight from themselves and their identity. Scattered throughout American society are Jews who want nothing more than to cease to be Jews and be accepted as Gentiles. This desire may take the form of an aching yearning toward something forever unattainable. They will then go through life always wistful, restless, suffocated. In other individuals this aspiration can become a consuming fire, an ardent ambition to be achieved at all costs. Then Jews change their names, dissociate themselves from their fellows, calculatingly conceal their origin and try to "pass." Then they school themselves to listen unprotestingly to anti-Semitic utterances, lest the slightest quiver of indignation on their part give them away. Indeed on occasion, and as an extra precaution, they may themselves take the lead in Jew-baiting.

There was a time, and that not so long ago, when dissident Jews had one sure exit open to them. They could turn apostate and formally enter some one or other of the Christian denominations. Since the Emancipation began, there have never been wanting some Jews to travel that road. Needless to say, conversions to Christianity have often been genuine, altogether unvitiated by escapism or self-contempt. Individuals on occasion have left Judaism for Christianity, inspired by only the highest motives, just as there has always been at least a trickle of Christian proselytes flowing into the Synagogue. With sincere conversions in either direction, I am not presently concerned. They are decisions of conscience achieved often only after a great and anguished ordeal. They deserve deference.

But some, perhaps many, perhaps even most of the Jews who enter churches fall far short from being as white as fleece in their motives. Whether consciously or unconsciously, they are much more interested in ceasing to be Jews than in becoming Christians, more eager to throw off what they were than to embrace anything in particular. That is why Jewish converts to Christianity follow a predictable pattern. Very rich Jews almost invariably join the Episcopal Church, and always its most fashionable congregations. Jewish intellectuals of a late Victorian design prefer Unitarianism or Congregationalism, the communions of that Yankee New England with which they long to be identified. Bourgeois Jews and especially their wives are likely to elect Christian Science. The Catholic Church attracts on the one hand Jews who, badly scared by anti-Semitism, feel that only a strongly organized communion and one zealous on behalf of "the souls it has acquired" is likely to offer them significant protection. Again, it draws to itself tired Jewish intellectuals, ex-Communists disillusioned with Marxism, weary rationalists whom reason has failed, the uprooted and unpossessed Jew who is looking for a tradition, for authoritative guidance, for a dogma to trust—

who would in sum be ripe for Orthodox Judaism, except that it is regrettably Jewish, whereas the Roman Catholic Church is so immaculately and blessedly Gentile.

Of this sort of formal bowing out of the Jewish group by way of conversion, there has been much less in very recent years. Experience has revealed that it does not work. The Jew who became a Christian of whatever sect has pretty generally remained a Jew in everyone's thinking, his own, that of Jews, that of Gentiles and even in that of the clergyman who baptized him. No church, it has been demonstrated, has been able to shield its converts of Jewish origin against full-blown anti-Semitism. And some have not even tried. All in all, refugees from Judaism have learned to their sorrow that a baptismal certificate offers less of safety and acceptance than they had supposed.

This means that the problem of the escapist Jew has grown more acute and painful, more nearly desperate. For now he has no way of crying quits to his Jewishness, of purging himself of it. He is tied to an identity he does not want and cannot slough off, which, therefore, he is likely to resent the more fiercely. This is the last and final stage in the disintegration of Jewish self-respect. With it we leave the normal and enter the realm of the psychotic and diseased. We come to the lowest depths of our constricting cone, to its apex, the point at which the Jew hates himself, other Jews and Judaism, because they are all Jewish.

For source material on the psychopathology of the Jewish personality, I turn to the volume entitled *Judischer Selbst-Hass (Jewish Self-Hatred)* by Theodore Lessing, pacifist, defender of the Weimar Republic, philosopher and Jew, who was murdered by Nazi assassins in 1933. In this book Lessing sets himself to an analysis of Jewish anti-Semitism, to a description of exceptional and flagrant instances of the sick Jewish soul. Of the variety of case histories he adduces, one or two will serve as specimens. Here, for example, is one: "Arthur Trebitsch, born in 1879 in Vienna, of Jewish stock, gifted as poet, philosopher, and student of political science, author of approximately twenty books and countless essays, was until his death on September 26, 1927, the wildest persecutor of Jews." Then follows the fantastic story of a handsome, blond Jew who was convinced of the existence of an international Jewish conspiracy against Aryanism, who chose as his comrade-in-arms anti-Semites like Eric Ludendorff, who ended his days obsessed with the fear that Jews had conspired to take his life.

No less astounding is the parallel tale of Otto Weininger, at twenty-three the author of the brilliant and sensational work, *Geschlecht und Charakter* and at twenty-three a suicide, largely because being a Jew he did not wish to continue to live.

But the most awesome passage in Lessing's book is found in a diary which he quotes. Dated as of 1920, written by a woman whom he describes as wellborn, beautiful, wealthy and talented, this document reads in part:

"I force myself not to think of it. To no avail. It thinks in me, thinks by itself, consults neither my wish, nor will, nor the natural drive to avoid the painful, hateful, deadly. It is always present, always in me: *this consciousness of my descent.* As a leper or one diseased with cancer bears his nauseating ailment concealed under his cloak and yet is conscious of it every instant, so do I bear the disgrace and shame, the metaphysical guilt of my Jewishness.

"What are other pains, disappointments and restraints which come from without compared to this hell within? To have to be what one detests! To be *compelled* to be, yes, to be compelled. Devices, extenuations and self-deceits do no good here. I am conscious, clearly, pitilessly: Jewishness is a matter of *being.* It cannot be shaken off. As little as a dog or pig can cast off its doggishness or swinishness, so little can I tear myself from the ties that bind me to that stage of existence that lies between man and beast— the Jews.

"Were I a murderer, a thief, had I committed the most pitiable, most execrable act—I should nevertheless stand guiltless before the Eternal. But never, so long as I live, will I be able to strip from myself the curse of my identity; never can I deny the sin of my Jewishness; the eternal metaphysical original sin weighing upon me as heavily as mountains. I know myself as cursed and damned. . . . "

There is more in the same tenor but this specimen quite suffices. Through this frothing, insane outpouring, one glimpses the bottomless pit, the tip of the cone, the lowest level in the Inferno of Jewish self-contempt.

How is the failure of morale, so grave a menace to the happiness and wholesomeness of spirit of the individual Jew, best to be averted? One's first impulse is to look for deliverance in de-Judaization. After all, it is because Jews are Jews, members of a minority group, that they are exposed to this psychic peril. Very well then, a snap judgment would seem to indicate, let them cease to be Jews. Let them cast off whatever is distinctive in their identity and heritage; let them lose themselves in the peoples among whom they live.

We shall, in the next chapter, appraise the practicality, indeed the very possibility of this tactic. As a procedure in psychotherapy—and this is our immediate point of reference—it is not only inefficacious, it is downright dangerous. It would seek to heal a wound with a hair of the dog that inflicted it; to neutralize a poison by administering more of it. The sick Jew is in his plight because, unable to make peace with his Jewish identity, he has been in flight from it. Now he is told to run harder. Even if he succeeds against all probability in getting away, the upshot of such a course is inevitably the intensification, rather than mitigation, of his difficulties.

A second counsel often recommended is that Jews establish their worth so firmly on their individual merits that no anti-Semitic blast will be able to move them. The reasoning behind this recommendation runs roughly as follows: because he is a Jew, a member of a minority, the Jew is likely to develop a sense of unworth and with it a whole train of dire consequences. Very well then, let him reinforce the sense of his self-esteem by achievement, possibly, indeed preferably, by achievement unrelated to his Jewishness. Let him be a good citizen, a devoted husband and father, a constructive businessman, a gifted musician, a brilliant mathematician, an epochal servant of humanity. Then when his morale is being shaken by anti-Semitism he can look to his attainments and, his sense of worth restored by them, can readily recover his psychic balance.

Now every human being ought to make the most of his talents, ought to be as useful and creative as is possible to him. And the consciousness of duty done, always pleasurable, may in the case of Jews often have a further utility, as a revivifier of self-respect. But in the main, this too is not the way out of the psychic impasse.

First, because it tends to corrupt the normal expressions of personality with intimations of an ulterior and essentially irrelevant motive. One is a good citizen or writes verse or engages in social reform not only for inherent reasons but so that someday he may be able to say to himself: "I'm a decent fellow after all." Life's interests are often compensations for adversity, but it is not easy to keep them natural when they are twisted to serve that purpose.

More cogent, because the procedure suggested is as a rule unlikely to be effective. A person accused of being a thief and a cheat is not helped by a consciousness of his capabilities as a metaphysician. Charged with dishonesty, he must know of himself the one truth that is pertinent: that he is honest. It is his honor, not his intellect, that is under a cloud. Where he is attacked, in his integrity, there both before the world and himself he must be cleared. Nothing else, no matter how flattering to him, will really do.

By the same token a Jew who *qua* Jew is obsessed with a sense of inferiority does not neutralize his difficulty by recounting to himself distinguished but irrelevant attainments. It is as a Jew that he questions his worth. It is only as a Jew that his conviction of worth can be restored.

The proof of this thesis, that one can create and create and still despise oneself, is written large in the biographies of contemporary Jews. Karl Marx was certainly a man of large accomplishments and well aware of them to boot. Yet, as his essay "On the Jewish Question" reveals, he had an abysmal contempt for himself and other Jews on the score of Jewishness. The brilliant contributions of Sigmund Freud did not protect him against a marked case of *selbst-Hass*. Indeed he who was the first to identify as a clinical entity the syndrome of Jewish demoralization failed to detect it in himself.

The clearest demonstration in recent literature that achievement is often inadequate to relieve malaise over Jewishness is to be found in Leopold Infeld's autobiography significantly entitled *Quest*. Here a mathematician and physicist of undisputed capacities and well-earned prominence discloses how, despite all else, a man may be haunted and tortured simply because he is a Jew. Permanently haunted and tortured. For, though Infeld asserts that he has purged himself of the harrowing evil, he protests too much and too fervently.

There is, in other words, little hope for the solution of the problem of self-contempt either in flight from Jewishness or in recourse to irrelevance. The struggle of the Jew to maintain his self-respect must be fought out along Jewish lines.

All this is to say that Jews are the more likely to be capable of resisting adverse psychic influences and of preserving their self-esteem as they know and love the history and tradition that have made them; as they enjoy, are stimulated by and participate in Jewish life; and as, last of all, they are imbued with a persuasion of the meaningfulness of the whole Jewish enterprise.

In discussing how Jews might best deal with anti-Semitism, I made the point that among other things they require a revived and invigorated Judaism. Apparently no matter where one scratches the Jewish problem one uncovers in the end the same truth. The second major issue confronting American Jews—that of self-acceptance—has led to an identical conclusion. Both as a line of defense against anti-Semitism and for the health of his own soul, the American Jew needs not less Judaism but more.

8

The Ultimate Decision

ONE ISSUE HAUNTS contemporary Jewish life like an inexorcisable ghost. Only rarely is it couched as a formal question; hardly ever does it appear on the agenda of public meetings, Indeed, so far as overt expression goes, it is by general consent treated as though it did not exist at all. Yet its presence can be felt whenever Jews assemble to discuss their social problems. If Jewish organizations split wide open over apparently unimportant considerations, if their proceedings are more excited than seems warranted, this hidden point of controversy is very likely to be responsible. Certainly whenever it does come into the open, it wakes the whirlwind. For this is the first and the last question of Jewish life, predetermining all others. In many senses, it is *the* Jewish problem par excellence.

This ultimate decision is over the perseverance of the Jews as Jews. It consists in a choice between the House of Israel continuing in its historic enterprise or undertaking to liquidate itself and shut up shop.

It was John Stuart Mill who once pointed out that no proposition can be said to have been refuted until it has been refuted in its best form. By the same token a problem must at the very least be properly stated if any claim is to be made concerning its solution. So with the alternatives of Jewish survival or extinction. A sound judgment concerning them must derive from an understanding, not a misunderstanding, of the two terms.

Thus Jewish survival does not signify, as is often imagined, a return to the Ghetto. It does not imply that American Jews withdraw so much as an inch from the social, political and cultural interests of the American community; that they foster a private group existence contained within, yet isolated from the larger body politic.

Such a course would in the first place be foredoomed to failure. No minority can successfully quarantine itself against its milieu. What is more, a tactic of this sort would constitute a downright immorality. It would mean that Jews avail themselves of the advantages of American society without assuming responsibility for it. The Jewish survivalist is neither so stupid nor so unethical. On the contrary, he is eager to expose his Jewishness to all the winds of doctrine that blow across the American scene. He assumes that American Jews will participate to the full in our country's life, that they will speak English as their first tongue, will regard the American republic as the object of their sole political allegiance, and will take to their hearts the classic goals of American society.

Assimilation is something more and radically other than this adaptation. It is the full surrender of Judaism and the Jewish identity. No matter how Judaism and Jewishness be conceived or defined, the assimilationist, as opposed to the adaptationist, wants none of them. He wills to lose himself beyond recollection or recovery in the majority group, to expunge even the faintest traces of what his fathers were and he is.

Here then is the crux of the matter. Not whether Jews and Judaism shall make themselves conformable to American circumstance—to this proposition there is no demurrer in any Jewish quarter—but whether the individual Jew and the Jewish community shall seek to be swallowed up in oblivion, in a final and irretrievable de-Judaization.

To this question all assimilationists answer aye. There, however, resemblance among them ceases. Beyond their common conclusion they exhibit a wide range of tempers, motives and reasoning. One assimilationist, interested only in his own exit from Jewishness, does not care a continental whether other Jews follow his precedent. Operating on the principles of *sauve qui peut,* and the devil take the hindmost, he knows only that he finds being a Jew a thankless, pointless business, and wishes to be done with it.

Of a different stamp is the assimilationist who thinks not of himself alone but of his fellows also. For his peace of mind it is not enough that he undertake to quit, even that he make good his intention. He wants all Jews to make the plunge with him. In this he may be motivated by no more than elemental self-interest. What other Jews do cannot but affect him. Should they remain stubbornly Jewish and so forever remind the world of his own Jewishness, his course will be all the harder. But as often as not the assimilationist's solicitude is pure altruism. Having discovered a saving truth, he cannot hoard it. His is the obverse side of group loyalty, a perverted *esprit de corps.* As the suicide of an entire household is sometimes an un-usual instance of familial devotion, so his desire to join hands with other Jews in group self-extinction may reflect his sense of solidarity with them. Except that in this instance, he loves them, to quote Chesterton, with a terrible hate.

Assimilationists differ among themselves in a second respect. Some follow an assimilationist line without deliberation, even unconsciously. De-Judaiza-tion is for them a process rather than a doctrine. They are not, so far as they are aware, going anywhere; they are drifting. Without willing it they have lost all distinctive Jewish informations, interests and loyalties. In some in-stances generations have been required for this end; in others one lifetime has sufficed. But whatever the span, the results are the same: Jews ignorant of Judaism, observant of none of its practices, unrelated to its values, un-affiliated with its institutions, devoid of allegiance either to the group or its spiritual possessions—in sum, Jews in name only.

In exactly opposite fashion there are de-Judaizers by conviction and choice, Jews who, having determined against Judaism on grounds of either mood or reason, proceed systematically to implement their decision. They may, as we observed in the chapter prior to this, be emotionally driven. If so, their assimilationism will be quite different in tone from the easygoing sort that is born in inertia. It will be angry and determined, and when crossed, fierce and impatient. Here is the wellspring of the bitterness and rage that gush forth whenever Jews debate Jewish survival.

But though deliberate assimilation may be psychic in origin, it can have other, more rational and healthier sources. It can be, and often is, a reasoned position. For many Jews it represents a logical program, the consequence of an objective examination of the Jewish problem. In other words, a cogent and impressive argument can be made for assimilationism.

Assimilationists as a whole have not been overly articulate. The literature expounding their doctrine is very meager. And that understandably. For if they be assimilationists by drift, they are by definition unaware of their own nature. If they are sick-souled escapists, they will be reluctant to pause over the Jewishness from which they are trying to flee. And the intellectually persuaded assimilationist, having decided against Judaism, is no longer in-terested in it, not even to the extent of telling the world why he is not interested in it. Hence it is difficult to find a flesh and blood assimilationist who has articulated candidly and systematically the credo by which he lives as a Jew, or to put it more accurately, wishes to cease to be one. Yet, we shall understand assimilationism more readily if we personalize our presentation of it. Let us therefore conjure up a Jew who embodies conscious, deliberate de-Judaization in all its forms. He will be a myth, or more accurately, a composite. But he will serve our purpose.

Mr. O, as we shall call him, advances two lines of argument, one practical, the other idealistic, both converging on the common conclusion that Jews would be well advised to discard their differential heritage. First of all, and as a matter of prosaic actuality, Judaism has lost all meaning and significance for great numbers of American Jews.

Judaism and the Jewish group are then in process of dissolution; which, he holds, is just as it should be. For the Jewish tradition in his eyes is thoroughly obsolete. Its beliefs and practices are either outmoded or else are shared by all the traditions of the Western world and hence, regardless of their origin, in no sense distinctively Jewish.

Convinced that all of Judaism—doctrine, practice and culture—is either worthless or replaceable, Mr. O quite intelligibly favors its dissolution. Let Jews and Judaism disappear, he contends. Nothing will be lost; much will be gained. The individual Jew will be relieved of the burdens of his minority status; he will be spared the assignment of preserving an ancestral religion which has lost its meaning. He will be emancipated to dedicate all his creative energy to American life. Last of all, a surface of friction within the community will be eliminated. Now Jews and Christians rub against and irritate one another. Let the Jews cease to be Jews and an old social tension will be relaxed.

What is commended by common sense is dictated by idealism also. Mr. O is likely to be one of those who look forward to the elimination of all religious, cultural and perhaps ethnic differentiations from the American people. He recognizes the right of creedal communions and minority cultural groups to their special beliefs and interests. But all along, it is clear, he regards the final dissolution of all differential elements as the optimal and ideal eventuality. For him, quite obviously, America is a melting pot that should in the end yield a homogeneous society.

He may go further to urge the obliteration of all lines of demarcation among men, regarding the variety and multiplicity of religious communions, cultures and peoples as a superfluity and a misfortune. In other words and among other things, he is an assimilationist because he is fired by the Utopian vision of an undifferentiated mankind. To him, de-Judaization is of the nature of an ideal. In their self-extinction, the Jews would blaze a trail for others. Nothing in their life career could possibly become them like leaving it.

To these three propositions, therefore, the assimilationist argument reduces itself:

1) Judaism has lost its value for Jews and for mankind; it is either obsolete, or else whatever in it still possesses meaningfulness is available to Jews in the religions and cultures of the non-Jewish world.

2) Both the Jews and society will be better off for the dissolution of Jewry —the former because they will be freed from the insecurities and frustrations of a minority identity; the latter, because a surface of friction will be eliminated.

3) Assimilation is to be commended on ideal grounds. The Jew owes it to America to have no special interests of his own. Indeed it may even be his obligation to mankind to renounce his heritage and so hasten the achievement of an undifferentiated mankind and a homogeneous world culture.

This is the assimilationist plea. Now, how does it stand up under critical scrutiny?

First, as to its practicality.

The issue is no sooner raised than the assimilationist case is immediately bankrupt. It proposes a program that cannot be executed. If it is often difficult to live as a Jew, it is next to impossible to quit being one. An occasional Jewish individual of unusual endowments or in an extraordinarily favorable position may make good an exit from the Jewish group. The great mass of Jews will have to remain what they are, regardless of their preferences in the matter, if for no other reason than because the Gentile world insists on it. They may change their names and their faces, cut themselves off ruthlessly from Jews and Judaism—all, if experience is a guide, to no avail. They may even adopt Christianity formally. Yet, as Gwethalyn Graham has testified in her perceptive novel *Earth and High Heaven,* they remain Jewish. They are Catholics or Episcopalians or Unitarians but somehow also and inexorably Jews.

How this can be, we shall inquire in the next chapter. There we shall discern that in addition to religion and culture, there is a third ingredient to Jewishness. For the time being and until we define it more precisely, let us call it a social identity. In any event it is the most stubborn and intractable element in the whole. The awareness of it hangs on in Gentiles, and in Jews too even when they would prefer not to think of it. Forgetting, after all, is not a matter of will. The Jew remembers or, given the present state of the world, is reminded. This is the upshot of millions of precedents not only in Europe but in the United States as well: try as they will, Jews win through only rarely to being swallowed up in the generality of men.

If, despite all experience, the Jew persists in ridding himself of his Jewishness, the result is likely to be only de-Judaization without assimilation. He works his way not into the oblivion of Gentile acceptance, but into a limbo, peopled by other Jews who like himself do not wish to be Jews. Once he has reached this point, he is indeed in an unenviable situation. For he does not want to be what he is and cannot become anything else. In the meantime he has exposed himself to multiple perils. He has invited upon his soul the blight that derives from the inability of men to accept themselves and to make the most of what they are. In addition he stands naked and defenseless before the world's hostility. Continuing to be penalized as a Jew, he has stripped from himself all the protections and compensations which a positive Jewish life might have afforded him. He drinks the dregs of a Jewish identity but of the wine not a drop.

It will come as no surprise to the reader to be told that I, the author, am no assimilationist. And yet, passionate survivalist as I may be, I am not happy over the fact that Jews cannot quit being Jews. In the first place, as a student of Jewish history I know that in every generation some Jews have dropped out of the ranks, and Jewry has not only survived the loss, it has probably been the better for it. Again, I do not see why there must be between 4,000,000 and 5,000,000 Jews in America. Neither in Scripture nor in Rabbinic literature is such a number ordained, certainly not in logic. I would then far rather have an American Jewry of 2,000,000 persons who really want to be Jews, who are excited and stimulated by the prospect, than a community twice as large, but half of which is either cold or hostile to its destiny.

Still again, while I am deeply pleased when other Jews choose to remain Jews in a large and significant sense, I resent the exercise of compulsion against anyone. Believing in liberty for all, I insist on the freedom of my fellow Jews to leave my company and abandon the historic Jewish enterprise, no matter how much it means to me. I know furthermore that a society which will not permit Jews to give up being Jews is also one that will make life difficult for all Jews, regardless of their attitudes toward Judaism. And last of all, it has been my experience that Jews who are forced back into Jewry are pretty generally doubtful acquisitions for the Jewish community. They participate in it unwillingly, are indifferent to its aspirations, and rebellious against its very existence. What useful purpose then can they possibly serve Jews and Judaism?

Wherefore, I have never been one of those Jewish survivalists who rub their hands gleefully over the unhappy plight of their de-Judaized fellows. In all earnestness, I would have been happier had matters turned out otherwise; had any Jew so disposed been free to walk out. The world however has neglected to consult me. In any event and regardless of anyone's preferences, the assimilationist program founders on launching against the rock of actuality.

But there is more to be said against it. It is not calculated to do much for Jewish morale. Quite the reverse. Its purport being "cease to be what you are," its effect is very likely to be an aggravation of the psychic disquiet already so widespread among Jews. Indeed, the whole proposal is not altogether cleanhanded ethically. Present it as you will, assimilationism is in the end a yielding to a blind prejudice, a knuckling under to the drive for social homogeneity. In the last analysis it means that the Jew says to the world: "You will not let me be in peace as I am, in my distinctiveness; very well then, I shall give up my difference and take on the approved general pattern." This, even if it were good policy, as it is not, is transparently very questionable morality.

But most of all I reject the assimilationist program because, far from agreeing that Judaism is obsolete and devoid of meaning, I am convinced that it has large and abiding significance for Jews and for the world. To abandon the Jewish heritage appears to me an act of wanton waste, a tragedy of spiritual vandalism. It disposes of Jewish problems only as suicide resolves personal problems—by expunging not only difficulties but values and potentialities as well.

Nor do I agree that America or mankind will be the better off for the disappearance of the Jewish group. The assimilationist, I am convinced misreads the issue. He notes that diversity, religious, cultural, ethnic, national, is often a stumbling block in human affairs. Hence he leaps to the

conclusion: make plain the way, remove diversity because of the obstacles
it creates.

But variety among men is natural and desirable. It is not only inevitable,
it is beneficial that there be dissimilar religious communions, cultures and
peoples. Such a condition is, first of all, a datum, a fact of being. So, furthermore, life is richer and more colorful; so one person or group stimulates and
prods another; so one good custom is kept from corrupting the world. What
is wrong with difference is not difference, but men's reluctance to allow and
encourage it, and to cultivate it creatively.

But enough of rebuttal. Let me put the survivalist case not as a refutation
of its antithesis. Let me rather state it positively as a thing in itself, with an
élan of its own. And once again, as with assimilationism, I propose to make
use of a specimen position—in this case the one I know best and most intimately, my own. What follows then is a declaration of the faith of a Jewish
survivalist. As such it may repeat at moments propositions we have already
established or may foreshadow fleetingly conclusions at which we are yet to
arrive. The reader I hope will forgive both the echoes and the anticipations.
The survivalist position ought be recorded somewhere in its integrity. And
this is as good a time as any, and the best imaginable place.

Perhaps I ought to indicate, too, that despite an apparent atypicality in my
situation, the argument as it will now unfold is broadly representative. For,
though I am a rabbi and hence in one sense not a fair sample, there are
enough Jews who are not rabbis who feel as I do to make my confession
expressive of multitudes.

What do I get out of my Jewishness to justify the expenditure of time
and energy upon it? How am I the better off for my adherence to it?

From the Jewish heritage, I derive my world outlook, a God-centered
interpretation of reality in the light of which man the individual is clothed
with dignity, and the career of humanity with cosmic meaning and hope;
a humane morality, elevated in its aspirations yet sensibly realistic; a system
of rituals that interpenetrates my daily routines and invests them with poetry
and intimations of the divine. To be sure, and as I shall relate subsequently
in some detail, I have had to do some tinkering on the traditional apparatus.
Despite this, it is a goodly patrimony I have received, goodly in faith, in
ethic and in folkway.

Now I might conceivably have won to analogous riches without the

Jewish past. Analogous perhaps, but in no case identical. For like all historic religions, Judaism has a character of its own. Its uniqueness—and the word carries no implications of superiority—consists of many special features peculiar to it. For example, it assigns an extraordinarily large role to study as a religious exercise, and to understanding as a key to salvation. Again, salvation is conceived as an objective not for the individual only but for society as well. Still again, Judaism, in contrast with most Christian confessions, is relatively unconcerned with matters of creed. It is less interested that Jews shall believe alike than that they shall strive to realize the same ideal objectives. . . .

In brief, though I share with liberal Christians large areas of affirmation, mine is a special position, which simultaneously satisfies me and serves also as a foil, goad and stimulant to other persuasions. Besides, the materials of Judaism lie at hand, ready for me to use. It would be uneconomical not to exploit them. Finally, I have observed that those Jews who do not acquire their religion from the tradition of their group quite generally do not get it elsewhere. American civilization, be it remembered, is in itself largely secular. Such Jews then, as often as not, simply go through life without a sustained *Weltanschauung,* an organic ethical code, and patterns of ritual.

Beyond this, my life is enriched by the accumulated treasures of over three millennia of Jewish history—a large literature in which I read extensively, not as an outsider but with a sense of belonging; music for me to sing, art for me to enjoy. I have the privilege of companionship with the great personalities of Jewish history. At my disposal is a second fund of folklore when I spin tales to my children. Mine literally is a double past—the American and the Jewish. My horizons are distant, not in one direction but in two. I am twice anchored in traditions, and hence twice secured against the peril of being rootless and "unpossessed."

And because my Jewishness is something positive, anti-Semitism looms less large in my life than in that of many of my fellows. I am not hagridden by it as they are. To them it is the whole of what is otherwise a senseless identification; to me it is an unfortunate, a tragic incident in an inherently worth-while enterprise. Like them, I am prepared to do anything I can to resist it. I, too, man the walls. But I have shrines, libraries and family altars to defend as well as jobs, legal rights and memberships in clubs. And I know that while much will be taken from me in the event of defeat, my Jewish heritage will still remain to sustain and give me direction. The de-Judaized

Jews, on the other hand, recognize quite clearly that they will be left with nothing. Little wonder that their preoccupation with anti-Semitism approaches a hysteria.

I am furthermore quite confident that by virtue of my attitudes, I am less susceptible than escapist Jews to infection by self-contempt. I am undeniably exposed to the same psychic influences that play over them. But in my case, as I have already indicated, participation in and appreciation of the Jewish tradition operate as immunizing elements. I am not tempted to flight from myself, nor bitter because I know in advance that it will prove futile. I cannot despise my identity: it is associated with a process I enjoy and respect. Not the least of the significances for me of a meaningful Judaism is its contribution to my mental health.

But is not the survivalist program provocative of anti-Semitism? Is it not "self-Ghettoization"? Does it not set Jews apart and by their differential behavior incite the hostility of non-Jews? In response, two observations must be recorded. In the first instance, I have in all actuality never for a moment practiced withdrawal from the general life of America. Nor have I ever felt an impulse or need to do so. For what is there in the cultivation of a religion and a historic tradition to militate in the least against full participation in the common political and spiritual life of our country?

And it is barking up the wrong tree to ascribe anti-Semitism to the attitudes of Jews toward their Judaism. The Jew-baiter does not resent Jews because they maintain their traditional Sabbath or sing their ancient folk songs in their homes. Nor is he more kindly disposed toward them if he learns that they have departed from the ways of their fathers. He feels as he does for reasons we have elsewhere analyzed. The relation of Jews to their Jewish heritage is rarely if ever one of them.

Is it practicable, this prospectus of inhabiting two worlds—a Jewish and an American? In this query, two questions are contained—one theoretical, the other pragmatic. The first asks: Are Americanism and Judaism ideally and ideologically compatible? To answer this question one must define the nature of Judaism and the Jewish identity. This is something we are to discuss in the very next chapters. I do not wish to anticipate the results of our investigation. There are terms that need to be clarified, a substructure of reasoning that must first be laid. Only then will the conclusions we are to reach be intelligible and helpful to the reader. Let us therefore, holding the matter of theory in abeyance for a brief while, turn attention to the second question: whether as a matter of actual experience one can be comfortably both a Jew and an American.

If I may judge from my own life—and that of many Jews who share my viewpoint—the enterprise is amazingly undifficult. Let it be recalled that I acknowledge only one political allegiance—to America; just as I profess only one religion—the Jewish. Here there is certainly no cause for conflict. Beyond that, I have two heritages—the American and the Hebraic. English is my language and that of my children. I was educated in the public schools of my community. The history of America is my history. But Hebrew is my tongue too, and Jewish history my background also. Lincoln and Jefferson are my heroes together with Moses, Akiba and Maimonides. They all get along in my imagination most companionably. When I read Van Wyck Brooks on New England in its flowering and autumn it is in my own literary past that I am being instructed. I have studied Spiegel's *Hebrew Reborn* with the same sense of identification. I sing Negro spirituals, American ballads and Hasidic or Palestinian folk songs with equal ardor. On the Fourth of July I set off fireworks and attempt to transmit to my children an appreciation of the significance of the occasion. With equal earnestness I kindle Hanukkah lights and discuss with them the meaning of that festival. At no time am I conscious of strain between the two worlds. I move from one to the other with such naturalness that I am scarcely aware of the change in spiritual locale.

The process is immensely facilitated by the essential sympathy in spirit between the two traditions. Both are democratic. Both emphasize the worth of the individual and his right to freedom. In both there is passionate devotion to the ideal of social justice. And the vision of the more abundant life is a secularized parallel of the ancient Jewish dream of the Kingdom of God on earth.

Incidentally it should be noted that America approves, or to put it more modestly, has no quarrel with my enterprise. For it is the essence of our political theory that the state exists so that the individual may find fulfillment where his conscience and intelligence direct. If then some American citizens believe they require a special religion and tradition for their salvation, America has no objection—provided always that the divergent interests do not operate adversely to the shared political and cultural life. Indeed, in a very real sense, it can be said that to this end American democracy exists, that Americans may be free to seek self-realization as their spirits dictate.

But I am not fair to either Judaism or Americanism when I say of them only that they are mutually compatible. In my Jewishness, by very virtue of its differential quality, indeed in all the diversities religious and cultural exhibited by American life, I see a breath-taking promise, a unique and unparalleled opportunity.

It is out of differences meeting in reciprocal understanding on a shared soil that cultures bloom most luxuriantly. History is replete with precedent for this statement. The age of Pericles, the Renaissance, the eras of Chaucer and Shakespeare were all, in no slight measure, the consequence of cross-fertilization of civilizations. The botanist has long known that plants grow best when they pollinate one another. He has for many centuries been doing deliberately what Nature has been wont to do hit or miss. Those who are devoted to the ideal of an America in flower could, it would seem, properly follow his precedent. We ought to preserve both the common government, language and culture which all groups share, and also the secondary diversities; and then, as a matter of planned policy, arrange techniques for their mutual meeting. Out of such husbandry of the spirit may well emerge a cultural life richer than any the human past has known.

III

PROBLEMS OF THE TRADITION

9

A Matter of Definitions

WERE LIFE COMPLETELY reasonable this book would very properly have begun with definitions. After the precedent set by Plato's *Dialogues* and Spinoza's *Ethics* we should at the very outset have dissected and clarified our key terms, "Jew" and "Judaism."

Life however is not altogether rational. Sometimes it is so imperious in its demands for action that men have no choice except to be up and doing at once, postponing to more auspicious moments the analysis of basic concepts.

But questions of theory cannot be put off forever. When the urgent task has been disposed of, the hunger to understand reasserts itself. Besides, there are some courses on which one cannot embark at all unless first the way has been charted by the intellect.

At just such a juncture we stand now. We have dealt with those issues that brook no delay. At the same time, we have concluded that Jews ought to strive to preserve their Jewishness and to make it meaningful. Definitions begin to matter mightily. Not to the assimilationist. Whatever Judaism may be, he wants none of it. The survivalist, however, must know what he is affirming, the nature of that which he seeks to perpetuate.

What then are the current conceptions of Judaism and the Jewish group?

QUESTION 1: Are the Jews a race?

ANSWER: No.

DISCUSSION: If "race" means a group of human beings who by virtue of a common ancestry share biologically inherited traits, then Jews most certainly do not constitute a race. To make the point more clear—"race" as applied to humans is the analogue of "breed" in reference to animals. There are of course breeds of dogs, distinguishable from one another in physical characteristic, mental aptitude, and, so to speak, canine spirituality. And their differences derive almost entirely from heredity. In this, the only precise sense, "race" is altogether inapplicable to Jewry.

In the first place, as Scripture itself attests, Jews were from the beginning of mixed ethnic origin. So Abraham is said to have brought with him to Palestine "the souls which he had acquired" in Mesopotamia. The Israelites on their way out of Egypt were accompanied by a "mixed multitude." Ancient Jews intermarried with the peoples native to Canaan. King David himself was by the testimony of the Bible descended from Ruth, a Moabitess. During the days of the Second Jewish Commonwealth, Jews engaged in proselytizing among the pagans with a high measure of success as is attested by the Talmud, Greek and Roman authors and the New Testament. All through the Middle Ages at least a trickle of conversions to Judaism continued. Hence the rigorous decrees issued by one church council after another against Judaizing individuals and tendencies. All in all, history suggests that far from being a "pure-blooded" group, contemporary Jews are pretty much a compound of all the peoples among whom they lived.

This conclusion is corroborated by anthropological research. There is not a single anthropometric standard which applies to Jews either universally or especially. Jews differ from one another in the shapes of their skulls, in the color and texture of their hair, in the pigmentation of their skin, in stature and, despite a folk misconception to the contrary, in the configurations of their noses. Nor does one need highly refined scientific tests to establish the physical diversity of Jews. Simple observation will reveal how dissimilar they are.

To be sure, Jews do exhibit certain attitudes and aptitudes which, if not universal among them, do occur with sufficient frequency to constitute "typical" traits. Among these may be included an attachment to learning, peaceableness and aversion to violence, concern with philanthropy, commercial acumen and intensity of family relationships. Considering these qualities, some observers have posited a psychic rather than biologic racialism in the Jewish group. A much simpler, less mystical explanation is available. Social influences account adequately for any qualities which Jews exhibit with especial frequency or intensity. Between their tradition and their historic status little room is left for hypotheses as to hereditary traits.

QUESTION II: Are the Jews a religious communion?
ANSWER: Yes, but not exclusively so.

DISCUSSION: The Jewish religion is, of course, the central and constant motif in the career of the Jews as a fellowship. Centuries ago a faith, ethical system and ritual pattern flowered in ancient Palestine. This religion, the inspiration and prized treasure of prophets, rabbinic sages, medieval philosophers, saints and mystics, of modern teachers and of countless obscure men and women in all generations, has run through Jewish history like a golden thread, tying past and present together and binding scattered Jewries into an organic unity. In it Jews have ever discerned their prime *raison d'être;* to it they have always consecrated the best of their energies. To the world this has been the main distinctiveness of the Jewish group.

Religion then plays a large role in Judaism and in the life of the Jews; but it is by no means the whole of either. Jews, as a body, are more than a creedal communion, more than an *ecclesia* or church—as is readily apparent from the following considerations.

Thus, if Jewry were purely a religious sect there could be no irreligious Jew. Jews being Jews altogether because of theological commitments, anyone incapable of those commitments ought to be no Jew. Yet there are persons, atheists, agnostics or skeptics, who by their own testimony, in the opinion of other Jews and in the judgment of mankind are Jews.

Consider by way of illustration so distinguished a figure as Albert Einstein. Universally Dr. Einstein is taken for a Jew, by himself, by other Jews, by the world and, with especial vindictiveness, by the Nazis. Now to be sure Dr. Einstein's world outlook can, given some latitude, be termed religious. Even then his *Weltanschauung* differs markedly from that taught by the Jewish tradition. Yet he is a Jew. On what score? Can it be by virtue of a faith he does not profess?

That theology is not the whole story can be seen further from the presence in Judaism of many clearly nonreligious elements. The Jew inherits from his Jewish past the Hebrew and perhaps the Yiddish tongues, a literature, secular as well as sacred, a law code that covers all of life, not merely its ecclesiastical facet, music, art, folkways, and what not.

Again there is in Judaism no formal creed to which Jews are asked to subscribe. Whereas every Christian denomination expects of its communicants that they make some specific profession of faith—the Apostles' Creed, or the Augsburg or Westminster Confessions for example—Judaism not only makes no such demands, it has never issued an official, authoritative statement of its theology. Or to put the point bluntly: every religious communion must define itself in creedal terms. Judaism has never done so. *Ergo,* it is not purely a religious communion.

Finally, to appeal to everyday experience, what is the point of the question: "Is so-and-so a Jew?" Is it being asked whether he accepts a particular theology? Hardly. That may be part of the meaning but certainly not its core. Not something doctrinal but something social is the nub of the inquiry. Wherefore, we write Q.E.D. after the proposition that while religion is vital in Judaism, the nature of Judaism and Jewishness is not exhausted by it.

QUESTION III: Are the Jews then a culture group?

ANSWER: Yes, that too in part.

DISCUSSION: Comprised within Judaism, as we have just observed, is a multiplicity of nonreligious elements. Indeed, some of the most significant manifestations of the contemporary Jewish spirit are of this character. The poetry of Bialik and Tschernikowski, the art of the Bezalel school, the new folk festivals of Palestinian Jewry, the compositions of Ernest Bloch are recognizably Jewish in inspiration and manifestly cultural in character. Culture therefore is one of the several ingredients of Judaism.

While "culture" describes part of this aspect of Judaism, it is too limited to catch the whole. Beyond the intellectual and the aesthetic which the word suggests are other elements—things, movements, causes and institutions of all sorts and devoted to the widest variety of purposes. "Culture," appropriate so far as it stretches, does not cover enough. A better concept is "civilization."

It must not be supposed that these elements, the religious on one side, the cultural or civilizational on the other, exist separately. On the contrary, they flow together into an organic unity, interpenetrating one another so thoroughly that it is difficult to discern where one leaves off and the others begin. Thus the Hebrew language, a cultural component, is integral to Jewish worship. Again, observances are very often matters of theology and folkway at one and the same time.

In Western civilizations, the religion of a people, generally Christianity, can at least in theory be differentiated from its culture. It is more difficult, indeed impossible, to draw such a line in Judaism. So, in the end, Judaism emerges as a *religious civilization.*

We now have our definition of Judaism. But what makes the Jewish identity? Is a Jew simply one who inherits, accepts and lives this religious civilization? There are Jews aplenty alien to the religion and civilization alike. To be sure, it is a very exceptional Jew who is not in some way, shape or manner touched by being Jewish. At the very least he is likely to belong to some Jewish association or to support some Jewish cause. But *rara avis* though he be, an occasional Jew can be found who does not participate in the Jewish religious civilization even to this limited extent. Yet, by universal consent, he is a Jew. Transparently then there must be, over and beyond religion and civilization, still a third motif in Jewishness, the residuum that persists when faith and culture are subtracted.

QUESTION IV: Do the Jews constitute a nation? Is this the plus that must be added to the religious civilization?

ANSWER: Yes and no, depending on how "nation" is defined.

DISCUSSION: If "nation" is taken to mean a political entity, and to embrace notions of sovereignty and citizenship, then it is totally inappropriate to American Jews who owe political fealty only to the American commonwealth.

At first glance we seem to have disposed of the word; actually we are by no means done with it. For though "nation" in the sense of political entity is unsuitable to present-day American Jews, it does fit their ancestors, it applies even now to some Jewries abroad; and, under a construction different from that we have so far assigned to it, it is applicable to American Jewry also. Let us examine these points.

First, as to the past. All through their history until modern times, Jews universally considered themselves and were considered none other than a nation. Certainly, during the days of the First and Second Commonwealths in Palestine, they neither questioned nor had occasion to question this conception. Even after the destruction of the Second Temple and their dispersal throughout the world, they continued to view themselves in the same light. They were, they felt, a nation in exile, but a nation.

This judgment was confirmed by their experiences. Not only culturally and religiously but politically as well they formed a people apart. They did not normally enjoy citizenship in the lands of their residence. Quite consistently and generally with the consent of local governments they regulated their group life by their own traditional law codes. They were in all actuality an *imperium in imperio,* one nation embedded in others. Non-Jews too envisaged them in this manner, and that not only in the Middle Ages but up to the very threshold of the nineteenth century. So, George Washington addressing an early American Jewish community, referred naturally and without hesitation to the "Hebrew Nation."

With the French Revolution, however, a radical change set in. First in France, subsequently elsewhere, Jews were enfranchised. Participants now in the civic affairs of various lands, they automatically transferred political allegiance from their own group to territorial governments, surrendered their private jurisprudence and became citizens like non-Jews round about them.

Nevertheless, the concept Jewish Nation is still very much and very properly in evidence. There are in Eastern Europe countries composed of various ethnic, national and cultural groups, conspicuously the Soviet Union, Poland and Romania. Unlike the United States, these are multinational and multicultural lands. Their citizens owe political loyalty to central governments, and yet in law and fact may be at the same time members of some one of the minority cultures or nationalities. In such settings, the Jews tend to conform to the general pattern. They too are Russian or Polish citizens as the case may be, but Jews also, and that not only in religion but in *nationality* as well.

In the case of Palestine, by international covenant the Jewish Homeland, the Jews constitute in aspiration and actuality a *nation* in the process of maturation, one that may in the not too distant future sprout into full autonomy and perhaps sovereignty as well.

"Nation" and "nationality," even when suffused with political connotations, are far from obsolete in modern Jewish affairs. On the contrary they are respectively the only congruous words for Palestinian and East European Jewries. On the other hand these concepts, so long as political connotations attend them, are quite unsuited to the Jews of the Western democracies whose Jewishness, whatever else it may require, asks no political allegiance.

Now, there is another totally nonpolitical significance to "nation." The term is used often and legitimately to denote not governmental or territorial entities but historic groups of human beings who share a past and its values and the will to persevere as a unit. In this sense the word is applicable to American Jews also.

The temptation so to apply it is strong. We have long been looking for a concept to describe the plus in Jewishness beyond religion and civilization. Here is one concept that has standing in history, that covers certain Jewries perfectly, and with some tailoring can be made to fit all. Little wonder then that many students of Jewish life use and defend the term. Others, more wary of being misunderstood, have tried their hands at variations of it. So Professor Salo Baron prefers "nationality," and Dr. Mordecai Kaplan "nationhood."

In vain! Try as one will, specify reservations as one may, "nation" for most Americans, Jews or non-Jews, has inescapable connotations of political sovereignty and citizenship. To employ it is to invite confusion. It would be wiser to look for some other word suitable not only to Jewries abroad but to the one at home.

QUESTION V: Our problem remains: the Jews are more than a communion and culture group. That plus cannot, or should not, be verbalized in "nation" and "nationality." How then can it be characterized?

ANSWER: The Jews are a *people*. This is the third ingredient in Jewishness.

DISCUSSION: A people is a body of persons who partake together in a social past and its heritage, a present and its problems, a future and its aspirations. To outsiders it appears as a distinct, identifiable historic entity. Viewed from within, it is marked by a sense of kinship and shared interests among its members. It is in sum a *Kultur-und Schicksalsgemeinschaft*, a fellowship of tradition and destiny. "People" then expresses a broad reality, yet political sovereignty and allegiance are not essential to it. Wherefore, both in what it says and leaves unsaid it fits the Jews.

This is the element which goes with religion and culture in Jewishness— the peoplehood of Israel. And this is the motif that persists when the others have been dissipated. By virtue of this a Jew may renounce the Jewish faith and repudiate Jewish culture, and remain both subjectively and objectively a Jew by identity. He is still part of the Jewish people.

Now too it is clear why Jews may be a minority nationality in Central and Eastern Europe, an emerging nation in Palestine, and a religio-culture group in Western democratic lands. For it is of the nature of a people to be protean, to take on different forms in different settings.

The truth that various Jewries can be dissimilar in status needs to be underscored. Men are prone to forget that circumstances alter cases, that what takes on one shape in one setting, may very easily appear under another guise elsewhere. Having formed a particular image of something, we are likely to insist on its universality. This fallacy of a single pattern crops up again and again in discussions of the Jewish situation. Always it muddies the waters and confuses the issue.

Thus, American Jews who justifiably regard themselves as a community of religion and culture can be stubborn in insisting that other Jewries conform to their design. That is why some of the American Jewish delegates to the Versailles Conference objected to minority nationality status for certain East European Jewries though that was what the representatives of those Jewries were asking for. Hence too many American Jews protest the use of the word "national" in connection with the Jewish Homeland in Palestine. In the opposite direction Palestinian and East European Jews naïvely apply to the American scene envisagements of the Jewish group appropriate to themselves. Habituated to such notions, they speak easily of the Jewish nationality and nation only to be taken aback when their American brethren furiously repudiate the terms.

In all these instances the same process of oversimplification is at work. Each type of Jewry develops a conception relevant to its own situation, makes of it a Procrustean bed, and then busies itself with cramming other Jewries into it. The error is understandable; it is nevertheless to be avoided. To this end the first step is the recognition of Jewish peoplehood. For, once this is perceived, diversity of status for diverse communities follows with unstrained naturalness.

We have spoken of Judaism and Jewishness as consisting in a religion, a civilization and a people. For purposes of analysis we have presented each pretty much as a thing in itself, as something that might conceivably exist without the others. This mutual isolation of our three elements is, however, a device of the intellect, not an actuality. We have already noticed how closely religion, culture and civilization are interwoven. Equally tight is the connection between "people" and the others. Judaism resides in the Jewish people. Without human beings to be Jews and to foster the Jewish tradition, the religious civilization could not be. In the same fashion the people is a people almost altogether by virtue of the religious civilization. The Jewish identity, though it may exist by itself, is most normally the product and embodiment of the faith, culture and civilization. In these it has its source; in these it finds its meaning.

The point I am now trying to make is not original with me. It has long been known that Judaism is a matter of three motifs, fused into an organic unity. Witness an epigram struck off by a medieval Jewish mystic who said: "God, Torah and Israel are One." In the light of our discussion, it should not be difficult to discern what he meant. He was affirming that Judaism is a matter of Faith, of Tradition and of Peoplehood, and that all three are inextricably bound together.

10

A Gallery of Jewish Portraits

ETWEEN MODERN JEWS and their medieval forebears many differences
can be discerned. None, however, cuts deeper than this: whereas the
Jews of times gone by shared a philosophy of Judaism, those of today
disagree over philosophies. The shift from singular to plural is deliberate. It
reflects a great revolution.

Jewry in the past acknowledged only one ideology for Jewish life. On this,
individual Jews might ring changes, stamping it with the configurations,
each of his own personality. Furthermore it was at no time formulated
officially. No synod of rabbis ever sifted out and proclaimed the basic affirmations of Judaism.

The one great theory of medieval Judaism remained permanently un-
crystallized; it was always subject to private variations. But it was there, a
climate of shared conviction, an all-pervading atmosphere of idea and value,
the strongest bond linking one Jew to another and all into a spiritual unity.

Now, consider by way of contrast the contemporary descendants of these
medieval Jews. Not only do they have no single rationale for Judaism, there
is scarcely a point on which they are not divided. They quarrel mightily over
ideological issues and, therefore, over questions of practice and policy as
well. To confound confusion, there are those—and their number is legion—
who have no consistent point of view but are not therefore silent. Anyone
who imagines that all Jews think alike should eavesdrop when they discuss
the philosophical premises of their group life.

Theories, like biological species, have their origins. Since those now extant
are all collateral descendants of what was once the universal philosophy, we
would do well to examine that in some detail.

The parent system had its origins in Scripture. It took on recognizable form in the first centuries before the beginning of the Christian era. It achieved its maturity in the Middle Ages. It persists among millions of Jews to the present day as the grand archetypal doctrine of their being. It can be summarized as follows:

1) All Jews believed in God, in His governance of the world in conformity with a moral law and a design of universal salvation. Over how God was to be conceived there might be divergence of opinion; on His existence and mastery over all things agreement was absolute.

2) All Jews believed in the Election of Israel, in the doctrine that, at a specific moment in history, God had chosen them from among all peoples to receive His special revelation and to serve as protagonists in the drama of redemption.

3) All Jews believed in Revelation, that God had made His nature and will known to men, but nowhere so completely and perfectly as in Judaism and its sacred texts. Scripture in its entirety and to its last letter was assumed to be of divine origin. Revelation, however, overflowing the Bible, inspired the whole tradition. As one ancient rabbi put it: "Whatsoever any diligent disciple shall at any time seem to innovate, lo, this is as though it had been spoken at Sinai." But since Judaism was broader in scope than religion, since it embraced not only theology, ethic and ritual, but history, law, literature, folklore, social institutions and a miscellany of other interests, it was in effect their full way of life that Jews held to be God-impelled.

4) All Jews believed in the permanence and immutability of Judaism. This followed relentlessly from the preceding article of faith. For God is not man. The manifestation of His will is neither imperfect, so as to require emendation, nor is it a temporary expedient. "He will not change nor modify His doctrine" was a universally accepted postulate.

5) All Jews believed in the incalculable worthwhileness of Judaism. A divine revelation, it was to them the supreme truth accessible to man, the appointed instrument for human deliverance. Without it no Jew could achieve salvation, nor could the Jewish people as a people be redeemed. As for the Gentiles, for them, too, Judaism had vast meaning. Not that non-Jews were damned. In this respect medieval Jewish theology was infinitely more liberal than contemporary Christianity. While the Church insisted, *Extra ecclesiam nulla salus,* that outside itself there was no salvation, Judaism taught, "The righteous of all peoples have a share in the world to come." But though Gentiles did not have to become Jews to be saved, Judaism

contributed to their salvation. For, being the true, the God-given way, it was destined inevitably to become the universal religion. Meantime it was the chief cornerstone in the mounting edifice of the Kingdom wherein someday all mankind would be housed.

6) As has already been indicated, all Jews believed, and non-Jews agreed, that Israel constituted a nation.

Such in substance was the ideology by which Jews once lived. Whatever its merits in logic, it functioned splendidly in practice. It furnished Jews with simple intelligible answers to the deep questions of their being. It not only resolved their intellectual problems, it fostered loyalty to the group and the will to self-sacrifice on its behalf. All in all, it is no small part of the answer to the riddle of Jewish survival.

Then came the French Revolution. The Ghetto system under which Jews had lived for centuries was shattered. New circumstances prevailed, among them two of incalculable moment. Political emancipation converted the Jews from aliens into citizens of the lands of their residence. Simultaneously the wall of their spiritual isolation was breached; they were exposed to the thought-life of the world from which for half a millennium they had been sheltered. Both changes were fraught with momentous consequences.

The shift in political status made a problem of the nature of the Jewish group. For, as Jews were either accorded citizenship or led to expect it, as they won or looked forward to the rights and securities enjoyed by other men, they realized very early that their habitual thinking on Judaism was no longer good enough. Could they, with a clear conscience, accept citizenship now proferred them and still continue to regard themselves as constituting another nation? The conception of the Jewish nation, long taken for granted, was suddenly troublesome. Loyalty to Judaism could no longer be pinned to the now moot nationhood. It fastened itself to what remained— religion. Of a sudden, for many Jews, Judaism became a creedal communion only.

A different combination of influences drove other Jews in the diametrically opposite direction. Emerging from Ghettos belatedly and all in one step, Jews plunged into the modern world. And a strange world it was to them, what with the philosophies, sciences and arts that had grown up during the centuries of Jewish immurement. In many Jews theological conviction proved too weak to stand the shock. The old faith crumbled. But when religion is removed from Judaism, nationhood and culture are left over. These then became Judaism to those Jews who could no longer be religious but were still loyal to their group.

So the nineteenth century split the historic single philosophy of Judaism into two mutually contradictory propositions, one asserting the centrality of religion, the other of nation and culture. As it happened the division was not only ideological, it was in a rough fashion geographical as well. Western Jewries tended to redefine themselves in terms of religion; Eastern, in the idioms of people and culture. And that for readily understandable reasons.

In Britain, Germany, France and the United States civic emancipation ran a full course. The idea of a Jewish nation came therefore to seem unwarranted. What is more, the prestige of religion in these lands remained large; diversity of communions was normal—two circumstances that further encouraged the Jews to envisage themselves as a sect. Again Jews were eager to avail themselves of their enlarged opportunities. To this end a creedal conception of Judaism was most helpful. It stripped the Jewish tradition down to theology, ethic and ritual. It enabled Jews to travel light, unburdened by too much Jewish paraphernalia.

In East European lands, on the other hand, the emancipation was long delayed, if indeed it ever came. Here Jews lived in large numbers and compact masses. Here old patterns of thinking tended to hang on. Here too a multiplicity of nationalities was as normal as, indeed more normal than, a diversity of religions. Czechs, Slovaks, Magyars and Croatians all inhabited the Austro-Hungarian Empire; Poles, Ukrainians, Georgians, Finns and many others made up Czarist Russia. Peoplehood, nationality and culture rather than communion served in this area as the bases of group difference. Like their Western brethren, Eastern Jews argued by analogy from others to themselves. Only it was a different analogy, one which inclined them toward self-definition in terms of people and civilization.

First cut asunder, the historical outlook was next splintered. To the examination of each of the fragments we shall now proceed. The materials however are difficult, consisting in abstract concepts and thin-spun arguments. The reader will, I am certain, find the going easier if the presentation is personalized, each point of view being presented through a protagonist, some real American Jew who embodies it.

THE RELIGIONISTS

Messrs. A and B, Dr. C and Rabbi D all believe that Judaism is in essenc
a religion. They find themselves therefore on the opposite side of the fenc
from Messrs. X, Y and Z who are all secularists. Our religionists furthe
hold in common a number of specific theological doctrines and ritual prac
tices—as is only natural when the same religious tradition is variousl
expressed. But if they stand together on many things, they differ, as will soo
become apparent, on many others.

Mr. A—a specimen Orthodox Jew.

Mr. A is a personable and cultivated young gentleman, at quick glanc
altogether undistinguishable from other Americans, Jewish or Gentile, o
his age, education and social position. On closer scrutiny, his thinking, hi
household and his daily existence disclose beliefs and observances strang
not only to non-Jews but even to most Jews of his acquaintance. For Mr. A
is genuinely an Orthodox Jew.

Be it observed at once that he does not conform at all to the vulgar mis
conception of the Orthodox Jew. English is his native tongue. He is no
recent immigrant, his great-grandfather having been born in this country
His strict adherence to the Jewish tradition derives from filial piety and
personal conviction, not from ignorance of the American scene or inadequate
exposure to it.

He is Orthodox because he accepts as true the basic premises of Orthodoxy
—that the Jewish tradition represents a divine relation and that it is im
mutable.

By this faith his life is transfigured. No matter where his mind may go
venturing, he looks for final intellectual authority to Scripture and Rabbinic
literature. Here, for him, is the supreme verity, the sure guide in the way a
man should walk. Unlike his secularized friends, he need not grope toward
notions of the good life and then doubt them when once they are reached
Accepting the authority of the tradition as indisputable, he knows what is
good, what evil and in what salvation consists. His heart is anchored firmly
the die of his spirit has been cast.

He is, as would be expected, scrupulous about Jewish rituals. He recite
the prescribed prayers each morning, afternoon, evening and on retiring a
night. He observes the various festivals devotedly. Nor is his performance

f the commandments mechanical or merely dutiful. On the contrary, it glows with ardor. As he goes his round, he is inspired by the thought that he is fulfilling God's will, is binding his own destiny to the millennial career of Israel, and is filling his days with the poetry of God-ordained and time-hallowed designs.

Between his Americanism and his Judaism—the latter embraces for him not only a faith, ethic and ritual but also a culture and a recognition of the peoplehood of Israel—he sees no incompatibility. Indeed there is none. This is his religion, to the free exercise of which as an American he has an indisputable right.

His life pattern however is not without its serious problems. While as a whole he is spiritually tranquil, there are times when he is troubled intellectually. He is a literate person, not unacquainted with biology, comparative religion, anthropology and psychology. Much in these sciences challenges his basic faith. So diffused is the opposition that every next book or magazine article may plunge him into a desperate pitched battle of the spirit. In this respect he is, for all his traditionalism, far removed from the temper of medieval Jews. Their Judaism was effortless. It had the smooth, easy flow of an outlook disputed neither by Jews nor their environment. His faith demands the exercise of will and determination.

Then he must overcome practical difficulties. The Law lays down many requirements not easy to comply with. Since he will not labor on the Jewish Sabbath and Festivals, he has had to find an occupation that would enable him to rest when almost everyone else was at work. This he has somehow contrived to do. But what of his children who are now growing up? Will they be equally fortunate? What is more, on the Sabbath he may not turn on an electric switch nor ride. He takes these restraints in his stride, but on occasion they cause him and his family no slight discomfort. Again, because of dietary regulations, he is all but prevented from dining at the homes of his friends or in public restaurants.

Some obstacles he has been unable to surmount. He does not wear a beard and earlocks, though both are commanded by the Law of Moses. Nor has his wife cut off her hair to don the wig specified by the tradition as proper to chaste women. He has compromised, as he is well aware, on many points in which ideally he ought to have been unyielding. Conditions have at times been too much for him. Nor is there any device consistent with his premises by which he can abate extreme requirements. Life may change, circum-

stances may alter, but, in theory at least, Orthodox Judaism cannot yield a
single point. Some latitude there is. The Law can be variously interpreted
or applied. But the free play allowed is very limited. Mr. A's Orthodoxy
may stand or break; it cannot bend.

The misgiving that haunts him most persistently is over his children. Try
as he will, he cannot shield them against ideas and social situations adverse
to his commitment nor against the examples set by their playmates, not only
Gentile but Jewish. His great fear is that they will depart from the way he
walks, either repudiating his postulates or rebelling against the hardships he
gladly endures or simply refusing to be different from almost everyone else.
Against such eventualities he is putting up a game fight. The odds, as he will
confess with sad candor, are against him.

Mr. B—a typical "old-line" Reform Jew.

Mr. B, an attorney and distinguished figure in his native Midwestern city,
represents splendidly what I will here call "old-line" Reform Judaism—to
distinguish it from the new school of Reform which we shall discuss later

To understand Mr. B one must know something of his grandfather who
came to America in the early fifties of the last century.

The first Mr. B was born in a Rhineland village to parents who, like all
Jews about them, were thoroughly traditional in thought and observance.
When he left his native soil for the New World, he was substantially an
Orthodox Jew. But he had no sooner arrived in America than his Jewishness
underwent transformations. He was at the time little more than a boy,
without well-established patterns of behavior. His parents were not with
him to restrain him. Nothing in his new setting suggested the past or reinforced loyalty to it. He was very busy during his first years as an American
getting acquainted with a strange language and a strange world. And he
had a living to make. He simply could not bother with cumbersome Jewish
practices. His habits of observance very speedily became disjointed. He did
the best he could, maintaining only the more important forms, adapting
these as best he could to his new situation.

At the same time he began to read American newspapers and magazines,
to attend lectures, to make contact with intellectual movements abroad in
the land. Old doctrines dropped away, leaving his religion a theism, firm
in tone but undogmatic.

Unlike his theology, the ethic in which he had been reared came through not only untouched but strengthened. All his days he took for granted ideals of probity, kindliness, philanthropy and social responsibility. And never for a moment did he hesitate in his allegiance and pride in being a Jew. All in all, for a person who had passed through a revolutionary migration, he emerged surprisingly unscathed.

Early in his sojourn in America a powerful influence came into his life, one so potent that we must pause over it. For, unless it is reckoned with, neither Mr. B grandfather nor Mr. B grandson is understandable.

To the synagogue which the first Mr. B helped establish, Rabbi M came to serve as minister. Like his congregants, Rabbi M was born and reared in Germany. But whereas old Mr. B ceased to be Orthodox only in the New World, Rabbi M was a Reform Jew before he boarded ship. Indeed this was the major reason for his decision to leave his native land.

At eighteen Rabbi M was a student in Germany preparing for the rabbinate. His background and experience to that point had been completely traditional, his education exclusively Hebraic and in content and spirit little different from that of his Ghetto ancestors. Then modern ideas penetrated his medievalism. He began to question not the God-faith of Judaism, a point on which he never wavered, but some of its special doctrines: the literal inspiration of Scripture, the validity of the rabbinic tradition, the bodily resurrection of the dead, the coming of a Messiah and the restoration of Israel to Zion. Simultaneously he concluded that some details of Jewish ritual were both irksome and meaningless—the dietary laws, for example, the rigidity of Sabbath observance, the exclusive use of Hebrew for worship, the absence of instrumental music from the Synagogue.

An acute sociological problem descended onto him also. The tradition referred frequently to the Jewish nation and to its future restoration in Palestine. But he did not feel himself as anything else than a German. How then could he in conscience regard himself as a member of a Jewish nation? And was not such an idea dangerous? Would not anti-Semites make capital of it? Besides M had no desire to return to Palestine, not even under the banner of a Messiah. Like most of his German Jewish fellows, he preferred Germany.

Beset by doubts, haunted by problems, he turned for guidance to the most progressive rabbis of his day. To them his dilemma was no novelty. It was the universal burden of young German Jews, one which they themselves had carried. Their first instruction was that he supplement his rabbinic education with secular learning. They imparted to him further a fresh, radical theory of Judaism.

From them he learned that Judaism was to be conceived as a religious communion solely, akin to the Lutheran or the Roman Catholic; that Jews were Germans who differed from their fellow citizens only as these fellow citizens differed from one another, in theology and denominational affiliation. By them he was taught to view the Jewish religion as the end product of an evolutionary process, divinely inspired, to be sure, but in general, not in detail. Wherefore, it was the privilege, nay, more the duty, of each generation to cast off discredited beliefs and outmoded practices. Doctrines were to be maintained only if they stood the test of reason; rituals only if they proved convenient and edifying.

But, M asked his mentors, since Judaism was not a literal revelation, why should it not be abandoned for other religions which taught the same basic truths? After all, it was neither easy nor materially advantageous to live as a Jew.

To which question, the doctrine of the "mission of Israel" was advanced by way of answer. The Jewish people, M was told, exists to fulfill a divinely ordained function, the imparting to the world of the knowledge of God and of His will. To this end, Israel must persevere.

From these premises flowed implications which Rabbi M's tutors, and he after them, drew rigorously. Rituals now were held to have value only as means to ends. It was right therefore to deal with them freely, modifying and abandoning them almost at will. The Hebrew language was relegated to a subordinate position. For, if the sole purpose of Judaism be to instil religious values, obviously that tongue suits worship best which the worshipers understand most readily. Jewish culture, except as it contributed to faith and ethic, became an illegitimacy. The dream of Israel restored in Zion was repudiated. God after all can be obeyed anywhere and the "mission" theory required the dispersion of the Jews among the nations, not their return to Palestine.

Fired by this revolutionary theory, M was ordained and became the rabbi of a synagogue. But as soon as he spoke his mind from his newly won pulpit, a storm of protest broke loose. Radical Reform had been born in Germany; most German Jews, however, were still rooted in the tradition. Rabbi M's congregants were deeply shocked by his ideas. For a while he continued to labor and preach, hoping to win over his people. He failed and, growing discouraged, turned like many of his colleagues to America.

The new scene proved more congenial. Mr. B and his contemporaries had long been ripe for just such an outlook as Rabbi M maintained. As they heard him expound his doctrines, their confusion dissolved, their gropings took on direction, they began to act resolutely and purposefully. Together rabbi and layman recast Judaism. The theology of the past was strained and restrained until it was clear rationalism. Worship was Anglicized, modernized, curtailed, stripped of markedly oriental and medieval elements. Personal observance relaxed. Anything in Jewish practice that seemed unintelligible or out of place in modern America was purged away. There emerged in the end the Judaism that found classic expression in the so-called "Pittsburgh Platform" adopted in 1885 by the Central Conference of American Rabbis.

This is the Judaism in which Mr. B, grandson and our contemporary, was reared. In many respects a better Jew could not be conceived. He is a devout person and a good human being. He is proud to be a Jew, and gives of both his energy and money to Jewish causes. He is furthermore an observant Jew, at least he is observant by the standards of his group. He attends the synagogue quite regularly on Friday evenings, though never on Sabbath mornings, invariably on Rosh Hashanah and Yom Kippur and occasionally on the lesser festivals. In his home he practices some of the traditional domestic rituals, those recommended by Reform Judaism and according to the modifications it has sanctioned.

And yet, as he will admit in moments of candor, much is wrong with his Jewish life.

In the first place, he is confused about the nature of Judaism. His grandfather's grandson, he thinks of it as a religion. But in an inchoate fashion he is aware of the inadequacies of such a conception. Everything we have already argued against the definition, he has experienced in everyday actuality.

Nor is he happy over the "mission" theory, ostensibly his rationale for the preservation of Judaism. He is more than a little uncomfortable over the notion that Jews must teach the world religion and ethics. The whole idea strikes him as somewhat arrogant. Most of the Jews he knows do not seem particularly suited to such an assignment. And he has heard tell that Jewish theologians in our day are much more the beneficiaries than the benefactors of Christian religious thinkers. Last of all, he is well aware that Reform Judaism, though it has spoken much of the mission, has done nothing to implement it. His Jewishness therefore is dedicated to a purpose that neither he nor anyone else seems to take seriously.

Again, the Judaism projected by his philosophy runs thin in practice. Stripped of much of custom and law, of the Hebrew language, Palestine and Jewish culture, it is a tenuous business at best. It holds his loyalties but not those of most of his contemporaries nor of his own children. He suspects that the times require a broader, stouter vessel than that on which his grandfather embarked.

And he is torn too over Zionism. His theory disallows of notions like a Jewish Homeland. But he has been too deeply impressed by Jewish Palestine as a haven of refuge and the site of a Hebraic revival to deny it his support. He contributes to Zionist causes, but hesitantly, with a bad conscience and a host of reservations. Nor is it only on Palestine that his ideology embarrasses him. He is in the same ambivalent mood toward the Jewish Community Center of his city and toward other Jewish agencies that are social or cultural in character but not religious. On all these his head says "Nay," but his heart "Aye."

All in all, the theory and prospectus evolved by Rabbi M and adopted so eagerly by the first Mr. B is neither in logic nor experience good enough for the Mr. B of our day. Yet, like all human beings, he is a creature of habit and prefers to hobble along with an inadequate doctrine and program rather than, at this late date, to go adventuring after better but strange viewpoints.

Dr. C—a representative Conservative Jew.

Dr. C, physician, professor at one of the great medical colleges in his field of specialization, is the son of a learned, deeply devout, Orthodox Jew of East European origin. From his father he caught early in life a fervor for traditional Judaism. What is more, his sense of the historical is keen, a quality that also inclines him in the same direction.

Despite all this, Dr. C discovered on attaining intellectual maturity that he was incapable of thinking or practicing as did his father. His education, especially his intensive training in the sciences, compelled him to recast ancestral tenets. He found it possible, for example, to believe in the inspiration of Scripture but not in its literal inspiration; in the worth of Judaism but not in its immutability. Furthermore, the exigencies of his life have forced him to depart from prescribed observances. As a physician and man of affairs, he has had to compromise to a measure on Sabbath regulations, on kosher foods and what not else. In each case he has given no more ground than has been exacted. If he can manage it he gets away from his consulting room on Saturday mornings to attend synagogue worship. And when he dines in public restaurants, as perforce he must, he makes such a selection from the menu as to avoid the graver violations of the dietary codes. Nevertheless he is not and does not claim to be what his father was.

But if Dr. C can be Orthodox neither in thought nor in practice, he refuses to be Reform. Aware of peoplehood and culture in Judaism, he has no sympathy with a definition in religious terms only. The untraditionalism of Reform offends him.

In his reactions, Dr. C is by no means alone. Many Jews feel as he does. Out of their dissatisfactions with the parties both of the left and the right Conservative Judaism emerged some forty years ago.

What is this Conservative Judaism? In practice it is a kind of middle-of-the-roadism, halfway, so to speak, between Orthodoxy and Reform. This in a nutshell is the program. As to the theory, it is regrettably difficult to put it precisely. Truth to tell, Conservatism has still not formulated the philosophy on which it stands. Its nearest approach to an ideology is the phrase "historical Judaism," a key idiom of its original founders. This would seem to mean two things. First, Judaism is a *historical* phenomenon, that is to say, it is possessed of a rich and valuable past. In this sense, "historical Judaism" underscores the traditionalism of Dr. C. It means that Jews ought to preserve their heritage and, so far as they can, as it was transmitted to them. "Historical Judaism" has another significance. Judaism, it implies, is a phenomenon *in* history, a growing, evolving organism. Wherefore, though it holds to its past, it must change in conformity with a changing world.

The main difficulty with Conservatism, as Dr. C will readily admit, is that it never outgrew its origins. Beginning as a repudiation of Orthodoxy and Reform, it has continued negative in character. It is something which consists in not being either of two other things; a device, not a doctrine. As such it functions fairly well in endorsement of the past. Where it breaks down is as a guide to progress. Professing the necessity for modifications, it throws no light as to the form they ought to take. The result is that Conservative Jews have in this respect been left to their own ingenuity. Some have made sweeping changes in the tradition, others virtually none. The consequence is near bedlam. And what is true of individuals applies equally to synagogues. Dr. C has in the last decade been affiliated with two congregations, both Conservative, but one near Orthodox in its worship, the other liberal almost to Reform.

The confusion and lack of character that mark Conservatism derive in part from the fact that it has been content to let the slogan, "historical Judaism," do service for a philosophy. They stem however in considerable degree from a neglect of even that slight ideology. On its face "historical Judaism" endorses the remaking of the tradition. Unfortunately the leaders and official agencies of Conservatism have failed to live up to their preachments. Affirming tradition *and* progress, they have in half a century failed to commend a single departure, no matter how slight, from old patterns. From all practical purposes they might as well have been Orthodox.

So they dissipated a great opportunity. At the turn of the century, as Dr. C often points out, there were in America masses of Jews who with proper guidance might have been led in an orderly march from the Orthodoxy that was already failing to a balanced, adapted Jewish traditionalism. The guidance was not forthcoming. What might have been a disciplined movement became a stampede. Much of the favorable occasion is gone. Very many of those Jews are now lost beyond recapture. It is Dr. C's hope that before the last sands trickle away Conservative Judaism may seize what is left of its golden moment.

Rabbi D—"new-line" Reform Jew.

Rabbi D, the son of a Reform rabbi, was raised on the ideas and among the leading personalities of Reform Judaism. Nevertheless he early dissented from his environment both on intellectual and pragmatic grounds. To some extent his father anticipated this development. For Rabbi D senior was a *rara avis* in his day—a Reform rabbi who was also a Zionist and Jewish culturalist. Whatever the influences that played upon him, the present Rabbi D found himself incapable of subscribing to "old-line" Reform as embodied in the Pittsburgh Platform. He could not agree to its definition of Judaism, or to the limited program that followed from it. Especially was he unhappy that Reform left no room in its scheme for Zionism.

For some years Rabbi D stood much alone among his colleagues, urging on them without conspicuous success a revision of ideology, greater emphasis upon Jewish culture, heavier traditionalism in observance and an acceptance of Zionism. With time, however, he found allies, especially among the younger Reform rabbis, who, having been recruited in the main from Orthodox and Conservative homes, came to their ministries with strong leanings toward the tradition. The change that took place in the rabbinate was paralleled among laymen, both those of German ancestry who, like Mr. B, had grown discontented with the older dispensation and those of East European origin who began to enter the Reform Synagogue in increasing numbers, carrying with them a heavy freightage of historic attitudes and attachments.

All through the first decades of this century the center of gravity of Reform Judaism moved steadily right. Defenders of the Pittsburgh Platform became a minority; advocates of its revision, the majority. In 1937 a rewriting of basic principles was effected. At its convention in Columbus, Ohio, the Central Conference of American Rabbis supplanted the hitherto authoritative Pittsburgh Platform with a new pronouncement. In the later statement Judaism was defined not merely as a religion but as the "historical religious experience of the Jewish people."

So the concept of Judaism was made to include not only creed and ethic but also culture and peoplehood. The new formulation furthermore, without endorsing Zionism, legitimatized it for Reform Jews. At the same time, it reached out unmistakably for a greater measure of the tradition.

This revision in the philosophy of Reform is too recent for judgment as to its significance and effectiveness. All depends on whether Rabbi D and his like-minded colleagues can reverse the century-old trend of Reform; whether, having convinced one another, they can induce the laity to follow their leadership.

THE SECULARISTS

Messrs. X, Y and Z are, like A, B, Dr. C and Rabbi D, earnest Jews who devote much attention and energy to the concerns of Jewish living. But here resemblance between the two groups ends. For Messrs. X, Y and Z are secularists. Not that they are all antireligious. Only one, X, can fairly be so characterized. Yet all three alike discern the core of Jewishness to consist in culture and nationhood rather than in creed and ritual. They are, in other words, lineal descendants of those who, when the great archetypal pattern broke up, found the rationale for Judaism in elements other than the religious.

Mr. X—a secular Zionist

Mr. X, a journalist by profession, has for many years been one of the leading figures in contemporary Jewish life. His approach to Judaism is very
simple. To him the Jews constitute a people living under a variety of social
circumstances. In America they are citizens of the land of their residence,
yet bound also to their fellows abroad by a common past and shared destiny.

Of this people large portions are not happily situated. In Central and
Eastern Europe Jews are persecuted. Everywhere they are subjected to extraordinary psychic strains; everywhere their traditional culture is disinte-
grating. A triple threat then imperils the people to whose survival Mr. X
is committed—the threat of extermination, or, if not that, of intolerable social
conditions; the threat of a deterioration of morale; and the threat last of all
of the stagnation and ultimate demise of the Jewish heritage. These anxieties, social, psychic and cultural, have made Mr. X a Zionist.

Most of X's fellows in Zionism are religious persons whose religious persuasions are a prime factor in their Zionism. Since they are prepared to
work for his objectives, Mr. X is quite ready to accept their co-operation.
But it is only fair to say that he and many secular Zionists with him have
no sympathy with the Jewish religion except insofar as it serves to convert
Jews to Zionism. In his youth, Mr. X came under the influence of the ration-
alistic skepticism so widespread in this country a half century ago. Perhaps
he was temperamentally ripe for such a conclusion; it did not take him
long to decide that all sects including the Jewish were thoroughly benighted.

To make matters worse, the religious leaders of his native community
were indifferent to the Zionist program of which he was already an adherent.
The Orthodox Jews, while they nurtured the hope of a Palestine rebuilt,
believed that only the Messiah could redeem Israel, and denounced the
young Zionist for seeking to force the hand of the Almighty. The Reform
Jews, because of their ideology, were even more hostile. His quarrels with
Jewish religious groups over Zionism strengthened the secularism of his
naturally secular soul.

Pretty much the whole of Mr. X's Jewish activity is confined to two enterprises—the amelioration of the social position of Jews everywhere, and the
advancement of the Jewish settlement in Palestine. The two projects furthermore are, in his understanding, one. To Zionism X looks for a solution of
all critical problems of the Jews. He expects masses of European Jews to
find deliverance from anti-Semitism by migration to Palestine. There they

will not only achieve political and social normality but, as a people resident on their own soil, will be released from psychic disadvantages. He counts also on a great renaissance of Jewish culture as a consequence of Zionist effort and achievement.

To him, and to many like him, Jewish Palestine is the alpha and omega of the Jewish problem, its solution so far as there is one. If so romantic a thought can be ascribed to one as hardheaded as he, it is to him what the Messiah was to his believing forebears—the instrument of Israel's redemption.

Mr. X's approach to Judaism has been the butt of sharp criticism. Some of this is entirely unwarranted. He does not expect, as has been charged, that all the Jews of the world shall move to Palestine. As a realist he knows that that little land could under the most favorable circumstances house only a portion of world Jewry. He is aware furthermore that the great majority of Jews will insist on living permanently in the dispersion. But he does believe that even those Jews who cannot or should not turn to Palestine will benefit by it.

Once the Homeland is established, Mr. X predicts, Jews everywhere will cease to be regarded as freaks, as the one people in the world that has no home of its own. They will be instead instances of a normal phenomenon, members of a people possessed of its own land who still elect to live outside of it. They will be helped psychically and culturally as well. As for Jews who choose to remain in the Old World, for them too the Homeland will be a boon. It will drain from Central and Eastern Europe masses of Jews, so easing pressures against those who stay on in Europe.

With one recrimination in particular Mr. X is violently but justifiably impatient—the accusation by some Jewish anti-Zionists that he is somehow deficient in Americanism. He knows, as they know, that he admits to only one political affiliation, the American. His concern over the problems of European Jews, his interest in the establishment of a Jewish Homeland no more affect the integrity of his American patriotism than do similar efforts by Irish Americans on behalf of Ireland or the attachment of Scandinavian Americans toward their lands of origin. Certainly Louis D. Brandeis was an unimpeachable American. And yet Mr. Brandeis was not only a passionate Zionist, but a Zionist of Mr. X's stripe.

To one criticism of X's position there is substance, a charge leveled not only by anti-Zionists, but by religious Zionists also: that he is living his

Jewish life vicariously, on the basis of what other Jews are doing and will do in Palestine.

Mr. X, since he is not a religious Jew, does not enjoy the satisfactions of Jewish belief or practice. Though he expects Palestine to foster a revival of Jewish culture, he exerts himself not at all to stimulate such a renaissance in America. In what then does his Judaism consist? Essentially in the things he does for other Jews, mainly Jews abroad.

Mr. X represents a doctrine, but one marked by such glaring deficiencies that in all fairness to secular Zionism another brand must be presented.

Mr. Y—a secular Zionist culturalist.

Mr. Y, an educator, is like Mr. X a Zionist, and that for the same reasons and to the same ends. But unlike X, he exhibits no antagonism toward religion in general or Jewish religion in particular. On the contrary he is quite kindly toward creeds and rituals. His sympathies however are so inchoate, he does so little about them, he pins his Jewishness so solidly to people and culture, that he too must be characterized as a secularist. The two men then share a common definition of the Jews and a common program for Judaism. Yet in one important respect one has an advantage over the other. Mr. Y is interested in Jewish culture not only for Jews in Palestine but for those in America and most pertinently for himself and his family.

To him, Jewish culture is integral to Jewish life, no matter where Jews live. The Hebrew language, music, art, literature, mores and folklore are everywhere indispensable to Jewish existence. While he expects the Homeland to be the heart and nerve center of Judaism in the future, while he grants that Jews elsewhere will draw on Palestinian achievement, he insists that every Jewry must try to be creative on its own. Salvation, as he sees it, cannot be vicarious. Indeed the very worth-whileness of Jewish Palestine for Jews in the dispersion will be determined by the vigor of their Jewishness. They can be helped only after they have first tried to help themselves. Subscribing then to X's prospectus, he supplements it with the doctrine that American Jews must tend their vineyard also.

Hence, while Y is much exercised over the rehabilitation of European Jews and the rebuilding of Palestine, he does not exhaust his Jewishness in these outlets. Jewish education concerns him mightily. He is zealous to foster Hebrew literature, music and art on the American scene. Nor is he thereby less devoted to the American civilization. As he sees it, his two cultural interests supplement and stimulate each other. That there are gaping voids and lacks even in Y's prospectus for a Jewish career we shall disclose in the next chapter. But at the least, his Jewish life, unlike X's, is not all extroverted; it has insides, a content of its own.

Mr. Z—*Diaspora culturalist.*

Born and reared among what were once the teeming Jewish masses of Eastern Europe, Mr. Z is vividly aware of the peoplehood of Israel. By profession a man of letters, he very naturally rounds out his notion of the Jewish people with culture. On religious matters, he is a complete indifferentist. By virtue of this, by further virtue of his conception of Jewishness as a people-culture complex, he is indisputably a full-blown secularist.

Mr. Z speaks of the Jewish people as frequently and fervently as Messrs. X and Y, but unlike them he is no Zionist. Insofar as Palestine offers asylum to homeless Jews, he assents. But this is in his eyes a coerced agreement, exacted only by a crisis in Jewish affairs. For normal circumstances, he would say that the Jews are a dispersed people who ought all to live out their lives where they find themselves. He envisages the Diaspora not only as permanent but as self-sufficient. A Homeland in Palestine is to him no more than a concession to *force majeure*.

Mr. Z's convictions about Jews are strongly influenced by his memories of Eastern Europe. There the Jews constituted and were recognized in law as a minority nationality, with a distinct group civilization of their own. In these terms he would like to envisage American Jewry. But it has not escaped him that such notions, however suited to multinational states like the Soviet Union or Poland, are inappropriate to uninational commonwealths like the Western democracies. Reluctantly then, he has abandoned the conception of minority nationality for American Jews. What remains of his position is therefore pure culturalism. For himself Mr. Z prefers Yiddish as the tongue for this purpose, but he will concede to Mr. Y the legitimacy of Hebrew also. And since the knowledge of both languages is on the wane, he is ready, though unhappy over the turn, to accept English as the medium of distinctively Jewish expression.

Now Z has not only compromised on minority nationality for American Jews, he has retreated long distances on the status of Jewish culture. Habituated to thinking of it as the primary civilization of Jews, as indeed it was pretty generally in the East of Europe, he now concedes that in the Western world it can hold at best a secondary position. When in the past he was asked by Zionists whether a tradition could be expected to live on indefinitely under such disabilities, whether a Homeland was not thereby made imperative, it used to be his practice to point to the Jewries of Poland, Russia and Romania as the assurances of full creativity. When the same questions are put to him of late, he has no answer. He shakes his head, and sighs.

On our gallery, several comments are in order by way of farewell.

It should be observed in the first place that equal attention has not been given to all the subjects. Some have been painted full-length and in detail; others have been drawn with the fewest possible lines. This diversity of treatment has been dictated in part by the comparative importance of the persons who stood for portrayal. Mr. Z for example is representative of little more than a handful of Jews, Messrs. A, B, Dr. C, and Mr. X of multitudes. The inequality is also a consequence of the architecture of this book. The positions taken by some of our models will concern us again elsewhere and at considerable length. In such instances, it has seemed the part of economy to resort to sketching.

Again, it must not be supposed that our seven subjects exhaust Jewish ideological types. They image only the most basic and representative. Not only do other theories exist, they exist in all sorts of combinations and permutations. Thus there are variants of Zionism according as it is, or is not, associated with specific religious orientations and economic doctrines. Diaspora culturalism manifests analogous diversity. And, *mirabile dictu,* there is an Orthodoxy that is not only Zionist but Zionist-Socialist.

Nor must it be taken for a tragedy that Jews are so divided over theories and programs. Diversity is a good. Certainly it is a boon to the artist who without it would have only one subject on which to try his skill. It is, I have already argued, of benefit socially. Jewry is no exception, being all the richer because more than one canvas hangs in its ideological gallery.

Last of all, it must not be forgotten that in the background behind our pictures stand large numbers of Jews who cannot be portrayed because their lineaments are too disjointed and indistinct to be caught. These are the Jews who have no settled opinions, or at best only fragments of conviction on Jewish matters; the multitudes who, never questioning that they are Jews, have never thought through to consistency what they mean by the assertion or what they want from it. Over their souls and minds the ideological struggle is being waged. Because of them it is charged with bitterness. For as they go in the end, the future of Judaism will be determined.

11

A Tenable Theory

LIKE THE PERSON who was amazed to discover that quite unawares he had been speaking prose all his life, the reader may be surprised to learn that for the past two chapters and more he has been thinking in the idioms of a particular philosophy of Judaism—that known as Reconstructionism. Thus our discussion of definitions and ideologies was Reconstructionist in its premises, its spirit, and, most important of all, in its conclusions. As a matter of fact, there is scarcely a nook or cranny in this book in which something of Reconstructionism does not lurk. Indeed, it is mainly in this quality that the partisanship of this partisan guide consists.

It would be possible to state this particular rationale for Jewish life in the abstract, as a sequence of theoretical propositions. Thanks to its highly systematic character, it lends itself readily to such treatment. But the device of personalization employed in connection with other ideologies commends itself even more pointedly now. For Reconstructionism is in every essential feature the creation of a single thinker who evolved it step by step in the course of a lifetime of questing. The record of the travail of this individual is therefore the best introduction to his conclusions. Besides, his intellectual career is invested with the *multum in parvo* quality of a symbol. It means more than itself. It may be seen as a recapitulation of the groping of modern Jews on Jewish matters.

Mordecai M. Kaplan, the author of Reconstructionism, was born some sixty-odd years ago in Eastern Europe. That fact is of prime relevance for the understanding of his mind and spirit. His first world was that of medieval Judaism, virtually untouched by modernity. The society of his childhood still conformed closely to old patterns of observance, still thought unswervingly in terms of the grand archetypal Jewish outlook. No one in that environment disputed the divine Election of Israel, the revelation of

Scripture, the general inspiration of historic Judaism; its permanence and immutability; its immeasurable and transcendent worth; and the truth that the Jews constituted a nation and a church, a people, religion and culture all at the same time.

In his early youth Mordecai Kaplan's family came to America. The change of spiritual climate was however much less drastic than might have been expected. The son of a devout and rigidly conforming rabbi, living almost exclusively among Jews, and these of uncompromising Orthodoxy, he was still for all practical purposes insulated against the New World. Only on his initiation into secular higher education did it break through to him. Then for the first time he experienced an ordeal of religious *sturm und drang*. But he contrived, although only after a struggle, to shore up his beliefs. When, having been ordained a rabbi, he came to the pulpit of a prominent metropolitan congregation, he was, so far as appearances went, so far indeed as he himself was aware, unimpeachably Orthodox in thought, sentiment and practice.

The structure of his faith had been repaired much less solidly than he supposed. Doctrines once entirely self-evident were now buttressed with complicated logical props and these in turn were often held in place only by will. The *Zeitgeist* enveloped him, forever challenging his commitments. All about him were books which in his mental eagerness he would not forego. There was in him the temper of a Socrates who had no choice but to follow the truth, though it lead to death.

Wherefore he commenced once again to examine the faith of his fathers. As he did so, questions, hesitations and doubts came alive within him. Perforce, he read more and more widely, more and more freely. With time he ventured into every field relevant to his problem—Biblical criticism, metaphysics, psychology, sociology, ethnology and comparative religion. Nor was his concern primarily for himself. Even more fiercely, he was driven by anxiety for the Jewish tradition and the Jewish people. True, he was no longer sure what Judaism might be, nor why it ought to be maintained, but he loved it no less passionately.

When he considered his fellow Jews, his apprehension increased mightily. Transparently Judaism was losing its hold on them. Some, he discovered, were abandoning it because of the very riddles that tortured him. Others were impelled by less honorable motives: a sense of inferiority, a desire for social preferment, wanton disregard for anything not material. Whatever the causes, the position of the Jewish tradition in America was parlous indeed. Those who loved Judaism had to find answers for urgent, crucial questions. A theory had to be evolved consistent with everything worth while in the Jewish past and yet consonant with the best in contemporary thinking. A philosophy of and by itself could not save Judaism; it could not be saved without one.

To this objective Dr. Kaplan dedicated himself—the evolvement of a rationale for Judaism, a rationale that would be lucid, cogent and responsive to facts, and of such mood as to inspire Jews with a passion for Jewish living.

So began an intellectual odyssey destined, as it turned out, to last some decades. This we shall now proceed to trace, not in detail nor exactly nor chronologically, but rather after its largest movements and lasting advances. For the mind, even a mind as orderly as Dr. Kaplan's, does not operate after the fashion of Euclid's geometry. It wanders restlessly, arriving sometimes at conclusions before premises, losing itself often in cul-de-sacs. Syllogisms, whatever their uses, are hardly ever a true record of mental creation.

Early in the game, Dr. Kaplan recognized that he was not the first Jew to feel the challenge of modernity. Wherefore he turned to earlier thinkers and their thoughts in the hope that among them he might find something to guide him on his way. Although he spotted here a useful idea and there an inspiring intuition, none of the established theories turned out either as logic or as programs altogether acceptable.

Orthodoxy, whether spontaneous as with his father or effortful as in the case of Mr. A, was no longer possible for him. With those who could accept its premises, he had no quarrel. For himself his studies had rendered him incapable of affirming the doctrine of literal inspiration. He had come to believe what no Orthodox Jew could concede, that, like all living things, Judaism must either accommodate itself to new circumstances or die. For all his early training and emotional attachments, he was forced to conclude that for him Orthodoxy was neither light nor deliverance.

If Mr. A's position did not solve his problem neither did Dr. C's. While Conservatism appealed to him in that it held fast to the tradition and still endorsed change, he was disturbed by its long-continued failure to achieve a systematic ideology. Even more, he was dismayed at its consistent evasion of the obligation it professed—the authorization of urgent new departures in the tradition. Of all the parties in Jewish life this was in practice the most congenial to Dr. Kaplan; he never lost hope that it would find a doctrine for itself, and the courage to practice what it preached. But until that came to pass (and it has not happened yet, many years later) Conservative Judaism could not offer him what he sought.

As for the neo-Reform of Rabbi D, it had not even been conceived let alone articulated at the time of Dr. Kaplan's questing. And when it did come into being it was his beneficiary, not benefactor, showing numerous and often deep impressions of his spirit.

Of all the religious philosophies only one, "old-line" Reform, remained for study. Dutifully Dr. Kaplan examined it, but to no avail. In the first place, classical Reform offended him by its violent and wanton breach of historic Judaism. What it had abandoned was not only dear to him but, as he saw it, indispensable to the fullness and hardihood of Jewish life. A Judaism that had renounced the Hebrew tongue and culture, much of the age-old regimen of observance, and Palestine—that Judaism, he conjectured, would prove too pallid to survive.

Experience confirmed his hunch. Reform, in fact, was not sustaining itself. It seemed to prosper. Actually it was suffering desertions all the time but making up for them by drafts on Orthodox and semi-Orthodox groups. Its prosperity therefore was specious. It was living on its capital, slowly consuming its assets. This insolvency moreover ruled in the pulpit also. "Old-line" Reform Judaism was unequal to supplying its own rabbis. Occasionally young men, reared in old-style Reform temples, made the Jewish ministry their careers. The overwhelming majority of Reform rabbis were recruited from Orthodox and Conservative backgrounds. Not that other parties in Judaism were doing better in holding their adherents. All were in the same boat. But it meant only that all were unsatisfactory.

Worst of all, "old-line" Reform had not proved itself creative. It had enjoyed three-quarters of a century of opportunity under the most favorable circumstances. Reform Jews in America were the wealthiest and best-established elements in the freest Jewry in the world. Yet they had been quite sterile, incapable, it would seem, of giving birth to new Jewish values. By definition, the range of their interests was narrow, limited to religion, to biblical research, theology, metaphysics, ethics personal and social, the techniques of group worship and individual meditation. But even in these fields they had made little to grow and of that still less was first rate. But creativity, Dr. Kaplan was persuaded, was both the sign and the assurance of vitality.

On practical grounds, because of its consequences, Dr. Kaplan could not assent to the theory of Reform. Nor did the theory as theory overpower him with its cogency. At its core it consisted of the notion that Judaism was almost purely a creedal communion. That this formula is gravely incomplete has already been established in Chapter 9, "A Matter of Definitions." It remains only that I make an acknowledgment, by now long overdue, that the argumentation presented on the point is pretty thoroughly Dr. Kaplan's.

Having failed to find the rationale he sought in the religious systems, Dr. Kaplan turned to the secularists, Messrs. X, Y and Z. But they too disappointed him. Like the Reformists, they had blundered but in the opposite direction. The former, concentrating on religion, had suppressed the peoplehood and culture of Israel; the latter emphasizing nationhood, civilization and Homeland, either repudiated or minimized the Jewish religion. And Judaism without the God-faith and its concomitants appeared to Dr. Kaplan a self-contradiction and a blind alley.

A secularized Judaism was out of harmony with what Judaism had been throughout history.

A secularized Judaism, moreover, would be a clumsy thing, perhaps an impossibility, in practice. Religion is so much part of the Jewish tradition, so closely interwoven with it, that it is impossible to touch one without laying hold of the other as well. The Jew who cannot or will not make peace with Jewish theology, who undertakes to get along on peoplehood and culture alone, will necessarily be exposed to spiritual embarrassment. He will always be stumbling over the all-pervading religion. God is omnipresent in Judaism as in the universe. To refuse to recognize that He is about is to invite chagrin and discomfiture.

A secularized Judaism would indeed present an almost pathetic spectacle. It would require that the individual Jew exert himself to the full for Judaism, only to miss its major satisfaction. No matter what the forces that have motivated and still impel Judaism, religion is the first among them, as it is the focus of the best energies, the occasion of the fairest creativity. A Jewish existence without it is preposterous; it is to play *Hamlet* without the Prince of Denmark.

Secularism consigns the Jew to admiring Scripture for its style but not its content; to revering the sages of Israel for their greatness but not that which made them great; to fostering Jewish literature for every reason except its message; to performing rites for all sorts of purposes, cultural and social, except the ultimate purpose, the service of God.

A secularized Judaism, last of all, would deny to Jews the spiritual sustenance they require, which Judaism in its historic form stands ready to give them. Jews, like all human beings, need the light, solace, and stimulation which only a religious insight can afford. A dereligionized Judaism would therefore turn out to be a grotesquerie. It would in the end reduce Jews to the pass where they would have to go outside Judaism for those truths and values which Judaism created and gave to the world.

No, Dr. Kaplan discovered, there was no resting place for him in secularism. Yet his journey through that realm had not been to no avail. In the worlds peopled by X, Y and Z, he had made discoveries and learned lessons.

Thus the secularist systems underscored a principle neglected or obscured by the various religious ideologies—the principle of the peoplehood of Israel. They projected into prominence the cultural elements in the Jewish heritage. And they strengthened within him his predisposition toward Zionism. In all these attitudes Dr. Kaplan had been instructed by the tradition. They were now reconfirmed.

Most important of all, having explored two sets of defective ideologies, he now had a clearer notion of what an acceptable rationale must be. Thus he had discovered by trial and error the folly of theories based on fragments of the truth. He had learned the necessity of a definition that took cognizance of all the elements in Jewishness. Wherefore, before he had framed his philosophy, he knew in advance that it would embrace religion, culture and peoplehood, all three and all at once.

He had been persuaded further of the inevitability of change in Judaism. The attempt of Orthodoxy to save the tradition by keeping it static was, he now believed, foredoomed to failure. But the evolutionary character of the heritage was more than an actuality to be conceded grudgingly; it had come to appear in his eyes as an opportunity to be exploited. It converted Judaism from a *fait accompli,* rich, beautiful but finished, into something which, if Jews so willed, might be made richer and more beautiful.

Again he had grown determined that Judaism must be consonant with the best in modern thought. He had no confidence in either sociologies or theologies that refused to face facts or that required closed minds. With fundamentalists he had no quarrel. But so far as he was concerned, there was hope for Judaism only if it was in harmony with the great scientific conclusions of the modern era. This too had now become a precondition for his future philosophy. It must set forth the Jewish religion and tradition in such a fashion that a Jew could honor the Jewish heritage and his reason at the same time.

And he had learned, last of all, that the beginning of an acceptable theory and program was a tenable definition.

All the other ideologies having failed him, he now proceeded to build a seaworthy conception of his own. At this point he made his first major contribution to contemporary Jewish thought. His predecessors, whether out of hope or fear, had pretty consistently been beguiled into definitions that were wishful rather than accurate. Dr. Kaplan, on the other hand, set about contriving his formula by examining the reality he hoped to formulate. An obvious procedure? Of course. And yet, against the record of those who had gone before, a step little less than revolutionary.

Once he had adopted this technique, the rest was comparatively easy. By the simple device of looking at Jews and Judaism, he was led inevitably to our conclusions of Chapter 9: that Judaism is compounded of religion, culture or civilization, and peoplehood, all organically interwoven; that it is the evolving religious civilization of the Jewish people.

Now a valid definition illuminates the nature of its object and makes intelligible its relationships. This definition explains how a Jew can be irreligious and still remain a Jew. In any such instance the Jewish culture, or at the least the Jewish social identity, persists, though the religion has been dissipated. On the other hand, we now understand why the Jewish secularist has such trouble in extricating himself from the Jewish religion. Since religion penetrates the whole organism, it will turn up everywhere.

One perceives too why the social status of Jews may vary from place to place. For Israel is a people and, like all other peoples, manifests itself in diverse fashions. The "mystery" of the Jews constituting a nation in Palestine, a nationality in the Soviet Union and Poland, and a religio-culture group in the West is now solved. It is no more a mystery than the dissimilarity displayed by other peoples—the Irish or Swedes for example—in the many lands of their sojourning.

Last of all, the relationship between Judaism and Americanism is clarified, not by oversimplifying the nature of the former as is the wont of those who define it as a communion, but realistically, in full recognition of its complex character. The American Jews, to pronounce once again what is virtually a refrain in this book, have only one religion, the Jewish; one political allegiance, the American; and two cultures, the Anglo-Saxon and the Hebraic. In this last respect, they are by no means unique. Millions of other Americans are the recipients of fragments or sizable portions of second cultures.

There remains one touchstone on which Dr. Kaplan's formula must still be tried. A valid definition of anything must explain not only that thing, but also its opposite. So, a theory of light ought to account for darkness; a hypothesis as to life must illumine death as well. Wherever a polarity of ideas exists, an elucidation of one of the twin terms should elucidate the other. Dr. Kaplan's hypothesis is adequate as a description of Judaism. But if it is to pass muster, it must also make intelligible the antithesis of Judaism, its disintegration—that is to say, assimilation.

This negative but climactic test is failed by the alternative systems. Consider, to take one random example, "old-line" Reform. This theory is inadequate not only to the facts of Jewishness, but, what is less often perceived, to those of assimilation. By its terms, a Jew should cease to be a Jew as soon as he loses rapport with the Jewish religion. On its maps, the border between Jewishness and non-Jewishness runs along lines of theology. Those on one side should be Jews, on the other Gentiles. And a single step ought to separate one condition from the other.

Creed, however, is not the frontier between Israel and the rest of mankind. Nor does a Jew cease to be a Jew when he loses faith in a set of doctrines; nor all at once. De-Judaization is as much a matter of sociology and psychology as of theology; it is not an incident but a process.

In this respect, once more Dr. Kaplan's system stands up better than its rivals. It covers the facts of de-Judaization, and without any straining at the seams. Judaism, it makes clear, is a mansion of many chambers. He who has abandoned one, even if that one be the sanctuary, may still be at home in the others. Not until he is clear of the whole edifice, roof, cellar and even the eaves, can he be said to be out of it.

Now too we understand why assimilation is almost always gradual. Because Judaism is multiple in ingredients it is rarely brushed aside with one gesture. More generally its elements are dropped singly or in small bunches, over a time span ranging from years to generations. What is more, experience indicates that the discarding of Jewish appurtenances will tend to follow a normal and predictable sequence. Jewish culture—the Hebrew tongue, music, art, literature—go overboard first. Theological doctrines are generally next. Then ritual and folkway go aglimmering. Affiliation with Jewish organizations and institutions follows in line. The afterglow of traditional Jewish ethic—the passion for learning, philanthropy and social justice—fades away.

The last and hardiest element is social identity. Long after everything else has disappeared this is likely to hang on both in the consciousness of the assimilating Jew and in that of the world. Indeed there are tens of thousands of American Jews in whom this is all that survives, the last ember of what was once a great flame. If and when this too is extinguished, when, in other words, the individual Jew has ceased to remember that he is a Jew, when further all other Jews and non-Jews have forgotten with him, then is the process of de-Judaization fulfilled. Assimilation has been achieved.

Tap it then on whichever side you will, and it rings solid, this conception of Judaism as the evolving religious civilization of the Jewish people. It is true to the historic character of Jewishness, to the facts of contemporary experience. Even to the assimilatory process it seeks to inhibit. It was then a masterful feat of theorizing that Dr. Kaplan had contrived. But was it no more than that? Or is there in his carefully conceived formula that for which he had gone aquesting in the beginning—a guide to the Jewish spirit in its self-redemption?

12

A Creative Program

[In the next two chapters the "tenable theory" at which we have arrived is brought to bear on the issues internal to Judaism and the Jewish group—that is to say, on the problems of Jewish theology, ethic, ritual and culture, and, in another direction, on the question of the proper organization of the American Jewish community.

To persons concerned with the content of Jewish life, especially to Jews seeking a positive relationship with their heritage and identity, our discussion of these themes will be pretty much the climax of this book.

The more casual reader is advised that that discussion may be somewhat technical and difficult. It is suggested, therefore, that he skim Chapters 12 and 13, resuming his sustained reading with the section on Zionism, page 221.]

Parturiunt montes. . . . The mountains labor, and a definition is born; we toil mightily among ideologies, and father a conception. Judaism, we affirm, must be envisaged as the evolving religious civilization of the Jewish people. Well, what of it? How is the American Jew better off now that he has arrived at our particular formula?

To this extent, certainly, he is farther along. He perceives much more clearly what he is dealing with. It is, he now knows, no simple and static entity. Rather is it a complex, many-faceted organism, rich in colors, diverse in members and ever changing. What is more, he also has some pretty clear intimations as to what he has to do. For, definition is not only description, it implies courses of action.

THE REALM OF RELIGIOUS BELIEF

Religious faith, in the sense of a theistic world outlook, is in many regards the neglected aspect of the Jewish heritage. Here is a tradition that can be said to have been born with the emergence of a particular conception of

God; a people whose members by the thousands have endured martyrdom on behalf of their creed, whose greatest texts have been proclamations of faith, whose greatest heroes were saints. Yet, in its scheme of things today, the God-interpretation of reality is quite submerged. This not merely among Jewish secularists to whom irreligion is often a matter of conscience but even among professing Jews, indeed in the Synagogue itself. Thus Jewish preaching, as is notorious among those who know it well, tends to shy away from theology. Again, of all the voluminous contemporary Jewish literature, very little deals with issues of doctrine. Indeed, matters have come to such a pass that rabbis and Jewish theological seminaries must resort to books written by non-Jews for instruction in contemporary religious metaphysics and in the scientific interpretation of the Bible. In other words, the classic *Weltanschauung,* Judaism's major gift to the world, and the Book in which it finds purest expression lie fallow these days.

This neglect of religious interests among Jews is not only unprecedented in Jewish history, it is broader and cuts deeper than among Gentiles—a circumstance not hard to explain. For Jews, like Christians, have been exposed to all the influences which account for the general advance of secularism in modern times. In addition they have been affected by special factors touching them peculiarly. Their distractedness is one such. The Methodist as Methodist has a limited budget of denominational obligations. The Jew as Jew has all those plus all the items discussed in this book. Little wonder that he has little time or energy to devote to Jewish doctrine and practice.

A second, even more potent cause of inordinate secularism among Jews is their tardy entrance into Western society. Christianity took the intellectual revolutions—Copernican, Newtonian, Darwinian and Freudian—one at a time. Even so it suffered large dislocations under their impact. Judaism, isolated from the world for five hundred years, coming into the open only very recently, got their full weight all at once.

Nor in accounting for the retreat of the Jewish religion is it proper to overlook the psychic element. Many a Jew who is an *anima naturaliter religiosa,* who would normally arrive by himself at religious affirmations, cannot make peace with the Jewish religion, not because it is a religion but because it is Jewish.

Whatever the causes of the secularist drift in Judaism, Reconstructionism must resist it. Religion is, from its point of view, many things in one: an integral element in Judaism, indispensable to individual self-fulfillment, and a prerequisite for general social health. To this extent at least our definition helps us; it dictates a position on religion.

The formula goes further, characterizing Judaism as evolving—that is to say, as something that grows and unfolds, that sloughs off outworn elements and flowers into fresh expressions. God-faith and theology, therefore, must also evolve and be transformed in response to new insights and novel conditions. Another tangled issue is resolved: the question whether Jewish belief ought to remain fixed, as Orthodoxy argues, or be regarded as modifiable.

Other positions on the Jewish religion are, of course, possible and proper. Judaism has a legitimate fundamentalist wing as has Christianity. With Jews who, like Mr. A. in Chapter 10, are at ease in Orthodoxy, Reconstructionism not only has no quarrel; it has, so far as theology goes, no message.

It addresses itself rather to those who would like to make their peace with the Jewish religion but cannot; who, on matters of faith, stand at the temple doors "heart in, head out." To these it preaches adherence to the old, as it stands if possible, remade if necessary, and yet creation of the new. It insists, "On this lay hold, and from that withdraw not thy hand." In sum, it acknowledges the polarity, universal in human purposes, between tradition and progress.

This means, more concretely, three specific jobs. First, the Jew must establish a rapport with Jewish belief as it emerges from the past. Second, he must rethink, *reconstruct,* those elements which are unacceptable to the modern mind. Wherever the traditional and the contemporary are at loggerheads, every effort ought to be made to resolve the conflict with minimal damage to the former. But boldness is called for as well as conservatism, and one must be prepared to abandon as well as to preserve. Third, he must seek to make the Jewish faith creative once more, productive of novel insights, revelatory of hitherto unsuspected truths.

This balancing between the old and the new is less difficult than may be suspected. We have already noted that doctrine in Judaism has never been cast into crystalline, authoritative form. Hence it lends itself the more readily to being remolded closer to the needs of any given generation. Besides, there has always been latitude in Judaism. The individual has ever been relatively free to put his private configuration on the group outlook. Uniformity of religious opinion has not only never existed among Jews, it has rarely been sought after. There is, therefore, less radicalism than first appears in our proposal of a continuous, progressive reformulation of Jewish theology.

It can be carried off—this project of establishing a harmony between the Jewish tradition and modern thought. Thousands of American Jews, myself included, have done it. We see the universe through a God-faith which enables us to comprehend it the more thoroughly; which invests it with meaning and purposefulness; which lends intelligibility and sanction to our ethical values; which stimulates us toward moral self-realization and the broader service of our fellow men, and which, last of all, enables us to see our Jewishness as a part of a cosmic design unfolding on all sides of us.

This faith, to speak for myself, is a legitimate descendant of that cherished by my ancestors—so legitimate that I enter their world as preserved in writing and feel myself completely at home. This faith is, at the same time, a proper expression of contemporary thought—so proper that I am at ease in the science and philosophy of our day. Not that I do not run into metaphysical systems alien to my own. These I reject partly because they are incompatible with the Jewish tradition, but equally because, in my judgment, they are inconsistent with rigorous reasoning.

I would not be misunderstood. It is not my intention to suggest that in adapting Judaism to its world setting, one must make it a "religion of reason," an outlook composed only of demonstrable propositions, in which, furthermore, all undertones of mystery and mood have been muted. Despite Hegel, reality is not all reason; despite the classical rationalists, the human personality is not pure intellect. A religion confined to the logically establishable, and indifferent to the emotional hungers of men would both misrepresent the universe and feed its communicants stones for bread. Yet, to say that there may be more things in this world than are dreamed of in our philosophies is one thing. To maintain as an article of faith what is contrary to the intellectually probable is very much another. This is not belief but its abuse. Reconstructionism seeks to obviate it for Jews.

From our definition, then, flows as the first imperative the retrieval of God in Judaism.

THE DOMAIN OF ETHICS

The Jewish tradition is immeasurably rich in ethical values. Of these, the world at large is familiar with only one segment, the Biblical. But Scripture does not begin to exhaust the wisdom concerning human behavior which srael has amassed through the centuries. Into Talmud and Midrash, into nedieval pietistic works, a people that made a career of contemplating the ;ood life and living it distilled its precious experiences. For much that they liscovered analogues exist elsewhere. But some of the perceptions they chieved are unique; some of the fields they explored have never been sur- veyed by others. For example, Judaism contains a virtually unprecedented thic of scholarship and the life of reason, an extraordinarily balanced ap- proach to the body and its desires, an unparalleled awareness of the reci- procity between individual and social morality. Mankind would be much nriched were these treasures to be made public property. Unfortunately, und incredible as it may seem, many of the most important moralistic texts of Judaism still await translation.

Our concern at this moment is not with the world but with Jews. For hem, Reconstructionism projects a second major line of endeavor: the ecapture, reconstruction and refertilization of Jewish ethical vision.

The task to be undertaken in religion must be duplicated in morality, and vith pretty much the same techniques.

First: the rediscovery of the past. The Jews of our time must come to know their significant writings and the principles they teach.

Second: a great sifting. Our generation, as each generation in its time, nust scrutinize and appraise for itself the judgments and aspirations formu- ated by the past. What it finds alive, meaningful, permanent, it must take o itself. That which is valid in essence but not in form it must modify. That which has outlived its day, it must, despite all reverence for the past, out firmly aside.

Third: the repointing of Jewish morality. The key Jewish ethical insights possess the virtue of timelessness. But it is one of the deficiencies of things ternal that they have no special message for any given day. An aura of generality invests them. Always relevant, they never point particularly to any specific situation. The prophets of Israel were keenly aware of this. Whatever their moral abstractions, they straightway concretized them. So hey no sooner asserted nature to be the handiwork of the God of all men han they denounced "them that join house to house, that lay field to field ill there be no room." They went further, ordaining a jubilee year wherein he poverty-stricken peasant might again possess the field that had been sold rom under him. Talmudic Judaism strove after the same objective, the con- version of ideals into habit, law and communal practice.

A similar task confronts modern Jews. Theirs is the assignment of exploring their ethical heritage to discover its meaning for modern times, of focusing its light on the obscurities of our day, the issues of individual morality, of war and peace, property and persons, freedom and authority, capital and labor.

Last of all: the evocation of new Jewish ethical expression. According to an ancient rabbinic epigram, the voice that sounded at Sinai was never silenced. What this signifies is that the proclamation of moral truth never ends. Now genius is a sensitive plant whose budding cannot be predicted or forced. There is no way whereby any group can guarantee that it will produce scientists, musicians, metaphysicians of the first magnitude. But every society ought to hope for such a consummation. The Jews with their tradition of ethical questing and their present experience of pain and injustice constitute a promising seedbed for prophets, saints, priests and scribes of the good life. It becomes then their duty and privilege to foster the cultivation of moral perceptions and values. In the past their husbandry in the field proved not unfruitful; it may turn out equally productive in times to come.

THE ROUND OF RITUAL

To anyone, Jew or Gentile, who views Judaism from without, ritual must appear unimportant, and preoccupation with it a misdirection of energy. After all, of what consequence can it be whether a Jew does or does not drive his automobile on the seventh day of the week, whether he partakes of, or refrains from certain foods. Such thoughts may suggest themselves to persons who stand outside Jewish life, never to those at home in it.

For, as any informed and practicing Jew knows, observance looms large in the Jewish scheme of things. So it has always been, the practices of Judaism having been cherished for two thousand years with the utmost fidelity and joyousness. So, though far less generally, it is still. The typical professing Jew of our day like his forebears knows well and values highly the Sabbath Eve with its candles, braided bread loaves and cup of Sanctification; the Passover Feast with its multifarious ritual symbols; the ram's horn sounding on the New Year; the austere solemnity of the White Fast of the Day of Atonement; the keening chant of the Black Fast of the Ninth of Ab; the prayer shawl; the first binding on of phylacteries after one's thirteenth birthday; the Kaddish prayer and memorial lamp for the dead; the

Scroll of the Torah dressed in embroidered velvets and adorned with glisten-
ing breastplate and crown. These a Jew is likely to remember longest and
most poignantly; in these and through these, faith and ethic embody
and transmit themselves. This is for many Jews the countenance of Judaism,
well known and passionately loved.

Little wonder that ritual has been a storm center, not only in the remote
past but in recent years as well. When Reform emerged in Germany, it
exhibited many radicalisms. But the one that most offended the Orthodox
was its iconoclasm on observances. Indeed to this very day the line of demarcation between traditionalists and nontraditionalists consists, of all things, in
that the former wear, the latter doff their hats at worship. This is, of course,
not the whole story, but it is symptomatic. Again, when Dr. Kaplan published his volume *Judaism as a Civilization* with its many bold premises and
unconventional conclusions, the most violent protest centered on his recommendation that certain details of Jewish usage be modified.

The ritual problem in Judaism is composed of two distinct yet inter-
related issues: a social reality and a theoretical question. The social reality
is the progressive disintegration of Jewish observance. There was a time, and
that not so long ago, when virtually every Jew complied with the last
and least requirement of the Law. That day is gone forever. While there are
Jews who still adhere firmly to the traditional design, there are many more
who have departed from it, either in part or all the way. The process has
been gathering momentum through the years. The band of the observant
dwindles, the number of the nonconforming grows apace.

The theoretical issue concerns itself with the role of ritual in Judaism. Is
a system of practices essential or dispensable? If the former, must it be the
historic system unchanged or can it be some variation of it? If the latter, on
what basis ought modifications to be designed?

Reconstructionism insists that Jewish life requires a regimen of observances. By its theory, Judaism is a religious civilization. Every custom possesses therefore not one but two significances. Vis-à-vis the Jewish religion
it is a rite; in relation to the culture, a folkway. So, when a Jew sets out to
partake of a Passover Feast he effects dual purposes simultaneously. On the
one hand he celebrates God the Liberator in prayer, song and symbolism.
His behavior is cultic, almost sacramental. At the same time he is doing
something analogous to reciting the Declaration of Independence on the

Fourth of July. That is to say, he is reliving a significant moment in the past of his people, conforming to a social pattern of his group.

Whether as ritual or folkway, observance from the Reconstructionist viewpoint is indispensable to Judaism. For no religion can be complete or thrive without some pattern of rituals; and no society can exist let alone be vigorous without some fabric of mores.

But what shall be the shape of Jewish observances? The unabatedly traditional? Some variant of it? Or the overtly nontraditional?

Here again Reconstructionism is explicit. And once more its conception of Judaism as evolving provides the warrant for its answer.

It is of the nature of a growing thing that it holds on to its past, and yet reaches toward a future. He who cultivates anything, whether a historic theology, an ethic or a system of practices, must guide himself accordingly. Jews in other words ought not to play fast and loose with their past, lest they lose contact with it, the root and strength of their present existence. On rituals as on so many other themes, the presumption is always in favor of the tradition.

A presumption, be it observed, not a rule. There are observances which in the process of time, have been emptied of content; some, indeed, which challenged by modern realities, can be maintained only by a heroic effort and then to no determinable advantage. Other practices could be made more effective spiritually were they to be changed in detail. Then there are lacunae in the Jewish regimen, junctures of large significance in the life of modern men toward which religion ought to have something ritualistic to contribute. To such situations historic Judaism, the creation of another age, often has nothing to offer. Reverence may have its place, but so also has boldness, the courage to renounce, to remake, to innovate.

But is not all this an invitation to anarchy? The Jewish group has no central authority to supervise changes in observance. Is not our policy a sanction to each individual to do with the tradition as seems right in his eyes? Is it not a counsel of irresponsibility? What else can be expected from it except the wildest disorder?

Undeniably, grave perils attend our proposal. Yet is there any other course except to risk them? Is not anarchy already upon us? Save for the limited and ever-dwindling ranks of the Orthodox, most Jews have long since arrogated to themselves privilege of doing with Jewish observance as they please. Nor does Reconstructionism offer carte blanche to the individual. On the

ontrary, it has been careful to define precisely the criteria by which change
nust be directed.* What is more, it is working for official sanction for new
departures, preferably from established wings of Judaism such as the Con-
ervative and Reform, but, failing action on their part, from the Reconstruc-
ionist movement itself.

It is freedom, not license, that Reconstructionism commends. Besides,
what alternative is open to Jews who wish to live Jewishly but cannot be
Orthodox? They must venture trial, error and experiment in the hope that
eventually there may emerge a new norm of Jewish observance, a pattern
t once traditional and yet entirely acclimated to modern America.

Admitted that the whole enterprise has in it something of a gamble. If
o, it is a gamble which cannot be refused. Destiny forces it; there is no
ther prospect of success.

THE FIELD OF CULTURE

Creativity is the index of a community's vitality and its assurance against
imes to come. It is the badge of vitality, because to live means to create. It
s a guarantee against the future, because the more a society creates, the more
meaningful its existence becomes for its members, the more they in turn
will exert themselves on its behalf.

By this standard—the standard of new things in music, art and literature—
ow go matters with Judaism? A candid answer must bespeak both dis-
ppointment and satisfaction. In Palestine the Jewish spirit has turned in-
andescent. There a small but renascent community has poured itself forth in
a flood of self-expression, intense, and diversely colored. In Poland—prewar
Poland of course—a Jewry hobbled by intolerance and crippled by poverty
till managed somehow to sustain a passionate spiritual existence, both con-
emplative and creative.

The picture grows darker as one turns elsewhere. Prewar Russia, by every
expectation, should have been the site of a vigorous Jewish cultural life. Its
ewry had long been highly literate and devotedly traditional. Under the
Soviets, Jews for the first time in history enjoyed political equality and social
ecurity. The Jewish community, moreover, recognized as a minority nation-
lity, was protected in its own language and civilization; it was accorded
ven a distinct national home, in Biro-Bidjan.

---

* *Toward a Guide for Jewish Ritual Usage,* a pamphlet published by the Reconstructionist
oundation, New York City.

Despite these favorable circumstances, Russian Jewry as a whole has not done too well culturally. Broad and uncontrollable factors account for this in part—the fierce absorption of Russians in the gigantic economic plans to which they had committed themselves, the tendency exhibited by almost all minority nationalities to drift toward Russification, the war. Among the causes, however, must be listed the Soviet policy on Judaism, its hostility to the Jewish religion, to Zionism and to Jewish culture, except the Yiddishist, its consistent segregation of Russian Jews from Jewries abroad.

All this may be water under the bridge. Because of the exigencies of the war, because of natural developments, the Soviet Union has very recently abandoned its isolationism; has modified its procedure, if not its theory, on religion; and, for the first time since 1917, has permitted contact between the Jewries of Russia and of the world. Furthermore, there now appears to be a fair chance of a revision of Communist policy on Zionism, Hebraism and Jewish Palestine. All in all, Jewish culture in Russia may from now on get a better "break."

There is reason for optimism as to the cultural future of Russia's Jews. But it is—and this applies to all Jews on the European continent—remote not immediate. Everything else aside, the Jews of the Old World have been drained of blood and substance. Whatever strength remains they will need for survival and recuperation. Not for a long time are they likely to have energy to give to literature or art.

Of all Jewries only one in addition to the Palestinian can now be looked to for productivity. That one is, of course, the American, the largest and freest in the world, the only community of size that has not been ravaged by the Second World War. Here too the picture is somber in hue. American Jewry has been far less creative Jewishly than might have been expected in view of its advantages. And very sizable advantages they have been: freedom and security; economic resources sufficient to sustain cultural enterprises; a rich environment of American literature, music and art to buoy up specific Jewish interests; a Jewish community large enough to serve as a market to artists and a public to authors; an age-old Jewish tradition of devotion to intellectual pursuits. Like the vineyard of which the prophet sang, American Jewry is culturally "a choicest vine" planted in "a very fruitful hill." Like that, too, it has disappointed its cultivators.

In the nature of things, it cannot be proved that the Jews of America have been less creative than their background and circumstances warrant. The pirit, being neither ponderable nor measurable, does not lend itself to the striking of trial balances. And yet, even statistically, an impressive case can be made for the thesis.

The novel is perhaps the most characteristic of modern literary forms. How much a society does with it may be taken for a barometer of sorts. If so, American Jewry is far from well off.

I have before me a bibliography of novels of Jewish interest. The list does not pretend to be exhaustive; it does however contain every important piece of Jewish fiction done in English in recent years. Well over half the titles represent translations from the Yiddish, Hebrew or German. One-fifteenth were written by Christians, including, in one instance, an apostate from Judaism; another fifteenth by British Jews; one-twentieth by American Jews who, by background and education, are Europeans rather than Americans. Of the entire catalogue only twenty-one percent are indigenous to the American Jewish community. It is not irrelevant to add that none of these is of the first magnitude, comparable for instance with the "Joseph cycle" of Thomas Mann. On this record American Jews have been nearly sterile. They appear to even greater disadvantage when compared with the smaller and infinitely poorer Jewry of prewar Poland, or with the Palestinian community which, one-ninth of the size of the American, has been more creative not only relatively but absolutely.

Further evidence for our thesis is afforded by an extraordinary symposium entitled "Under Forty." * Inquiries were addressed to a number of distinguished, younger American Jewish authors concerning their attitudes toward Jewishness and Judaism, and the influence of both on them. They were asked, among other things, whether they had "formed a conscious attitude toward their heritage"; and whether the Jewish tradition had played any role in their literary development.

These questions, soberly put, were answered with equal sobriety. All participants in the symposium revealed themselves to be acutely aware of their Jewish identity. Some of them seem always to have possessed this awareness, others to have had it forced on them by anti-Semitism. No matter how acquired, it has been an influence in their lives. Almost to the man they agreed that by virtue of it they were the more sensitive to the dangers of political and economic reaction and to the minority problem in all its mani-

---

* *The Contemporary Jewish Record*, Feb., 1944.

festations. Conversely they were the more passionately committed to demo
cratic ideals.

Jewishness as identity quite clearly looms large in their thinking an
feeling; Judaism, whether as religion or culture, comes off badly indeed. O
the eleven respondents, seven deny it any place in their scheme of thing
One indeed goes so far as to deny that it can have any meaning for anyon
"There is," he writes, "much show and talk of affirmation, but only to th
end that the negative, or neuter, elements may be made more acceptable.
And as for the Jewish religion, "its function is to provide, chiefly for peopl
of no strong religious impulse, a social and rational defense against th
world's hostility." (Is it a coincidence that the author of these earnest bu
categorical assertions confesses that since childhood the word Jew ha
"struck straight to the unconscious where fear, shame, attraction and repu
sion are indistinguishable?") Only four of the eleven ascribe considerabl
influence on their inner lives to the Jewish heritage, and even these in var
ing degrees. To two at least, Judaism operates as a *fait accompli,* a childhoo
experience which, though never renewed, continues a potent memory. Th
reckoning ends then with only two of the writers regarding Judaism a
actively meaningful to them.

On the basis of my own observations, I am inclined to believe that th
distribution of attitudes among these eleven persons is not fortuitous, bu
mirrors with fair accuracy the standing of Jewish culture among the Amer
can Jewish intellectuals. That is to say, among them about two out of eleve
are concerned with specifically Jewish values. Ernest Bloch, Maurice Samue
Ludwig Lewisohn suggest themselves for illustration. Indeed, simultaneou
with the publication of the symposium and in the teeth of the contention o
one of its participants that there could be no worth-while Jewish expressio
in this country, several of the great orchestras of this country presente
Leonard Bernstein's *Jeremiah,* a work of distinctly Jewish inspiration. Un
fortunately one swallow, even a flight of swallows, does not make a sprin

Now, I wish to be altogether clear. I do not conceive of the American an
Jewish cultures as being mutually competitive. Nor am I fired to jealous
by the spectacle of Jews giving themselves to pursuits unrelated to Judaism
The artist has a full right to go where his spirit listeth. Nor is he under an
obligation to express himself through Jewish media. On the other hand, i
he does elect to do so, he is equally within his rights not only formally bu
essentially. Jewish interests are as thoroughly legitimate on the America

cene as any. The Jewish thread is a proper strand in the fabric of this land,
o weave with it an entirely American act. As I see it, then, the Jewish
artist has a choice between working on the larger loom or the smaller.
Whichever he selects, he is equally worthy of his hire.

My point right now is a simple one. In the life of the American Jewish
man of art and letters the Jewish identity and heritage are facts. As such he
ought somehow, somewhere, whether as nuances to other themes or as major
motifs, respond to them. And yet, as we have just seen, he will, if he is at
all typical, fail to do so.

Why? The answers are many. Ignorance of Judaism, psychic blockings
against it, lack of clear thinking about it, absorption in social issues so total
as to leave room for nothing else, all these, as the symposium demonstrates,
are episodes in the story. The nub, however, is that it must be so. Judaism is
the secondary, ancillary civilization of American Jews. With the inevitable-
ness of a body drawn by gravity toward a larger mass, they will drift
naturally in the direction of the broader field. Of creative artists no more
than a minority can be expected to seek self-expression in Jewish channels,
and of these only a minority in turn to do so consistently.

Whence it follows that the American Jewish community for all its size
and resources cannot be expected to sustain itself culturally. To put it
bluntly, it is going to have to live on the largesse of other, more intensely
Jewish Jewries.

But though Jewish arts and letters in this land cannot but be largely
derivative, the larger the volume of original output the better. In the first
place useful activity is not only a sign of group health; like exercise, it tends
to superinduce it. Again, no matter what the worth of importations, the
home-grown poem, song or painting, sprouting on the American scene, will
both savor of it and be relevant to it. The odds may be heavy against indigenous Jewish creativity. Despite them, the game must be played. Every
encouragement must be given by the American Jewish community to native
authors, playwrights, composers, choreographers and sculptors. Fellowships,
subventions and markets ought to be assured to persons of promise and
works of merit. As matters stand now, he who puts his hand to a Jewish
artistic enterprise will begin with difficulties in getting his piece mounted
and end with a limited audience. The least American Jewry can do is to
offset the crasser and more readily remediable disadvantages.

RECONSTRUCTIONISM AND ZIONISM

In the architecture of this book, Zionism is an unruly element. It cuts across all the lines we have drawn for the orderly division of our materials; it spills over into every field of Jewish interest. And all the time it is also an entity in itself. That is why it has been reserved for the fourth and last section of this volume.

And yet in advance of the special presentation that still awaits us, I should like to pause briefly over the Reconstructionist view of Zionism. Not that the latter derives from the former. Zionism is too large, complex and tumultuous a movement to be bound to any single ideology of Jewish life. But we are now exploring the practical implications of Reconstructionism. Our argument will not be complete unless we inquire, no matter how briefly, after its position on this vast and crucial issue.

To put the matter bluntly, Reconstructionism leads directly to Zionism. Given the premises of the first, the second follows relentlessly.

1) No program for the perpetuation of Judaism can be indifferent to the welfare of the people who are its bearers. Palestine has saved the lives of myriad Jews in the past, it promises to redeem many more in the future. On this score alone Reconstructionism must indorse Zionism.

2) There is in Reconstructionism a heavy bias in favor of the historical in Judaism. The love of Zion, the hope of its rebuilding, the dream of the restoration there of at least a part of the Jewish people are etched deep and indelible in the consciousness of the Jewish traditionalist. In effect it is next to impossible to accept the Jewish civilization without embracing Zionism at the same time.

3) The Jews constitute, as we have seen, not only a religious communion and a culture group but a people also. And every people ought have some place in the world where its peoplehood can find total expression.

4) Reconstructionism implies Zionism because of the needs of Judaism, because of the persistent disadvantages we have just surveyed under which Jewish culture operates everywhere. The second civilization of Jews, Judaism is constantly under the necessity of refreshing itself from a free-flowing source. Somewhere in the world it must be the dominant concern of Jews. In other words, a Jewish Homeland must be established.

Reconstructionism on all these counts is Zionist. But it does not therefore sanction all vagaries of Zionism. Thus it stands against the secularism of

Messrs. X and Y. Religious in its premises and objectives, it insists on the primacy of religion in every aspect of Jewish life. For, only when grounded in the historic Jewish faith and ethic can Zionism be vigorous and full-blooded, only when tempered by them can it be kept from nationalistic excesses, and only under their direction can it serve, as it should, the classic humanitarian purposes of the Jewish tradition.

By the same token, Reconstructionism offers no sympathy or asylum to the Zionism that sees only Palestinian Jewry and no other. There is a Zionist who is so thoroughly absorbed in his distant task that he forgets his Jewish obligations nearer to home. There is another Zionist who despairs of the possibility of Jewish life outside Palestine. Convinced that Diaspora Judaism is doomed, he concentrates his energies on the only Jewry that appears to him to have a chance. With such pessimism, Reconstructionism has no patience. It has confidence in the future of Judaism throughout the world. It objects to the notion that Palestine and the Diaspora are competitive and mutually exclusive. It holds such an alternative to be false and to obscure the job of modern Jews which is not a matter of "either . . . or" but of 'both."

THE NEED FOR KNOWLEDGE

Even now we have not squeezed from our ideology the last juice of implication. Two enterprises remain to be extracted. The first, a decision as to the organization of the American Jewish community, is so much a theme by itself that we shall reserve it to the next chapter. The other is, as it chances, no less than the chief cornerstone of the Reconstructionist program, that first and last thing from which all else proceeds, toward which everything reaches. I refer to its emphasis on Jewish knowledge, as broad and deep as can be achieved.

A concern over Jewish information and understanding is, needless to say, not the monopoly of any one school of thought. All survivalist ideologies are agreed that the Jew must be informed. It is only the assimilationist who can indulge in or tolerate illiteracy. The advocate of the continuance of Jewish life, be he secularist, religionist or Reconstructionist, can afford no such luxuries. By knowledge as much as by faith and works, Judaism in the past transcended the rigors of its lot. Only with these can it outlive its present crisis.

These days, unfortunately, ignorance of Jewish affairs is quite the rule among Jews. Modern Jews, educated on all matters of general import, are very commonly innocent of Jewish learning of any sort. They know no history, theology or sociology; not Bible, Talmud or prayer book; neither prophets, sages nor heroes. Literacy used to be law among them. Now, of all groups that possess distinguished traditions, they are perhaps the most untutored in their own.

Because knowledge is wanting, the people perish. I would not be guilty of oversimplification. Many of the ills that afflict Jews and Judaism are totally unrelated to what is present or absent inside Jewish heads. Thus were every Jew a Maimonides, anti-Semitism would still be his heartache and dark peril. But other issues, if they cannot be resolved by information, certainly cannot be resolved without it. The diffusion of knowledge and understanding may be nowhere enough by itself. But in many situations it is half the battle, or else a precondition without which the battle cannot even be joined.

For one must know himself, his foes and the lay of the land, or he will not fight intelligently. One must know who and what he is, that indeed he is a man and not a craven, or he will not fight courageously. And one must know what he is fighting for and why it is worth the effort, or he will not fight purposefully, resolutely.

Hence it comes to pass that the protagonists of the various survivalist ideologies who agree on so little besides are so much in harmony here. Because of varying premises and goals, they may differ to a degree on the goals of instruction, its materials and its techniques. Beyond these they are of one heart: Jews must be won to an understanding of their history, their tradition—religious, ethical, ceremonial, cultural, institutional—of their literary monuments, of the Hebrew tongue, of their problem, of the proposal for its solution, of their group purposes and ideals.

Everything I am trying to say about the indispensability of knowledge to the Jewish tradition has been anticipated by the tradition itself. In myriad epigrams and metaphors, the teachers of Israel from Moses on insisted that only as Jewry was informed could it be assured of life. But nowhere has this thought been stated more colorfully than in a legend spun by ancient rabbis.

When Moses descended from Mount Sinai, they relate, he held in his arms, as Scripture informs us, the tablets of stone engraved by the finger of the Holy One, blessed be He. And such was the virtue of the inscription hat it was not Moses who carried the tablets, but the tablets which carried Moses. So it came to pass that his descent over jagged rocks, on the verge of crags and yawning chasms, was effortless and safe. But when the prophet neared the mountain's base and caught his first glimpse of the Golden Calf, when God's words and the idol were brought into confrontation with each other, a wonder ensued. The sacred letters detached themselves from the stone in which they had been inscribed and vanished into thin air. Moses was left holding a blank, inert thing, too heavy for him. It is not true, the sages assert, that Moses threw the tablets to the earth, so shattering them. The fact is that he had to let them go or be crushed. The lettered stone which had carried Moses was, once letterless, too much for him to bear.

It is not difficult to discern what the ancient rabbis are trying to say in their parable: given knowledge and insight, Judaism sustains the Jew; without them it is a crushing burden, too heavy for even the strongest to withstand.

13

An Orderly Household

I
T IS RECOUNTED of Alice that when she first entered Wonderland she was
moved to remark, "Curiouser and curiouser!" So far as I can recall, it is
not related of her that she repeated the comment subsequently. Thus
Lewis Carroll reveals himself to have been a masterful psychologist. For it is
of human nature that with time and exposure one learns to take anything for
granted, even the howling topsy-turvydom that awaited Alice down the
rabbit's hole and behind the looking glass.

This observation is occasioned by a flagrant paradox, the contrast between
the wild disorder which prevails in Jewish public affairs and the complacency with which most Jews accept it. On the one hand, the Jewish community is so badly set up that it cannot cope with some of its most pressing
difficulties; on the other, so habituated are individual Jews to their condition
that many regard it as normal, and some will even defend it as desirable.

To be sure, there are enterprises for which American Jewry is well, even
admirably organized. But there are others in which confusion is the rule.
As I have intimated, combating anti-Semitism is one such; the determination of policies for the rehabilitation of European Jews is still another. One
would have imagined that on tasks as urgent as these, efficiency and group
discipline would be at the peak. The truth is that just because these issues
burn, disagreement over them is fiercest; organizational anarchy at its
wildest.

It ought to be added too that, bad as matters are today, they are incom-
parably better than they were a generation ago. The years have brought
gains. In the sea of chaos, islands of order have been crystallizing. One can
see that someday there may be a land bridge through the waters to distant,
desired shores. But right now, there is more ocean than earth. To put it
bluntly and without metaphor, the situation so far as Jewish communal
organization goes, while improved, leaves much to be desired.

This is thrice unfortunate—being bad for Jewry, for the individual Jew and for Judaism. It is bad for Jewry in that its gravest evils are incompetently dealt with, if not neglected altogether. The problems before the Jewish group may be too large and complex for its best efforts. But when strength is dissipated as at present, or not so much as tapped, the prospect grows bleak indeed.

It is bad for the individual Jew, who, even when he wishes to enlist in the struggle, often cannot find a place where his enrollment will be accepted. Or he may be left bewildered by the claims of contending parties. Only a rare Jewish layman these days knows his way through the maze of committees, conferences, societies and associations which together constitute what passes for an organized Jewish community. And it is an even rarer person who, aware of the true state of affairs, can preserve equanimity. Chaos is not only inefficient, it is disheartening.

It is bad, last of all, for Judaism. Discouragement on this score carries over into attitudes toward Judaism. To the typical Jew, everything Jewish is of a piece. Let him be disappointed in one respect and he will feel let down generally.

The present state of affairs cannot be said even to spare the Jew responsibilities. One might suppose that the less of organization, the fewer organizational obligations. The opposite is the case. A well-ordered society, like a healthy organism, is relaxed, economical of motion. Anarchy, like disease, is attended by feverish, pointless activity. So it comes to pass that for want of order, organizations are multiplied within American Jewry to the point that the body politic swarms with them. More, not less, is required of the individual by way of affiliations, dues, meetings, elections, agenda, conventions and controversies. Ironically but understandably, the greater the hubbub and ado, the less the aggregate accomplishment.

That it could not always have been so is self-evident. Judaism and the Jewish people could never have survived under such disabilities. In truth, throughout the centuries Jewish communities were, as a whole, efficiently and democratically administered. What is more, they generally conformed to a master pattern. Under this archetypal design, evolved through trial and error, all Jews of a town constituted a *kehillah,* or community. Once each year adult males elected an executive board to supervise every matter of Jewish interest. So every Jew was caught up in a single body which reflected his will and ministered to his needs.

Variations from this system and failures in it occurred from time to time. Sometimes the *kehillah* was captured by a clique, or dominated by rich householders. On occasion, it split open in controversy. At intervals, kings, bishops or town senates exploited it as an instrument for extortion. And recurrently, rich or influential Jews who enjoyed the favor of the royal palace or episcopal see presumed to speak for their fellows. The *kehillah*, like all human institutions, was imperfect and corruptible. It was, however, a commonsensical arrangement, and, on the whole, worked well.

How, out of such antecedents, American Jewry worked itself into its present condition of near insanity would make an absorbing tale. We shall not wait to hear it. Whatever else this book may be, it is not intended as a chronicle. Our interest is with the present, with the here and now of the American Jewry. That theme falls naturally into two sections: the local scene—that is, the individual community—and the nation-wide.

THE LOCAL JEWISH COMMUNITY

The Jews of any neighborhood partake of common interests and needs which can be satisfied only through co-operative effort. There is, then, no city or town of Jewish residence that does not have some kind of Jewish communal organization. Its form, however, varies from place to place, running a wide gamut.

There is, in the first instance, what may fairly be called the "rudimentary" Jewish community. Even this, the rawest and most primitive level of Jewish civic structure, exhibits sizable areas of co-ordination. Thus every Jewish settlement is equipped with one or more synagogues, and attached to them schools, cemeteries, men's and women's clubs. Either on the fringe of religious institutions, or more commonly independent of them, will be a miscellany of philanthropic agencies, social settlements, community centers, credit unions, local branches of national Jewish organizations and what not else.

Characteristic of the "rudimentary" community is the absence of co-ordination among its many organizations. The individual synagogue may be affiliated with a national body, but no formal bond will unite it to other synagogues in its own vicinity. Each is a law unto itself; each stands or falls on its own. Agencies for charity are not only unrelated to religious institutions, they are unassociated with one another. Inevitably they compete in fund raising, encroach on one another in function, display conspicuous waste and confusion.

The gravest ill likely to beset a community of this type is a plague of spokesmen. Like seven-year locusts, these are invisible until some crisis occurs. Then, as though from nowhere, prophets arise in Israel. The local rabbis very properly make themselves heard, but with them also leading merchants, prominent attorneys, persons of general prestige, and, for good measure, any Jew who likes the limelight. Usually, under such circumstances, little can be heard for the din, which is perhaps just as well. In acute and delicate situations, however, tumult can be a costly indulgence.

The next higher plane in organization is that represented by the "federation" community. At this level everything is as it was in the "rudimentary" stage except that local philanthropic agencies have been co-ordinated. Somewhere along the line, the Jews of a particular locality have been goaded into rebellion against at least the most obvious of their discomforts. Perhaps they have grown weary of appeals for contributions too numerous to be counted. Perhaps their sense of economy has been affronted by exorbitant expenditures on fund raising and "overhead." Perhaps they can no longer abide the spectacle of many organizations doing badly what one could do well. Whatever the reason, they have armed themselves with the authority and prestige of contributors and compelled their local charitable agencies to unite on fund raising and the clearance of programs.

The Federation of Charities where it has been attained represents a real advance in administrative effectiveness and public order, and hence indubitably in group morale. Its quite genuine virtues have beguiled some Jews into expecting more from it. There are those who look to it for central leadership on the problems of anti-Semitism. For such larger functions it is not adequate. In the first place, bound to limited aspects of Jewish communal living, it is circumscribed, inelastic. But more important, it lacks that democratic base on which any form of Jewish communal organization must stand if it is to possess authority and command discipline. Try as they will—and most Federations have tried valiantly—to find a popular base for themselves, inequality is inherent in their nature. They are money-raising agencies primarily. The larger contributor exerts the larger influence. As the local Federation is unfit to determine matters of policy beyond philanthropy, so the National Council of Jewish Federations and Welfare Funds is not an admissible spokesman for American Jewry on a national scale. This body, established to give information and guidance to local Federations and to co-ordinate their efforts, has discharged its duties admirably. It is, however, not adaptable to a broader role. The disabilities of its constituents are its limitations too. For, like the agencies on which it rests, it lacks a popular base.

On the next level of co-ordination stands the "welfare fund" community, which, to put it tersely, is simply the "federation" pattern extended to embrace not only local philanthropies but extramural as well. The two designs are so much of a piece that having discussed one, we need not delay over the other.

A radically different conception of communal organization is that embodied in the "Defense Council." Here the unifying principle is not the urge toward charity and social work, but, as the name indicates, the need to resist anti-Semitism, actual or threatened. Defense Councils can therefore exist alongside Federations and Welfare Funds or with almost equal ease in "rudimentary" communities. They represent one impulse only—the desire of Jews to pool their strength against the forces that threaten them. Hence it comes to pass that a Defense Council may be called into being by an already existent Federation or Welfare Fund. Again it may be no more than a self-constituted committee of "leading" citizens. In other instances, it may serve as a local clearinghouse for chapters of national defense organizations.

Whatever its form and the process by which it comes into being, no Jewish community should be without one. Unless, of course, it is prepared to submit to indignities. Reference has already been made to recent mishaps in cities like Boston and New York. Had the Jews of both places been properly organized, the situation in neither would have come so close to getting out of hand. A Defense Council is then a desideratum. The trouble with the device is that nothing is fixed either as to its shape or the auspices of its launching. In consequence, many a Defense Council lacks the endorsement and confidence of the Jews it presumes to protect.

The most highly developed scheme of local Jewish organization is the Community Council. One of the latest developments in American Judaism, it is designed to integrate action on matters of universal Jewish interest without impairing the inner freedom of individuals and groups. Most usually, the Council is composed of delegates of all the local Jewish organizations, each being represented proportionately to its membership. The normal

Council comprises in addition delegates at large chosen by universal ballot. So it repeats in miniature the make-up of the entire community. It is intended to be truly "representative."

The Council takes as its domain the general welfare of its Jewish constituents. By virtue of its representative character, it pre-eminently can claim the right to speak on their behalf. It is its function to plan and execute programs in defense of Jewish rights. Projects in vocational guidance fall properly within its purview. So also the compilation of vital statistics and sociological data, a function that too frequently goes by default. In some instances, Councils have launched community-wide educational enterprises, or have arranged for critical surveys by experts of existing pedagogic and cultural institutions. These large and important duties are as significant in what they omit as in what they include. Outside their scope, be it noted, are the internal affairs of synagogues and other constituent organizations, the ideologies on which they operate—in sum, all matters of conviction, whether personal or collective.

Approximately one hundred communities, from the smallest to some of the largest, have adopted some variant of the Council idea. The conception is still young, too young for definitive evaluation. But it is of interest to record that this latest development approximates very closely the *kehillah* pattern of Jewish history. The centuries would seem to have brought back an old design.

NATIONWIDE JEWISH ORGANIZATION

It is not only the Jews of a given vicinity who are partners in a given destiny. All American Jews, the 5,000,000 of them, partake of common problems and objectives. For some they are admirably organized; for others, passably; for still others, wretchedly or not at all.

Their religious interests have found fairly efficient institutional expression. The rabbis of the entire country are banded together in several ministerial associations, reflective of diverse ideological viewpoints. Orthodox, Conservative, Reform congregations are similarly federated. And each of these sectarian divisions maintains at least one seminary for the training of clergymen in conformity with its viewpoint. What is more, the major rabbinic and lay bodies co-operate in turn through the Synagogue Council of America, the spokesman, so far as one exists, of the over-all Jewish religion in this country.

Perhaps it ought to be added, lest too sanguine an inference be drawn, that the religious scene, while generally favorable, is not without its unhappy features. Thus in some wings of Judaism unity is still a consummation to be wished for. Orthodoxy in particular is splintered; there are no less than five general associations of Orthodox rabbis. Again, the Synagogue Council of America is a consultative body merely, requiring the consent of all its constituents on any controversial measure.

Last of all, because of these structural weaknesses, because also of widespread secularism among Jews, organized religion is much less influential in Jewish affairs than it ought to be. So, some great nationwide Jewish bodies accord it not even the most conventional recognition. A conspicuous illustration, drawn in this instance from a local setting, is to be seen in the Federation for the Support of Jewish Philanthropies of New York and Brooklyn. This, the largest Jewish charity in the world, makes no regular provision in its controlling board for representatives of synagogues or the rabbinate.

The best job of organization on a national scale as on the local has been done in philanthropy. In this field, American Jews are confronted by three staggering assignments: (a) the relief and rehabilitation of European Jewry, (b) the building of Jewish Palestine, (c) the adjustment of Jewish *émigrés* in America to their new scene. For each of these tasks, a great single instrument has been fashioned, respectively the American Jewish Joint Distribution Committee, the United Palestine Appeal, and the National Refugee Service. These three agencies moreover co-operate in fund raising through the United Jewish Appeal. To complete our account of the orderliness of Jewish charitable efforts, reference should be made again to the National Council of Jewish Federations and Welfare Funds, which supplies individual communities with information and expert guidance.

A similar instance of tight organization and of jobs done with maximal efficiency is afforded by the National Jewish Welfare Board. This body constitutes in peacetime primarily a clearinghouse and consulting service for Jewish community centers. In both World Wars it has been the official and accredited representative of American Jewry to the Army and Navy, ministering to the religious needs of Jews in the armed forces. Comprising rabbinical and lay elements, a veritable cross section of the group for which it acts, the Jewish Welfare Board is a brilliant argument for the possibility of Jewish integration and a heartening precedent of the benefits to be derived from it.

There are still other bright spots in the Jewish picture: the "wider scope" activities of the fraternal order of B'nai B'rith, its programs for young people, its Hillel Foundations on university campuses, its Anti-Defamation League; or, by way of further illustration, the professional societies of Jewish social workers and educators. With these, however, our tale is about told. The rest, if not chaos, is certainly not order.

Thus the occupational redistribution of American Jews is literally nobody's affair. Some work has been done in the related field of vocational guidance for Jewish youth, notably under the auspices of B'nai B'rith and the Jewish Welfare Board. Further, the Conference on Jewish Relations has executed a number of statistical studies of the occupations through which Jews derive their livelihoods. All these have their worth. The core of the issue still goes by default. No agency exists possessed of the resources and armed with the authority to determine the facts, to set a communal policy by their light and to carry it through to completion.

The same story repeats itself in Jewish culture. We have already made the point that the meaningfulness of Judaism, perhaps its very survival, may in the long run depend on the capacity of American Jews to foster creativity in their midst and to adapt to their own uses the productivity of other Jewries. One would expect much mobilizing of Jewish energies to these ends. These are the facts: a few farsighted individuals have set up privately endowed foundations for the encouragement of literary and artistic undertakings; the Jewish Publication Society, getting far less support than it deserves, continues to print meritorious books of Jewish interest; sporadically and without central planning, someone, all on his own, will translate into English some significant volume written in Palestine or Poland. Beyond this, a cultural rebirth of American Judaism is much like the weather; everybody talks, but no one, certainly no official agency, does anything about it.

Most tragic of all is Jewish disorganization in the face of the two most crucial Jewish problems of our time: anti-Semitism and the rehabilitation of European Jewry.

Consider the first of these. We have already examined and appraised the peril in which the 5,000,000 Jews of this country now stand. Whether their danger be remote or near, they dare not trifle with it. Seemingly, their peak strength and the best of their talents, channelized with the utmost efficiency, would be enlisted in the job.

Even this reasonable expectation is not being realized. The effort against anti-Semitism is under not one but four commands: the American Jewish Committee, the Anti-Defamation League of the B'nai B'rith, the American Jewish Congress and the Jewish Labor Committee. To confound confusion, it is quite normal that at any given time some of these bodies shall not be on speaking terms. They are forever jostling one another, competing for funds and prestige, indulging in mutual recrimination, laboring, all four of them, often where only one is required, and at other times operating at such cross purposes as to cancel one another out. Then too, some matters fall, so to speak, between too many stools and are simply neglected.

Recurrently, an outraged public opinion or the pressure of events forces this unruly quartet into some semblance of harmony. So in 1938, with anti-Semitism clearly on the increase in the United States, the four united to form the General Jewish Council. The avowed purpose of this new agency was to co-ordinate the activities of its constituents. A higher hope, too, was entertained that the Council might turn out in the end to be that one weapon which American Jewry needed for its self-defense. Little came of these great expectations. By 1941, when one of the member bodies resigned, the Council had long existed only in suspended animation. It has since given up the ghost.

Subsequently two of the agencies, the Anti-Defamation League and the American Jewish Committee, entered into limited understandings for fund raising and clearance of program. More recently, in the winter of 1943-1944, a new arrangement for mutual consultation among all four bodies was instituted in the form of the National Community Relations Advisory Council. To the present this agency has not only survived, it is functioning vigorously. Yet informed opinion runs that, though nothing could be more gratifying than its success, nothing would be more surprising.

That these four organizations are such uneasy bedfellows is not fortuitous. While personality clashes contribute, and far too heavily, to their mutual antagonism, the incompatability among them derives from deeper factors, from social stratification, economic interest and diverging attitudes toward Judaism and the Jewish identity.

To all generalization, including the generalizations in which we shall proceed to indulge, there are exceptions. Yet with rough accuracy, the four organizations may be described as follows:

The American Jewish Committee, the oldest of them, is supported by a relatively small group of wealthy and influential Jews of German origin, in the main either "old-line" Reform by persuasion or else assimilationist. It does not pretend to enjoy popular support or to express the will, democratically determined, of American Jews. Candidly representing the "rich and well born," it is studiously courteous, conservative and cautious. It prefers to combat anti-Semitism quietly and behind the scenes. It is in the main unsympathetic to Zionism, though not to the Jewish Palestine which Zionism is building.

The American Jewish Congress, which originated as a protest against the Committee, is middle-class in composition, East European in descent. Its adherents are predominantly Conservative and Orthodox religionists on the one side, and secular Zionists on the other. In any event, they are likely to be passionate about Jews and Judaism. Having come into being as a rebellion against an "oligarchy," actual or supposed, dedicated from its very inception to reflecting the mind of the masses of Jews, the Congress makes much of its "democratic" character, more indeed than the facts, objectively regarded, justify. But it does stand on a vastly broader base of popular sanction than the Committee. It is militant in dealing with anti-Semitism, and thoroughly Zionist.

The Anti-Defamation League of the B'nai B'rith is rooted in as near a cross section of American Jewry as can be discovered anywhere. The B'nai B'rith, a fraternal order just over a century old, cuts across all sectarian and partisan lines. Its tactic on anti-Semitism may be described as a mean between the Committee and Congress. While its membership is heterogeneous, it has with time taken increasingly positive positions on Zionism and the Jewish tradition.

The Jewish Labor Committee was founded by trade unionists and non-communist radicals. Originally reflective of all shades of the Jewish working classes, it has suffered from the defection of Zionist and religious elements. Right now it is strongly under the influence of "Bundist" *émigrés* from Eastern Europe, its orientation being pretty much that of Mr. Z whom we have already met. In other words, it is nonreligious, non to anti-Zionist, Yiddishist in culture with a heavy infusion of Marxist-socialist economics.

I present this sequence of vignettes not because I believe them to be adequate descriptions, certainly not because I am at the moment concerned with making a partisan point, but because I wish to exhibit how deep are the chasms in American Jewry. It is not caprice that divides the Jews of America in the face of their common enemy, but deep dissonances of mind, heart, interest and social position.

A passable apology may be invented for disorganization on self-defense. There can be no excuse for disunity over the rehabilitation of European Jewry. Here certainly the American Jewish community cannot be content with less than a single authoritative agency to determine and implement its will.

Until the summer of 1943, no such instrumentality existed. The Congress, the Committee, the B'nai B'rith, the Jewish Labor Committee, and, since Palestine was part of the picture, the various Zionist bodies—each expressed, generally in independence of one another, its special viewpoint on every episode in the passing scene. The immediate result was babel, a welter of conflicting interpretations, proposals and programs. The long-range consequences were the confounding and disheartening of American Jews; the frittering away of much of what they had to contribute to the alleviation of the lot of their brethren abroad; and, not least in import, the bewilderment of Gentiles, including officials of the various governments.

Such a situation was intolerable even to a Jewry long accustomed to almost anything. In August 1943 the American Jewish Conference was convened. Composed of five hundred delegates, one-quarter designated by all major national Jewish bodies, three-quarters elected by indirect popular vote, the Conference stood on a broad, democratic base. It could be accepted therefore as substantially reflective of American Jewry. That it was convoked at all was something of a miracle. The first step toward its establishment was taken by the B'nai B'rith; the next by an exploratory meeting of representatives of thirty-two nationwide organizations.

All along, it was a matter of common knowledge that much depended on the American Jewish Committee, its readiness to participate, and, once that point had been established, its willingness to abide by decisions. Not that the Committee was necessarily the most influential agency; certainly it was not the largest. But it enjoyed considerable prestige and without it unity would still not be attained.

The Committee indeed proved skittish and hesitant. It objected to calling the Conference an "assembly," a word that to its palate savored of the legislative and permanent. So the Conference came to be a "conference" instead. The Committee insisted further on the privilege of dissent from any of the decisions of the Conference. The whole business, to use a phrase whereby ancient Jewish sages designated an inordinate difficulty, was "as hard as the rending of the Red Sea." But it was carried off. The rough places were made smooth. When the Conference convened, the Committee was a participating agency.

The supreme test, however, was not yet. It did not come until the Conference came to consider the Zionist issue in general, and more particularly the prospect of a Jewish Commonwealth in Palestine. On all other points a consensus, even unanimity, prevailed. On this too sentiment was overwhelmingly in one direction. When the matter came to a vote, only four delegates balloted against the "Commonwealth" resolution. But here the Committee would not defer to the majority. It first dissociated itself formally from the resolution and then, when the Conference had adjourned, withdrew from participation in it.

Once before, in December 1918, the representatives of American Jewry stood in a similar pass. At that time Louis Marshall, president of the Committee, for the sake of Jewish unity and democratic procedures, bowed to a decision on Zionism unwelcome to him and his group. The present-day leaders of the Committee are made, it would seem, of different stuff.

The split in the Conference, occasioned by the resignation of the American Jewish Committee, seems to me to have large importance. It gives further evidence, should any be required, of the depth of the cleavages among American Jews who, in the face of the gravest tragedy in Jewish history, once again reveal themselves incapable of unity and self-discipline. It highlights the difficulties to be expected in all efforts at achieving integration of Jewish action. It has set in motion a whole chain of destructive consequences. Once again, not one voice speaks, but many, to the despair of Jews and the bedevilment of Gentiles. Another stinging, rankling wound has been inflicted on Jewish morale. The Conference itself has survived the schism, but so much the weaker and poorer in prestige, so much the readier a victim to centrifugal forces. The Committee is now an object of widespread popular resentment. And in the end, wretched Jews abroad will be forfeit in life, happiness and freedom for the wrangling of their brethren in the New World.*

Now we address ourselves to what is logically the next question. What shall be made of the facts we have surveyed? Of the organizations and organizational forms we have scrutinized, which are good and which evil; which ought to be fostered and which discouraged? What, in short, is the optimal pattern for the individual Jewish community and for American Jewry as a whole?

Before coming to grips with these questions, let us pause for a moment to set our sights. Let us first ask ourselves what a Jewish community should be like, to what standards it ought to conform. This point settled, we shall be able to pass judgment on the diverse designs of Jewish civic life.

A Jewish community, regardless of scope or scale, must conform structurally to the following criteria:

1) It must be comprehensive; that is to say, it must embrace all Jews who wish to be Jews and all institutions devoted to the continuance of Jewish group life. It must have room for diversity whether personal or collective, for religionists and antireligionists, for Zionists and anti-Zionists. Nobody, nothing that seeks to serve Jewish ends can be declared out of its bounds.

2) It must be equal to the jobs it will be called upon to perform. In the main these will fall in the domain of social status. An acceptable Jewish community is therefore one competent to deal with anti-Semitism, with the defense of Jewish rights, with economic discrimination and occupational redistribution. It must be capable too of discovering the composite mind of its constituents and of serving as their voice. Where the exercise of Jewish influence is indicated, it must be able to muster it and bring it to bear. In short, it must be able to do what needs to be done.

3) It must be economical, getting along with one committee rather than two, with few instruments rather than many. It must discourage the multifariousness and the overlapping now so common to Jewish public affairs.

4) It must possess authority. Its position among Jews and its constituent

---

* Thanks to the disunity created by the secession of the American Jewish Committee, American Jewry was represented at the United Nations Conference in San Francisco by *four* distinct groups of consultants invited by the United States State Department and by a number of uninvited individuals and "wildcat" organizations. What happened in San Francisco not only corroborates our conclusions but stands as a solemn warning to American Jewry in all its future approaches to the United Nations.

organizations must be such that they will wait for it to speak first on any theme of general concern, and, so long as it does not transgress its constitutional bounds, will abide by its decisions.

Jewry these days is a voluntary association. Whatever may have been its prerogatives in the past, it possesses in modern times neither the right nor the power to compel obedience. This is as it should be. Under the democratic axiom of the separation of church and state, government cannot tolerate coercion of the individual by any religious or cultural minority. And no one in modern Jewish life would have matters otherwise in this respect. But just because the Jewish community cannot and desires not to enforce its will, self-discipline on the part of Jews becomes all important. It is the only principle of cohesion. In its absence all co-operation and order disappear.

But the readiness of freemen to abide voluntarily by communal decisions depends on what they think about their group life. If they trust the community as fairly representative of themselves and their fellows, they will accept its leadership, suppressing their individual dissents. Otherwise, they will do as appears right in their eyes.

5) The Jewish community, therefore, must be thoroughly democratic. Only so can it possess authority and elicit discipline. To be more specific, it must be representative in structure and composition of the people it serves, and must strive in its decisions to mirror their prevailing sentiment.

The democratization of Jewish public affairs is a prize to be sought after on many scores. In the first place, democracy is a moral ideal to be pursued for its own worth. A traditional Jewish virtue, it belongs as of right in the conduct of the Jewish community. Last of all, as we have just observed, it is the only hope of introducing order in chaos, of silencing irresponsible and self-appointed spokesmen, of linking all Jewish hands for shared Jewish purposes. If the democratic method cannot do the trick, the trick cannot be done. To this principle there is literally no alternative, not in morality and not in practice.

6) The Jewish community should reflect the nature of the Jewish group. Jewry, as we have seen, is not a matter of religion exclusively, nor of culture, nor of peoplehood, but of all three together. Jews, therefore, cannot properly be organized except on the basis of all three component elements. This truth argues against the thoughtful proposal put forth some years ago by Judge Horace Stern of Philadelphia, that the Jews of each city be organized into a community through the federating of their synagogues. The recommenda-

tion fails to take cognizance of the broad diffusion of secularism among Jews. To establish a religious test for participation in the Jewish community would be in effect to disenfranchise a substantial number of its members. This is not a cheering fact for Jewish religionists; but it is a fact that had better be reckoned with. Aside from *Realpolitik*, Judge Stern's plan rests on the faulty premise that Jews constitute a religious communion. A truly congruous arrangement of their public affairs will take cognizance of other elements also.

But if religion alone is not an adequate substructure for the Jewish community, neither are secularized culture and peoplehood. The Synagogue as an institution must occupy a key position in the machinery of group life. Nor may the community concern itself only with the issues of peoplehood, that is to say, with problems of social status. It must in addition foster religious and cultural interests. These are integral to Judaism; they should therefore be embodied in the structure of the community; their advancement must be among its prime purposes.

Such are the criteria for optimal Jewish communal organization. Let the reader now apply them seriatim to all the local setups we have described, from the "rudimentary" onward. Is it not apparent at once that only the Community Council measures up to our standards? It alone is at once comprehensive, equal to its task, structurally economical, democratic and accurately reflective of the essential nature of Judaism and the Jewish group. As it chances, the scheme has spread rapidly in recent years. Even New York City, megalopolis of Jewry and citadel of disorder, has begun to experiment with the concept in a number and variety of neighborhoods. The idea is obviously satisfying a need. Were it still disembodied, without a single incarnation to the present, it would remain the only pattern to be commended as right in principle throughout.

The nationwide problem is more complex and obdurate than the local. Here two necessities intertwine: that of dealing immediately with specific, pressing problems, and that of constructing a permanent agency to represent American Jewry against any and all future contingencies. The first is a job of here and now, of improvising hastily with the materials at hand. In the second we can devise and build at our leisure, and with an eye to durability.

Anti-Semitism, by way of conspicuous example, is not a matter safely to be deferred. It must be attacked at the earliest instant and with whatever forces happen to be available. We may not approve of the character and spirit of the armies on our side, but if they are ready to fight we owe them our plaudits and support. This is no time for Jews to spurn allies. The Committee, the Anti-Defamation League, the Congress, the Labor Committee, have long been in the thick of the struggle. The sensible Jew will swallow his reservations, and, though doubtless with unequal fervor, wish them all Godspeed. He will, if he is very sensible, manage to enlist in one or another.

At the same time, he will seek to establish better liaison among them and, if possible, to persuade them to set up a centralized high command. This means the exerting of constant pressure against recalcitrant agencies. Every contribution of energy or funds ought to be an occasion for the reading to the recipient organization of a lesson in co-operation. The columns of the Anglo-Jewish press must echo this preachment, as ought public discussion. The leaders of the competing organizations will have to listen eventually. And should they be so strong-willed as to disregard universal sentiment, they will scarcely dare to flout the contributor on whom all else depends. This then is a job immediately at hand: the strengthening at once of the National Community Relations Council, the currently promising intermediary, the winning for it of increased authority until either it or some other body yet to be established becomes that much-to-be-hoped-for central high command.

On the second of the urgent communal problems, the question who shall speak for American Jewry in postwar policy, vast progress has been made of late. The American Jewish Conference is just such a body as our criteria imply. True, the secession of the American Jewish Committee has shaken it. But that blow, while harmful, has not been fatal. Besides, in the light of our discussion, the responsible Jew has no alternative except to support the Conference. For it alone is comprehensive and orderly; it alone has at least a chance of being strong enough for its assignments; it alone is based on democratic procedures, and, hence, possesses the moral base for authority.

Every assistance then to the Conference! Let it be made clear both to Jews and non-Jews that aside from it none holds a mandate to voice general Jewish opinion. So the prospect is better than fair that at long last one agency may come to be accepted by all as representative of American Jewry on Jewish problems in the postwar era.

But both the National Community Relations Council and the American Jewish Conference are jerry-built, set up in a hurry to provide shelter against impending storms. Nor can they be reconstructed as permanent edifices, the former because it rests on four pillars that simply refuse to stand together, the latter because it is admittedly no more than an *ad hoc* and temporary lodging; both alike because, designed for limited specific purposes, they do not cover vital areas such as occupational redistribution or cultural creativity. Something other is needed, better planned and executed, more comprehensive and erected not by individuals or limited groups, but by the will of all its owners and tenants.

But is there anywhere any development to lend substance to the dream of such a structure? As it happens, there is. Unheralded and unsung, Jewish Community Councils have been spreading across the country from one locality to the next. In them may lie the key to the nationwide organization of American Jewry. As soon as enough communities, or, in the case of metropolitan centers, enough neighborhoods have established Councils, a National Council of Jewish Communities can be set up. In this, local Councils would participate in proportion to their populations. Representation might be accorded further to significant religious, cultural and social parties.

Such a National Council would measure up to the criteria, practical and ideal, we have set ourselves. Possessed of a popular mandate, it would soon tower above and dominate all factions. It could become the abiding, over-all social framework of the American Jewish community, supervising all common interests, and either subordinating to itself, or dispensing with, the many agencies now in operation.

Such an institution, be it observed last of all, would be solidly grounded. Jews, interested in the better ordering of their group business, have in the past proceeded much after the fashion of political liberals launching third parties. They have, as it were, always nominated candidates for the presidency, but neglected wards and precincts. That is to say, they have always begun at the top, by trying to throw a superstructure over existing organizations and leaders. This mistake is avoided by the National Council of Jewish Communities here proposed. Our design starts where logically it should, at the bottom, and works upward.

This proposal anent Councils, both in its local and nationwide application, is meeting with no slight opposition. It is assailed especially on the grounds that it is (a) secularist, (b) un-American, (c) Jewish self-Ghettoization, (d) authoritarian in the sense that it seeks to coerce Jews.

None of these contentions holds water.

It is not secularism to recognize that Judaism is more than a religious communion and the Jewish group broader than a church. Nor is it secularism, unless realism be secularism, to acknowledge that there are irreligious Jews. The plan before us involves no depreciation or denial of religion. On the contrary it allows full representation to synagogal institutions and interests. Besides, a sane arrangement of the Jewish community cannot but aid the Jewish faith. Jews are much more likely to be sympathetic to Judaism if they are pleased over, rather than disgusted with, the Jewish household in which they live.

Nor is there greater merit to the criticism of our proposal as un-American. The government of the United States has no interests beyond those of order and public morality in the internal affairs of religious or cultural bodies. So far as it is concerned, such bodies may be ruled by Popes abroad, Houses of Bishops at home, Conferences, Assemblies, Conventions or what have you. Jews, then, who have special interests in common have a right to organize themselves as they see fit, as have Catholics, Mormons, Elks, Atheists, the Daughters of the American Revolution or the members of the Pulaski Society. Under our American system any group may pursue any purposes it elects, as long as they are not illegal or immoral. Indeed, this is the end to which democracy exists—that people will be free to strive after goals of their own choosing.

And as for the contention that Councils, local or national, would coerce and enslave free Jewish Americans, this is farcical. Membership in the Jewish group remains optional as ever, compliance with any decision still a matter of individual choice. To be sure, a saner organization is more likely to elicit self-discipline and conformity. But the principle of voluntarism is not thereby affected. Just as little basis exists for the claim that our prospectus involves self-Ghettoization. No Jew, by virtue of it, will associate less with his fellow Americans, or will be a jot farther removed from American culture. His life will go on as always, except that his special Jewish interests will be better attended to.

This, indeed, is the whole point. There is not the slightest trace of secularism, un-Americanism, self-Ghettoization or authoritarian compulsion in our proposal. What is involved is whether Jewish public affairs shall be efficiently or inefficiently run, democratically or by usurpation, co-operatively or disjointedly. It is all as simple as this, whether the House of Israel in America is to be orderly or disorderly. Between two such alternatives can anyone hesitate?

IV

PROBLEMS OF THE HOMELAND

14

Zionist Theory

ASIDE FROM ASSIMILATIONISM, Zionism represents the most controversial issue in Jewish life. Opinion concerning it is sharply divided, debate over it surcharged with passion That the project of establishing a Homeland for the Jewish people in Palestine should be a storm center may seem inexplicable, for the enterprise has proved its utility and practicability. It has provided to hundreds of thousands of Jews who might otherwise have perished under Nazi oppression not only deliverance from death but an opportunity to live free and creative lives. On the worth of the Jewish settlement in Palestine scarcely a single responsible and informed Jew cavils.

To be sure, there was a time some decades ago when this too was strongly questioned. It was argued that Jews needed no Homeland of their own. Jewry, the contention ran, enjoyed freedom everywhere except in Czarist Russia and some Balkan states, and there too the emancipation was on its way. And as for those European Jews who elected or were compelled to emigrate—they could turn to the Western world, South Africa or Australia, lands eager for new settlers and far richer in resources than Palestine. The early opponents of Zionism held further that whatever might be its sentimental merits, the proposal to settle modern Jews in the Holy Land was totally unrealistic. Palestine, they pointed out, was a little, arid, neglected territory inhabited by a half-starved and backward population. It was questionable whether European Jews could live in the land at all and wrest from its sterility more than the meagerest livelihood.

Such objections to Zionism have evaporated completely. The march of tragic events has reduced them to nullities. The apparently secure and solid foundations of the Jewries of Europe have been revealed as resting on quicksand. In our time the entire structure has collapsed, burying in its debris millions of Jewish lives and great and ancient Jewish communities. Since

1933 hundreds of thousands of Jews have been compelled to seek avenues of escape—only to find doors of virtually all lands closed before them. Had the basis of Jewish settlement in Palestine not already been laid, many of these now living happily there would since have perished. What is more, the ability of Palestine to absorb immigrants has far exceeded the estimates of the critics of Zionism. Six hundred thousand Jews have entered the country in the past twenty-five years; and, according to the judgments of scientific students of the problem, there is room for millions more.

In the light of all these considerations, the staunchest Jewish opponents of Zionism no longer question the worth of Jewish colonization in Palestine, its necessity and its practicability. Why then should controversy persist? When Zionists and non-Zionists agree on so much, over what do they differ so vehemently? The truth is that Zionism is more than a project for the settlement of Jews in Palestine. It is about this "more," consisting in ideological premises and in ideal objectives, that the opposition centers.

The roots of modern Zionism are many and complex. In great measure, it derives from an ancient group yearning, dynamic with the accumulated aspirations of a long succession of generations. It came into being at the moment when the Temple of Jerusalem was destroyed and the masses of Jews banished from their ancestral soil. Their dispersion had no sooner begun than they commenced to pray and labor for its ending. To them the prospect of Judaism and the Jewish people apart from the soil which had nurtured both was unimaginable.

Their refusal to accept the decision of events reflected more than an emotional tie to a particular place, more too than the reluctance of men to make their peace with a new and disadvantageous turn of events. It sprang at least equally and perhaps to an even greater degree from religious conviction. The Bible asserted an organic relationship between the people and the land. The ordinances of the Law of Moses, for example, assumed the inseparability of the two. And the prophets affirmed not only that the time would come when Israel would live securely and gloriously on its sacred ancestral soil, but also that until that time arrived deliverance could not be achieved for mankind as a whole. The world required the truths of Scripture for its salvation, and it was out of Zion that the doctrine would go forth and the word of God from Jerusalem.

The attachment to Palestine of the first generations of the dispersion was perpetuated in those who came after them. At every public service, morning, afternoon and evening, in each private devotion whether in the grace after meals or on retiring at night, Jews prayed for their return to Zion. Two of the most solemn services of the ritual calendar, the Seder feast of Passover, and the day-long worship of the Day of Atonement, closed with brief but fervid supplications to God for that event. And it is no accident that what are perhaps the greatest pieces of Hebrew poetry from the time of Scripture to the modern era were the Zion odes of Judah ha-Levi—the verses he dedicated to the glory of the Holy Land. Constantly throughout the long centuries Jews from all over the world traveled great and perilous distances to visit Palestine, to live in it, to die and be buried in its sacred ground—so that at all times a Jewish community, whether large or small, was to be found within its borders.

Intense as was his longing for a Zion restored, the medieval Jew almost never attempted to implement it by direct action. He was so enmeshed in circumstances and so weakened by them as to despair of his powers. Even more, the very tradition which encouraged his hopes discouraged efforts to realize them. For it was God, Scripture related, who by direct intervention would gather the dispersed of Israel and replant them in their land. For man to assume the divine prerogative would be blasphemy, an arrogant effort to force the hand of God. Hence, though there was always a trickle of returning exiles, nothing on a large scale was done about the restoration of the people to its land. The dream was almost a trance.

Only with the coming of the Emancipation was the hold of this spell on the Jewish spirit relaxed. Many thousands of Jews in Western lands repudiated the vision altogether—and that on various grounds. Some assumed a negative attitude because under their new condition they had come to regard themselves not as a people but exclusively as a religious communion. Others cried quits with the hope of their fathers because, having assumed the rights and duties of citizenship in the lands of their residence, they felt themselves unable to persevere in an attachment to another land. Still others discarded the old aspiration because, enjoying the enlarged and, as it seemed, continuously enlarging privileges of freedom, they did not relish the thought of transfer from places they knew and loved to an unfamiliar corner of the Eastern Mediterranean.

In Eastern Europe where Emancipation was tardier and Jewish traditionalism stronger, the dream of the return persisted with virtually unabated vigor. Even where it seemed to have perished, it was often dormant rather than dead. The momentum of the past is always a powerful force. Time-weighted notions and aspirations may seem to have vanished, while actually they persevere in the subterranean reaches of the individual unconscious and in the vague inarticulated values of the group. For multitudes of Jews in the modern world all that was required to rekindle the love of Zion was a spark struck off by events.

Into the making of Zionism has gone not only the drive of the ancient tradition but the weight of recent developments both within and without the Jewish group. Like all social phenomena, Zionism is composite rather than simple in derivation. It represents the interweaving of at least four distinct strands of thought. These are now organically united. Genetically they were diverse and for purposes of analysis they may very well be kept so. None of them can be considered the creation of one individual; none had a lone innovator or sole spokesman. Yet a single personality stands out so pre-eminently in the inception of each that it may well be ascribed to him. So treated, modern Zionism may be said to consist in four elements—the Herzlian, the Nordauist, the Ahad HaAmist, and the Gordonian.

THE HERZLIAN MOTIF

Theodore Herzl, (1860–1904), playwright, columnist and foreign correspondent for the Vienna *Neue Freie Presse* was for most of his tragically brief life a de-Judaized Jew. Yet under his assimilationist exterior moved memories of childhood experiences, bits of traditional Jewish folklore and folk value ready to burst into flame at the application of the spark to which we have alluded.

The spark was supplied by the Dreyfus trial. Herzl was shocked to the depths of his being by the deep and virulent anti-Semitism which first selected an innocent Jew as the scapegoat for a reactionary conspiracy and then charged all Jews with responsibility for his supposed crime. Like most middle-class Jews of his generation, he had taken it for granted that anti-Jewish prejudices were destined to extinction. Emancipation would continue its progressive, almost inevitable expansion until it had completed itself in the full acceptance of Jews. But when in France, the home of the Declaration of the Rights of Man and of the first enfranchisement of Jews, so much anti-Semitism persisted one hundred years after the Revolution of 1789, there was reason to re-examine the sanguine assumption Jews cherished as to the continued improvement of their position.

The conclusions at which Herzl arrived in virtually one flight of intuition were that the security of European Jewry was more apparent than real, that riding the wave of political liberalism and industrial expansion, the Western world had emancipated its Jews, but that old antipathies still ran strong in the lower depths. Let reaction set in—and threatening signs of such a turn were already visible—let society go through a period of economic adversity, and the freedoms Jews enjoyed might crumble like an eggshell in a powerful and angry hand. The Jews of Europe were in the position of never being able to trust the ground under their feet. Such a position, Herzl insisted, was intolerable. It put inordinate strains on the Jewish personality and exposed Jewry as a whole to a constant peril.

For this impasse, Herzl became convinced, there could be only one hopeful and constructive resolution: the Jews must become a people like all other peoples; that is to say, they must have a land of their own in which a large part of their number would reside, to which any Jews who were the victims of anti-Semitism could turn with the assurance of a cordial welcome. Jews who lived in liberal countries, who did not desire or had no reason to leave them, would of course continue as citizens of the states in which they resided.

Even they would be benefited by the realization of his proposal. Given a Jewish National Home, they would cease to be an eccentricity. The taint of the gypsy, who lives everywhere and has no home of his own, would be wiped from them. In the eyes of the world they would now appear additional instances of a normal phenomenon, like Frenchmen or Britons settled and naturalized abroad who still enjoy a dignity and assurance deriving from their fatherlands. Finally, a Jewish state, Herzl believed, would be an anchor to the windward. Should a tempest break over Jewry, it would afford refuge and safety.

Parallel to this train of reasoning on Herzl's part ran another. The achievement of a Jewish National Home was to be attempted by political methods. Open covenants openly arrived at was a cardinal principle in his thought. He saw little utility in Jews migrating as individuals, without official assurances, into whatever territory might be selected as the site of colonization, in the hope that once there were enough of them, a Homeland would be automatically attained. At any moment the government controlling the area of settlement might decide to refuse entrance to additional Jews, thus nipping the enterprise in the bud. What was required was an agreement with some state whereby the right of Jewish immigration and ultimately of national self-determination would be assured. This insistence on negotiation with governments and on guarantees makes the Zionism of Herzl "political," and is in many respects his unique contribution.

At the time when Herzl arrived at this twofold conclusion as to the need of a Jewish National Home and as to the method of winning it, there was much of which he was ignorant. He did not know, for example, that his thinking had been anticipated, notably by Leo Pinsker in his brochure *Auto Emancipation* and by Smolenskin in his essay *Eternal People*. Nor did he have more than the vaguest notion of the problems of Jewish culture—the ground of the Zionism of Jews like Ahad HaAm. Unaware further that Palestine still held a special position in Jewish emotions, he did not initially specify it as the site of his proposed National Home.

He did not appraise properly the difficulties in his way. Having busied himself in protracted negotiations with the Turkish government, he did not realize that the largest obstacle would turn out not the corruption and sloth of the sultanate but the opposition of the Arabs of Palestine, then oppressed to the point of despair and silence. At the beginning he miscalculated entirely the potential sources of support for his idea. For some time he tried to convert Jewish philanthropists to his program. Only after months of heartbreaking and futile labor did he see that the masses of Jews, especially the teeming millions of Eastern Europe, were his natural supporters and allies. Only, in other words, after he had tried and failed elsewhere did he go to the people with his dream. Only then did he organize his concept on a popular and democratic basis.

The man, in other words, suffered from serious deficiencies and limitations, not all of which were overcome by subsequent growth. Despite them he remains a titanic, heroic figure, a giant in vision, a martyr in self-sacrifice, beautiful and romantic in bodily appearance as in spirit, a natural leader of men who wore himself into the grave out of devotion to the truth he conceived.

It has often been said that his largest contribution to his people was his personality. Such a statement underestimates him as a thinker. Ultimately Herzl is important for those doctrines which constitute the Herzlian element in Zionism—the prophetic insight into the radical insecurity of European Jewry, the bold leap from this observation to the need for a Jewish National

Home, the insistence on political guaranties and legal security as the fundaments of the enterprise, and the discovery painfully won that the word could be made flesh only through the will of the people democratically organized.

THE NORDAUIST MOTIF

Contemporary of Herzl, and among the first converts to his cause, Max Nordau (1849–1923) was one of the brilliant intellectuals of the Paris of his day. Physician, essayist, journalist and author of searching analyses of man's social behavior, he was an extraordinarily rich and attractive human being. His adherence to Herzl's program was therefore a source of great encouragement to Herzl himself and a major contribution to the prestige of the movement in its incipient stages.

Like Herzl, Nordau was won to Zionism by a recognition of the instability and precariousness of the Jewish position in the Western world. But as a careful reading of his addresses to the various Zionist Congresses will reveal, he was moved by another consideration, related to the first yet distinct from it. He was a student of social motivations, of the complexities of human conduct. In the books which made him famous in his generation, he can be said in a measure to have foreshadowed some of the discoveries of psychoanalysis. Given this interest in personality, he was especially sensitive to the presence in Jews of subservience and self-repudiation, the psychic consequences of minority status. To a Jewish National Home Nordau looked for healing. Jews who would take up residence within it would now breathe a more wholesome emotional atmosphere. Freed from dependence on Gentiles, they would exhibit the ease and self-respect natural to people who know that they are where they belong.

Jews who remained in the dispersion would also be benefited by the realization of the Zionist program. As Herzl expected the establishment of a Jewish state to improve the social position of Jews outside it, so Nordau was confident that it would bolster Jewish self-respect everywhere. Though outside Palestine Jews would continue in their pre-Zionist condition, they would be the surer of their worth because of the existence and achievements of their people's Homeland.

This line of reasoning, though we have associated it with the name of Nordau, was by no means exclusively his. Aspects of it had been anticipated by the Socialist-Zionist Moses Hess. It appears transiently in the writings of

Herzl and more fully developed in those of Ahad HaAm. But it finds its completest expression in early Zionism in Nordau and may properly be associated with his name. The question of authorship apart, this chain of theorizing has become a permanent element in the Zionist ideology. One of the results which Zionists expect from their program is the distillation of a healthier spirit within Jews everywhere.

THE AHAD HAAMIST MOTIF

Both Herzl and Nordau turned to Zionism in response to adverse circumstances affecting the Jew but in origin external to him. Ahad HaAm's Zionism, on the other hand, sprang almost entirely from the inner needs of Judaism as he construed them. For this role of serving as spokesman of the internal Jewish values, he was by background and temperament peculiarly suited. Asher Ginsberg (1856–1927), or Ahad HaAm as he is more commonly known from his pen name, was born and raised in Czarist Russia. In his childhood he was something of a marvel for his Jewish learning. As a young man he came under the influence of contemporary world thought, particularly that of Herbert Spencer and the positivists. This experience disjointed the theological doctrines in which he had been reared, but it left unaffected his loyalty to the Jewish people, its cultural tradition and ethical values. Indeed his new philosophy can be said to have enriched his appreciation of Judaism, for it equipped him with a naturalistic, sociological viewpoint from which to consider and evaluate afresh Jewish practices and principles.

As one devoted to his people and culture, Ahad HaAm was profoundly disturbed over developments within the Jewish group. Everywhere the Emancipation was running a full course. Which was all to the good, except for its effect on Judaism. Many Jews had ceased to have any adequate knowledge of their background or any serious concern over it. Gifted Jews, absorbed almost totally in the wider scene, were too busy for specifically Jewish interests. The stuff of Judaism was running ever thinner for lack of new materials. People and tradition were slowly bleeding to death.

Nor did the fault lie, as Ahad HaAm analyzed the situation, in a failure of will. With the best resolve in the world, Jews could not prevent developments adverse to Jewish culture. The broader society surrounding the Jews offered larger and more attractive opportunities of self-fulfillment. Inevitably Jews gave it the first of their thought and the best of their energies. This was the tragic impasse, as Ahad HaAm saw it. Jews in the modern world as a matter of necessity and obligation made of Judaism a secondary civilization. But Judaism could not survive in such a position.

From this entrapment there could be, Ahad HaAm believed, only one exit. Somewhere in the world must be a place where Judaism could be the primary culture of Jews. For the Jews who lived there the cultural problem would simply disappear. They would live Judaism as naturally as they breathed. For the others Palestine would serve as a "spiritual center." Endowed with Jewish vigor, it would replenish the resources of those Jewries incapable of sustaining themselves. From its abundant strength transfusions of life blood would flow to the pallid, anemic communities of the Diaspora. Enriched by a steady stream of music, art and literature, they would themselves be stimulated to heightened creativity.

Such was the reasoning that made a Zionist of Ahad HaAm. As to the place best fitted, indeed alone eligible to serve as the cultural center, he had no hesitations. It had to be Palestine; there was no alternative. Other lands might be useful as havens of refuge or scenes of colonization but only Palestine with its historic memories and hopes could be the site of a rebirth of the Jewish spirit.

THE GORDONIAN MOTIF

Each of the three Zionist motifs that we have so far reviewed can with fair accuracy be associated with some individual. The fourth lends itself less readily to such treatment. If we call it Gordonian, after Aaron David Gordon (1856–1922), it is not because he was its originator, but rather because he was so perfectly its incarnation.

Briefly put, what I here call Gordonism is the determination on the part of Zionists that the Jewish community in Palestine shall embody the best social ideals of the Jewish and human traditions.

Since the days of the prophets Judaism has steadfastly cherished an exalted vision of social relationships. Reverence for the human personality, solicitude for the right of every individual to self-fulfillment, belief in the essential unity of mankind, and confidence in the coming of a Kingdom of God on earth—all these have ever been basic components of Judaism. Nor were they permitted to remain values to be professed but not realized. One of the major goals of Rabbinic Judaism was the conversion of these principles into legislation and social institution.

This age-old passion for social justice was from the beginning a powerful influence in evoking Zionist attitudes and in making them dynamic. As matters stood in the Diaspora, Jewish morality could make itself felt only through the individual. There was no chance of imprinting it on a whole community, of fashioning a society after its image. But in Palestine, where a new commonwealth was to come into being, that opportunity would be present. The most precious of Jewish values would at last be free to incarnate themselves. This prospect fired into passionate commitment thousands of Jews who might otherwise never have heeded the Zionist message.

Zionism's record of social achievement has justified the highest expectations. The movement was scarcely under way when an extraordinary policy was adopted on land tenure. It was determined that the soil, when purchased by public funds, was to remain the perpetual possession of the entire Jewish people. On it tenants might take up residence, paying a minimal, fair, equitable rental. But it was not to be bartered or sold, nor might anyone hold more than he himself could work.

Behind these unusual measures stretched a long history. In order to prevent the concentration of land in the hands of the few, and, in inevitable consequence, a rootless peasantry, the Law of Moses proclaimed boldly that the earth was the Lord's. On this premise it forbade the sale of land in perpetuity, providing for its redistribution at regular intervals.

These principles, reaffirmed by prophets and rabbis, were echoed in modern times by a variety of social reformers, notably by Henry George. When, therefore, the moment came for Jews to found their commonwealth, they naturally were guided by their tradition and systems of thought in harmony with it.

Analogous developments took place in adjacent fields. The doctrine of the right of the individual to self-determination and the legal rules in which Judaism embodied it flowed together with modern progressivism to evoke an advanced trade unionism. Organized labor in Palestine comprehends today all workers whether of hand or brain, and is concerned not only with their economic position but their social and cultural welfare as well. Similarly Judaism's historic ideal of brotherhood and mutual aid among men, stimulated by contemporary economic liberalism, translated itself into a cooperative movement, perhaps the most advanced and intensive in the world.

The climactic expression of this last tendency is the Palestinian commune. The country now houses a large number of rural settlements and some industries organized on the basis of voluntary collectivism. In these communes, all things, except the most personal of possessions, are the property of the group, which in turn is directed by the democratically determined will of all its members. The success of this noncoerced communism has up to the present been most impressive. Some predict confidently that the largest contribution destined to emerge from Palestine is just this new design for social living.

Of these developments Aaron David Gordon, as we have already indicated, was by no means the originator. And yet they all were strained through and transmuted by his personality. Gordon came to Palestine in his middle years. Behind him was a near lifetime of intense traditionalism and of painstaking reflection on social problems. Before him loomed a vision for the Jewish community in Palestine.

The first text he lived and preached was of the dignity of work, of the glory of field and workshop. No man, he believed, had the right to subsist on the toil of others, nor could he, unless he partook of elemental productive toil, be whole in spirit. "Hard black labor," as he characterized it, was both the obligation and privilege of every true human being. It was also a precondition for the health and fruitfulness of Palestinian Jewry in all its higher reaches, in art, religion, science and literature. For communities, like individuals, must be rooted in the earth and watered with sweat, or they will not flower.

If parasitism was one cardinal sin in Gordon's eyes, self-centeredness was another. Like the first, the second poisoned the character of man, sterilized and made unstable his society. Yet competitiveness, the race for personal advantage and self-gratification, was conventional to the Western world, the premise and by-product of its scheme of things. These immoralities, Gordon insisted, must not be transferred to Palestine.

A member of an agricultural commune in Galilee, Gordon practiced, wrote and spoke his message, directing it to himself, to those about him, to those turning from all the world to the land of their fathers.

Now, somewhat less than a half century since the formal inauguration of the World Zionist Organization, it is apparent that history has broadly validated the purposes of the founding fathers of the movement. If Herzl,

Nordau, Ahad HaAm or Gordon erred at all, it was in underestimating the cogency of their reasoning.

Herzl in particular has been justified by events far beyond his prophecy. He was right, tragically right, when he spoke of the radical insecurity of European Jewry. Everything that has happened from his day to the present constitutes one long, harrowing demonstration of that thesis. The hundreds of thousands of Jews now alive in Palestine, the millions who perished in Europe for want of asylum, all testify together to his foresightedness in insisting on a Jewish National Home. Nor must it be supposed that Palestine's role as a haven of Jewish refuge is played out. As was indicated in Chapter 1, masses of Jews will be rootless in the postwar world; for very many of these there will be but one open way, that broken for them by Herzl.

Herzl has been proved wise, too, in his insistence on political methods and political guaranties for his cause. Into the platform of the First World Zionist Congress he wrote that the Jewish Homeland must be "politically secured and legally recognized." This policy won its major triumphs in the Balfour Declaration of 1917, and the Mandate issued by the League of Nations in 1922. But its astuteness has been demonstrated time and again ever since. It has furnished Zionism with a *locus standi*, from which appeals might be addressed both to Great Britain and the world. Whenever the covenant made by the nations with the Jewish people is threatened with violation, the latter are not resourceless. Standing on the solid ground of treaties and pledged words, they can call the violators to account.

Similarly the notion of a popular organization on behalf of Zionism, though accepted by Herzl only tardily, has turned out to be sound. For it emancipated Zionism from domination by philanthropists. It shielded it against personal whims and prejudices. A folk movement, it could tap the energies and talents of a whole people. The cause would have been poorer, weaker, perhaps dead by now, had Herzl not been driven, out of disappointment with individuals, to address himself over their heads to Jews in the mass.

Needless to say, there are elements in Herzl's thought which the years have treated less favorably. Thus, he exaggerated the influence of a Jewish Palestine on the social position of other Jewries. Again, events have forcibly revised his envisagement of the political future of the Jewish Homeland, as we shall discover in the next chapter. Most important of all, he failed to perceive how great an obstacle Arab opposition would be to his ideal. Yet in the main, time has validated his intuitions.

Nordau too has proved a true prophet. The Jewish Homeland and the struggle to achieve it have indeed worked miracles on the self-esteem of Jews everywhere. Palestine has realized further Ahad HaAm's predictions. It fosters today a brilliantly revivified Jewish culture of the largest consequence to the Diaspora.

The Gordonian motif, finally, has vindicated itself by its fruits. Labor in all actuality has become a religion among Palestinian Jews. Under its sway shopkeepers have been turned into farmers, lawyers into mechanics and clerks into fishermen. The evil spell of the Ghetto on the economics of the Jewish group has been broken at last.

This is the theory on which Zionism has built its house, and this the measure of its achievement. Having contemplated them, we are ready for the question with which this chapter opened: Given the large and incontrovertible accomplishments of Zionism on behalf of Jews, on what grounds are some Jews openly and passionately against it?

In posing this query, I do not have in mind the ignorant who know nothing about Jewish problems, nor the de-Judaized who care less; nor extinctionists who, eager that Jewry disappear, regret its reinvigoration by the Homeland; nor the sick of soul to whom Palestine is a public reminder of the Jewishness they want forgotten. Such Jews will of course be anti-Zionist. I am looking for the balanced, nonpsychopathic, nonescapist opposition.

The first type of anti-Zionism originates, surprisingly enough, in that very religion from which springs so much of the initial impetus toward Zionism. For, while the traditional doctrine distinctly imparts the promise of Israel's restoration, it is quite explicit that it is the Messiah who is to bring that event to pass. By far most Orthodox Jews hold nowadays that human co-operation to the realization of this purpose is not inconsistent with the Messianic faith. Some, however—and they are very few in number—have decided otherwise, holding that man has no right to intrude upon God's devices. To them Zionism is an impiety, a usurpation of the prerogatives of Providence. No matter what ordeal Israel may endure, regardless of the promise, social and spiritual, implicit in the Zionist program, they will do nothing except pray, and wait patiently for God's own time and the Redeemer.

Any belief conscientiously maintained merits respect. Certainly we would serve no point by disputing this particular article. A dogma held on faith, it can be accepted or rejected, but not debated.

The second anti-Zionism emanates from Communism. It is part of being a Marxist to repudiate religion, first as contrary to the materialistic world outlook, and second as an opiate whereby exploited masses are drugged into passivity. So far as Zionism is of religious motivation, Jewish Communists can have no traffic with it. In addition, Communism traces all social evils, including the specific ills of Jewry, to the exploitive character of the capitalist order. It holds that for all the great public maladies of mankind there can be only one radical cure. Let capitalism be wiped out by proletarian revolution, and the diseases it fosters will be eliminated. On these premises, Zionism as a solvent of Jewish problems is not only a waste of energy, it is, even worse, a diversion of attention from the great issue to a detail, from heart to periphery.

The Communist party has been steadfastly a declared enemy of Zionism. Everywhere it has fought the Jewish Homeland, denouncing it for its religious motivations, as a capitalist trick to distract Jews from social revolution, and, ironically enough in view of England's handling of the Mandate, as a façade for British imperialism. Even the Jewish Communists of Palestine—and there are a handful of them—have been opponents of the very community which shelters them.

Of late, the Communist party shows some signs of a revision of its attitude on Zionism. Thus, during the summer of 1941 one of its Jewish spokesmen referred to Palestine as "an important part of our people—a community which is building an organized national life in that part of the world." When Palestinian Jews sent to the Soviet Union, as they did on numerous occasions, contributions for the relief of Russian war victims, the messages that passed back and forth were marked by cordiality and a hitherto unevinced mutual respect. Last of all, the Stalinist regime seems to be modifying its line on many scores. It is possible that someday it may reverse itself on Zionism also. But until that time has arrived, Communism must be taken as constituting a second anti-Zionism.

Perhaps it ought to be added for clarity's sake that Marxists are not necessarily anti-Zionist. On the contrary, Marxist-Zionists not only exist, but in large numbers and with considerable influence. Indeed, radicals of this and other stripes have contributed mightily to the Zionist movement. Especially is the social progressivism of Jewish Palestine in their debt. These, however, are non-Communist Marxists. Socialists, in other words, can be and often are Zionists; Communists, until the present, never.

Of sharply different character is the third type of anti-Zionism, welling mainly from middle and upper-class circles. Since Communism and extreme Orthodoxy can claim only the fewest adherents, this movement can truthfully be said to be anti-Zionism par excellence, the most influential and significant organized resistance. In thought and personnel alike it bespeaks "old-line" Reform. At its core stands a band of rabbis, all Reform and all protagonists of the unrevised Reform position.

When the Central Conference of American Rabbis, the official agency of the Reform rabbinate, adopted its new "Columbus" Platform; when, on successive occasions, it revealed itself overwhelmingly pro-Zionist, these men were left without an instrument for the expression of their viewpoint. In 1943, therefore, they established the American Council for Judaism, invited lay co-operation and proceeded to publish statements expository of their sentiments. These provide a reliable guide to the thinking of informed anti-Zionists.

Their first contention is that Zionism misrepresents the character of Judaism which they maintain to consist in religion only. This definition has already been the subject of a careful analysis (Chapter 9). The reader will no doubt recall that it proves on examination untenable in logic and uncreative in action. We need not pause over it again.

Of greater moment and cogency is the second objection of "old-line" Reformists that Zionism is secular in its instruments and purposes, and is therefore inconsistent with the religious character of Judaism. That the Zionism of some Zionists is secular is undeniable. But to assert that Zionism must be secularist is absurd. The religious sources of Zionism, reaching back to the prophets, refute any such notion. When, moreover, some ninety Reform rabbis, in founding the American Council for Judaism, declared Zionism to be incompatible with the Jewish religion, approximately nine hundred rabbis including over two hundred of the Reform group repudiated the statement, asserting in the strongest possible terms that Zionism represents a natural manifestation of historic Jewish religious conviction. And in actuality, the center of gravity of Zionist strength not only in America but everywhere in the Diaspora falls squarely among religious Jews.

Of a piece with this argument is another, closely related to it: that Zionism represents a retreat from and denial of the "universalistic emphasis" of Judaism. The Jewish religion, it is contended, ever since the days of the prophets has eschewed particularism, aspiring rather toward the brotherhood of all men under the Fatherhood of God. To establish a Jewish Commonwealth, whether in Palestine or elsewhere, would therefore contravene a glorious doctrine of the Jewish tradition.

Impressive as this proposition seems at first blush, it disintegrates under examination. Be it observed that the prophets, the first and most exalted universalists of history, were at the same time also ardently devoted to their people and its land. Nor were they thereby involved in self-contradiction. For they had dedicated their nation to the overarching goal of the service of all mankind. As their universalism did not require that individuals surrender individuality, so it did not demand that peoples cease to be what they are. On the contrary it seems to have been their conviction that each person and each nation serves God best by fulfilling its uniqueness, provided always that self-realization subserves the Divine Will and broadest human welfare.

In other words, objections to Zionism on this score misread Jewish universalism, a doctrine that involves not the elimination of the particular but its consecration to universal ends. Indeed, thanks to their blunder, the members of the American Council for Judaism are themselves ensnared in embarrassing inconsistencies. If they were as good as their word in objecting to particularism, they ought to urge the dissolution of the Jewish religion and the American nation, both particularist entities. Needless to say, they advocate neither. All in all it is difficult to avoid the judgment that once again the anti-Zionist party has thought loosely and spoken carelessly.

One grain of validity there is in the critique of Zionism as particularistic. It is the peril of all allegiances that they may become intemperate, immoderate, in a word, chauvinistic. This danger threatens Zionism, but in no greater degree than it imperils any other loyalty or interest. Wherever chauvinism appears, it is to be resisted—whether it be the chauvinism of self, egotism, or that of a group, jingoism. Zionists will be well advised to be on the watch against such a perversion of their ideal. But while the threat is ever present, it is not peculiar to this one cause, not a necessary nor even likely consequence of it.

Anti-Zionists protest further against "the political emphasis now paramount in Zionism." The pronouncements of the American Council for Judaism fail to interpret this phrase; it is therefore difficult to say exactly what it signifies. It may refer to methods for realizing the Zionist objective, or else to the objective itself. If to the former, that is to say, if what disturbs non-Zionists is the existence of a World Zionist Organization that negotiates with governments, the League of Nations and the United Nations, then it is hard to take the objection seriously. For since Zionism aims for a goal that requires the consent of governments, it obviously has no course except to deal with them. If this be "political," on what meat has the word fed that it should be viewed as so horrendous? Besides, most anti-Zionists applaud the practical achievements of Zionism and hope that Jews will be free to settle in Palestine in the future. Is it not naïve to approve of results but to object to the only instruments by which these results can be attained?

On the other hand, anti-Zionists may mean by "political emphasis" the goal of Zionism, that is the establishment in Palestine of a Jewish Commonwealth. On a number of scores they may object to self-determination for Jews in their Homeland. Since Palestine's political future is to come under discussion in the next chapter, we will defer to that place our examination of this argument.

Perhaps the gravest misgiving of non-Zionists is over the consequences of the Zionist program for Jews outside Palestine. More specifically, as American Jews they are apprehensive lest Zionism be somehow unpatriotic and un-American, lest it divide and hyphenate their civic loyalties. All such notions are grotesque. The American Zionist, if he is typical, has no intention except that he and his children shall live out their lives in America. His interest in Palestine flows from his concern for his fellows abroad, and for his own Hebraic heritage. In such a situation there is nothing to touch the integrity of the relationship of Jews to the countries of their citizenship. No matter what is now or may come to be in Palestine, the political obligations of American Jews to America will not be modified by the least jot or tittle.

That anti-Zionists are overly timorous in this respect is demonstrable from one simple circumstance: every president of the United States from Wilson to Franklin D. Roosevelt has endorsed Zionism; the Congress of the United States has declared in its favor time and again; great Americans of all walks of life, Wendell Willkie for example and Henry Wallace, have exhibited deep sympathies with it; and one of the greatest Jewish Americans, Louis D.

Brandeis, was a leader of the Zionist movement. Obviously there is no inconsistency in being an American and a Zionist at the same time.

Nor are American Jews unique in evincing attachment to their fellows abroad, or to the ancient land whence their people and faith stem. Methodists, Quakers, Roman Catholics and Christian Scientists maintain relations with sister churches and brother communicants all over the world. British, Irish and Swedish Americans are sentimentally attached to the lands of their origins and keenly interested in their fortunes. Nor is the Quaker, the Catholic, the Swedish or the Irish American the least compromised in his Americanism therefor. Our country, all of whose citizens are more or less recent immigrants, knows, understands and respects such solicitudes and affections. It recognizes too as part of its purpose that, as long as public order and unity are not breached, every individual shall be free to foster the devotions of his soul.

The final contention of the anti-Zionist is that Zionism endangers the status of American Jews by supplying the anti-Semite with an argument. Given a Jewish Homeland, they reason, and the Jew-baiter will raise the cry: "The Jews have their own country; let them go to it!" Such fears are almost incredibly puerile. When Eire and Norway attained political autonomy, was there to be detected the least impulse to drive either Irish or Norse Americans from this country? Ah, to be sure, it will be responded, but then there is no significant anti-Irish or anti-Norwegian sentiment in America, whereas of anti-Semitism there is a great deal. Granted! But then is not anti-Semitism logically and chronologically anterior to Zionism? Can the latter be blamed for the former?

The anti-Semite is an insensitive fellow, or he would not be what he is. He does not require the existence of a Jewish Homeland before he begins assailing Jews. And he does not care whether the Jews he attacks have places of refuge to turn to. Very simply, he hates Jews. This is the whole of his temper, totally unaffected by whether or not Jews settle in Palestine.

The fact of the matter is that neither Hitler, Gerald L. K. Smith nor any other of the breed became an anti-Semite because of Zionism, or made propaganda capital out of it; that in a word, Zionism has no role whatsoever in the creation and intensification of anti-Jewish prejudices. The fair-minded non-Jew is by definition not hostile to Jews, nor will he be affected adversely by the emergence of a Jewish Commonwealth. To the contrary, the achievements of Palestine may induce in him a heightened respect for Jews as a whole. And as for the bigot, he does not need pretexts.

There is then an anti-Zionist case, but not one article of it is truly tenable. Certainly, it does not begin to equal the argument in favor of a "politically recognized, legally secured home for the Jewish people in Palestine."

The present-day discussion of Zionism, moreover, is no exercise in pure logic, no feat of intellection isolated from actuality. Social realities, ugly and compelling, are implicated too. Pervading our argument is all the fearsome urgency of Jewish homelessness which we presented in Chapter 1. More then must be charged against Jewish anti-Zionists than that they reason loosely and badly, which forsooth they do. They have also been guilty of hideous miscalculations in the world of pragmatic decisions. Were it not for their antagonism or indifference, Zionism would have been much farther along by 1933, and millions who perished in Europe might today be alive in Palestine.

Now, to blunder is human and forgivable. But to persist in an error is not so easily to be condoned. Yet this is exactly the sin of many anti-Zionists and non-Zionists. One may pardon them for failing to see in 1920 what Herzl perceived in 1900. Obtuseness is not generally willed. But in recent years the Jewish scene could not be misconstrued. On the one hand, tens of myriads of Jews with the death mark on their foreheads, and on the other only Palestine ready and capable of delivering them.

Before such a spectacle the behavior of the Jewish opposition to Zionism becomes culpable indeed. Most anti-Zionists, if they were not persuaded by argument, yielded at least to a burning necessity and to the importunities of pity. But some temporized and hesitated. Others straddled the issue by terming themselves anti-Zionists but pro-Palestinian, a position made objectionable by the fact that many of its advocates worked harder at their anti-Zionism than their pro-Palestinianism. Some few Jews remained obdurate and unyielding, preferring apparently that Jews die rather than that a Jewish Homeland become an actuality.

When I have divested myself so far as I can of my partisanship, I am still saddened by the conviction that the hands of such American Jews are stained with the blood of their fellows.

15

Jewish Palestine

To say of a cause, as we have asserted of Zionism, that it is sound in theory is to affirm very little about its practicality. Many a concept possessed of logical consistency has broken upon the reef of hard reality. The question therefore now poses itself: granted that the Zionist case has been vindicated as argument, is it workable?

The response falls into two parts. The first is the testimony of experience. The second concerns itself with the obstacles in the way of the further incarnation of the Zionist idea. Are these insuperable, has the enterprise already attained its maximal embodiment?

First to the past. What has been the record of Jewish accomplishment in Palestine, and is it such as to justify further effort?

"The greatest colonizing enterprise of modern times"—such is the summary characterization of the Permanent Mandates Commission of the League of Nations, a judgment borne out to the full by the evidences.

Since the close of the First World War over half a million Jews have entered and successfully established themselves in Palestine. During the decade of 1933–1943, when Jewish homelessness was most acute, the country absorbed 280,000 immigrants. To sites unoccupied for centuries life and civilization have returned. Tel Aviv, a flourishing modern city of 200,000 souls, stands where for centuries, until almost yesterday, deserted sand dunes rolled. But not only has the Jewish population of Palestine grown prodigiously. Arab numbers have risen also from 664,000 in 1918 to over 1,000,000 at present. And this only in Palestine. In Transjordania to the East, in other near-by Moslem lands, there has been no parallel upsurge of vitality. Vivid testimony, affirmatively and negatively, to the beneficial effects of Jewish settlement.

Perhaps the most brilliant of Zionist accomplishments has been on and with the soil. In a countryside which knew only primitive methods of cultivation, Jews have established 276 farm colonies, sustaining 150,000 souls and exhibiting the most modern and advanced of agricultural techniques. They have improved the Jaffa orange and developed markets for it; have founded wineries and factories for the processing of farm products. In schools and experimental stations they have bred hardier and more productive plants, cattle and fowl. They have made large-scale and scientific enterprises of truck farming, dairying, the raising of poultry, the growing of cereals, citrus and deciduous fruits. Turning to the lakes and the Mediterranean Sea, they have revived the ancient Palestinian occupation of fishing. They have launched extensive projects of reforestation, planting millions of saplings upon hills long left denuded by wanton woodcutting, overgrazing and neglect. And all this on six percent of the land's area! Little wonder then that Walter Clay Lowdermilk, Assistant Chief of the Soil Conservation Service of the United States Department of Agriculture, summarized the whole process as "the most remarkable devotion to land and reclamation of land that I have seen in any country of the New or Old World." For centuries men had had reason to be skeptical of the Biblical description of Palestine as a "land flowing with milk and honey." Anyone, however, who has witnessed it as rejuvenated by Jewish effort and idealism knows that it once merited and can yet deserve again the tribute of Scripture.

Analogous, if not even more remarkable, developments, have taken place in industry. Jews have set up in Palestine approximately 2,300 factories and 4,000 workshops. Pre-eminent among these are the Palestine Potash Company which extracts minerals from the Dead Sea; and the Palestine Electric Corporation which supplies the land with power and light. Smaller enterprises also have demonstrated their ability to maintain themselves profitably. Among the products they turn out for sale in Palestine and throughout the Near East are building materials, machinery, metalware, textiles, pharmaceuticals and electrical equipment. One of the most interesting of the recently introduced industries is diamond cutting. Jewish refugees from Holland and Belgium have so successfully transferred their trades to a new scene that today much of the diamond cutting of the world centers about Tel Aviv. Of late, Jews have entered upon shipping and commerce. The establishment of a Maritime Training School gives assurance that, like their ancient fathers, modern Jews will be among "those who go down to the sea in ships." The prospects are good today, objective observers agree, that Palestine may become for the Near East what industrialized Holland and Belgium are for Europe.

These achievements, moreover, have been attained along with impressive gains in the welfare of the laboring classes. The Jewish workers of Palestine are organized into a General Federation of Labor, 126,000 members strong, and constituting with their families forty percent of the Jewish community of Palestine. This movement reaches far beyond the normal activities of trade unions. It establishes and directs agricultural settlement, co-operative enterprises in industry, transport and construction; educational and medical institutions, health insurance and unemployment relief. Most significantly, it fosters trade unionism among Arabs, in part out of convictions as to its necessity and rightfulness but also in self-interest. For, transparently, the standard of living of the Jewish worker is pegged to that of the Arab.

An advanced hygiene represents a further Jewish triumph in Palestine. Through Hadassah, the Women's Zionist Organization of America, the most progressive medical procedures have been introduced into the land. In the Rothschild-Hadassah-Hebrew University Hospital, the greatest in the entire Near East, in hundreds of local clinics, thousands of physicians and nurses are engaged self-sacrificingly in stamping out the age-old diseases of the Orient. In consequence, an American epidemologist can report: "The contrast between malaria incidence among the troops stationed in Palestine during the last war, or among those stationed now in Syria, and that among the forces at present in Palestine, is striking. Twenty years of malaria control have rendered Palestine the only country in this part of the world in which this infectious disease is of minor significance as a factor in troop morbidity." What is more, the Jews on principle make their medical resources readily accessible to Arabs. The results are to be seen in a sharply falling mortality rate among Arabs, in a marked improvement in their general health. It is no accident that Palestine of late has become a medical center for the entire Levant, the resort of the sick of many lands in their quest for relief and healing.

These achievements, industrial, agricultural and hygienic, have most recently "paid off" for mankind as a whole. When the cause of democratic freedom stood with its back to the wall, Jewish Palestine acquitted itself magnificently. Over 30,000 Jewish men and 3,000 women enlisted in the British fighting forces, to serve with distinction on many fronts. A body of approximately 35,000 volunteers may not seem impressive until it is recalled that in proportion to total populations, it is the equivalent of an American army of about 8,000,000. In addition to fighting men, the Jewish community has contributed to British forces in the Middle East engineers, sailors, physicians and nurses. Finally, it has been a by no means negligible source of supplies. Whereas in the First World War Palestine was dependent for food and industrial goods on import, this time, thanks to Jewish enterprise, it has been able to provide food, matériel, technical and repair services to Allied armies in the field.

No list of Jewish attainments in Palestine can fairly omit one of special distinction, the creation of new patterns of group living. In this respect too, in imaging forth the Gordonian ideal, the record is notable. The little land has become a laboratory for the testing of social innovations. The worth of these may someday far transcend the community that houses them. As Sir Arthur Wauchope, former High Commissioner of Palestine, commented: "We are all interested not only in the War but also in any social or economic changes that may take place after the War, especially those needed to bring about a more equal distribution of wealth. . . . If changes in our social or economic structure are to be discussed, then it is worth-while to consider the one example of such a system where people actually do live on an equal economic basis."

The expectations of Ahad HaAm have also been fulfilled. The Land of Israel is again a great seedbed for Jewish culture. The Hebrew language has been revived and modernized. A progressive school system has been established, equipped with technical and professional branches. Talmudical academies and institutions of religious instruction flourish. Crowning the whole stands the Hebrew University of Jerusalem with its monumental library, scientific foundations, department of liberal arts and institutes of Hebraic and Islamic civilization.

In no other land of the world is the population so universally literate and awakened culturally. The per capita publication of books and magazines would be amazingly high in a well-established community, let alone in one still in its pioneering stage. The Palestine Symphony Orchestra, under the baton of the world's leading conductors, has performed with distinction throughout the Near East. Theatrical troupes stage wide and exacting repertories of native and translated drama. In the enthusiasm, and under the stress of an intense group life, many old ceremonial forms have been recast into more relevant patterns, while new practices expressive of modern aspirations have sprung into being.

Finally, as the early theoreticians of Zionism hoped, the Homeland has remade the Jewish personality. That it has shattered the inertia of middle-class occupationalism, we have already asserted. But only statistics can reveal how basic the revolution has been. So, according to a study made in 1937, of 100,000 Palestinian agricultural and industrial workers over one-third had had no definite occupation in the lands of their origin, one-twelfth had been merchants, and almost one-fifth students. Of 25,000 persons living on the soil, less than ten percent had engaged in agriculture in Europe. Physical labor has come into its own in Jewish Palestine as in no other Jewry anywhere.

"The results can be seen," writes Philip S. Bernstein in *The Nation*,* "in new Jewish types—strong, self-respecting, unafraid. Psychologically and physically, they have much in common with the frontiersmen who cleared the wilderness and built the first settlements on the North American continent. The Palestinian Jews are the only Jewish community which under attack in this war has sunk its roots deeper into the earth, stood its ground resolutely, and demanded the right and the weapons to fight back blow for blow. It is not that they are heroes, but something in their attachment to their own soil gives them a quiet strength and courage denied to the harried, rootless Jews in Europe."

Such is the record of accomplishment of Zionism. Reviewing it, persons of good will have no choice except to seal it with approval and benediction. The adventure, however, is far from over. Palestine, to make again a point made before perhaps to weariness, will be called on for much more than it has yet performed. It must receive immigrants on a vastly increased scale. It must, if it is not to fail the hopes of Diaspora Judaism, turn even more productive of Hebraic values, more inventive of new social devices. And if it is to fulfill the Zionist design, nay more, if it is to realize itself, it must someday embody Jewish political self-determination.

Before these aims large obstacles loom and grave dangers impend. Some of these derive from disputed facts, notably whether Palestine is capable of absorbing masses of additional immigrants. Others express organized oppo-

---

* "Jews in Europe." Quoted by permission of *The Nation*.

sition, the antagonism to the Zionist program of almost the whole Arab world, the vacillations and more recently the near opposition of Great Britain. Over these riddles of fact and policy looms like an incubus the climactic enigma, result of the others and at the same time productive of them: what shall be the political structure toward which Palestine is to evolve? Shall Jewish immigration cease now; shall the country become an Arab state with a Jewish minority? Or shall Jews continue to enter the land? If so, they must in the not too distant future come to constitute a majority of its populace. What then will be the polity to be commended by morality and practicality alike?

Whatever the theoretical validity of Zionism and its past successes, no judgment as to its future can be reached until these questions have been resolved. It may be that Zionism is now up against an immovable, unbreakable wall. Or that it can advance only to the hurt and wronging of others—the Arabs perchance, or the British. If this be the case, Jews have no alternative except to bow to inexorabilities. They must, no matter how reluctantly, pronounce: "It is enough. We have wrought well, but our hands may attempt no more." But if, on the other hand, the obstacles turn out to be surmountable, and the course ahead to be free from transgression of the rights of others, then the Jews must prosecute the Zionist idea vigorously and to its completion. The incalculable suffering of European Jewry, the inner needs of the Jewish spirit allow no alternative.

THE ABSORPTIVE CAPACITY OF PALESTINE

On the ability of Palestine to accommodate a large additional influx of Jews, Zionists count heavily. Is not too much being expected from a little and none too fertile land? Palestine, Trans-Jordan excluded, covers a total area of about 10,000 square miles. It is the size of Vermont, only a little larger than Sicily. And of its area only half is regarded as cultivable. Within these narrow confines 1,580,000 human beings now live. This number includes an increase of approximately 800,000 souls achieved within twenty-five years. Has not the saturation point already been reached, or else, is it not by now in clear view?

Such misgivings are reasonable. They are not, however, warranted by determinable facts. Thus it is of record that ancient Palestine in the first century of our era sustained a population conservatively estimated at 2,500,000 * and more optimistically at 4,000,000.† If on a rudimentary agrarian economy and without modern industry the country could support so many inhabitants, historical evidences suggest strongly that contemporary Palestine is still far from its maximal population.

This presumption is strengthened by a number of considerations. Of the cultivable soil, only half is now being tilled. Furthermore, the land under the plow is as a whole worked primitively. With the introduction of more advanced methods, the absorptive potential of the country expands once more. Nor should the so-called uncultivable tracts be written off as dead loss. Jewish colonists have given abundant evidence of their ability to wrest a livelihood even from soil classified by the Palestinian administration as untillable. Indeed, approximately one-third of the land occupied by Jews has been reclaimed from swamp, marsh, desert and rock. Long regarded as hopeless, it has turned fertile with the application of the proper technique, whether irrigation by artesian well, terracing or drainage. Finally, should the plan of Walter Clay Lowdermilk suggested in his *Palestine, Land of Promise* be attempted, should the upper waters of the Jordan River be diverted to high-level conduits for purposes of irrigation, large areas now too arid for farming will be made fruitful.

But the absorptive capacity of Palestine, as of all other countries, depends on industry as well as agriculture. In this respect the possibilities of Palestine are virtually limitless. Already it has become the workshop of the Levant. New industries are constantly being launched and new markets discovered. In brief, with intensive systematic agriculture and an aggressive industry, the assumption of a much increased population is abundantly warranted.

How many more Jews can Palestine receive? No definitive answer to this question is possible for the simple reason that up to now the potentialities have expanded apace with immigration. The population has increased mightily in the last generation and the end is nowhere near in sight. Indeed were a million Jews to enter the land tomorrow, its inhabitants would be no more numerous than they were, according to conservative estimates, in the first century.

We are not dependent on guesses and doubtful comparisons. On the basis of the record and of realistic programs, sober, scientific calculations have

* *The Jewish People in the Time of Jesus Christ*, by Emil Schürer.
† *A Social and Religious History of the Jews*, by Salo W. Baron.

been arrived at. One of these is contained in an *Aide-Memoire on Post-war Emigration Needs of European Jewry and Resettlement Possibilities in Palestine,* submitted in February 1943 to the British Ambassador and the United States Department of State by a joint committee representing almost all nationwide American Jewish agencies. This report concludes that "taking into consideration known possibilities, Palestine . . . should be capable of absorbing another three million inhabitants."

These are Jews speaking; their pleading may be ex parte. Consider then the judgment of a non-Jew and a distinguished agronomist to boot. After long study, Dr. Lowdermilk decides that the country is capable of receiving 4,000,000 immigrants beyond its present population.* Now let us suppose that Dr. Lowdermilk, scientific agriculturalist though he be, has been un-moored by some wild enthusiasm. Let us cut his estimate in half. Five years ago, a figure of 2,000,000 might not have been large enough to embrace all the European Jews who will desire and need to go to Palestine. Today, alas, it will be enough.

ARAB OPPOSITION

The largest single obstacle in the way of the Zionist enterprise is the resistance it meets at the hands of the Arabs of Palestine and their fellows in neighboring lands. The entire future of Jewish Palestine, it may be fairly said, depends ultimately on the overcoming of this antagonism. To this end the world must evaluate it properly.

Let us first dispose of one bit of propaganda, seemingly a solid argument, in reality hollow and devoid of substance. I refer to the claim that Jewish colonization in Palestine has proved deleterious to Arab welfare. Were this proposition to be established, Zionists would morally be bound to renounce their plans. Obviously it is ethically intolerable that one group seek to solve its problems at the expense of another. The notion that the need for *Lebensraum* justifies aggression is a Nazi, not a Jewish, concept.

The fact of the matter is that Jewish settlement in Palestine has worked to the advantage, not the hurt, of non-Jews. We have already commented on the upsurge of Arab numbers in recent years. This is to be ascribed in the first instance to the lifting of standards of living resulting from the inflow of Jewish capital, enterprise and skills. It is the consequence also of a considerable *Arab* immigration from surrounding territories. Thanks to

---

* *Palestine, Land of Promise,* p. 227.

higher wages and better working conditions, Palestine has become a land of promise for others than Jews. Further, the value of Arab industrial establishments quadrupled between 1922 and 1937; the area of land under Arab cultivation in the same interval increased by over fifty percent. Because of the taxes paid by Jews, the British Mandatory Government has been enabled to finance road building, public works and health services such as otherwise would have been beyond its reach. The Arabs have been benefited not only by these but by elaborate educational facilities supported only in part by themselves.

Nor is there any basis for the charge, another staple Arab contention, that Jewish progress has been made possible only by dislodging Arabs from the soil. When in 1931 the Hope-Simpson Commission went looking for the multitudes supposedly made landless by the immigration at that time of 100,000 Jews, it found only 600 families, and of these many had received compensation from the Jews but had preferred not to use their funds for the purchase of new farms. When, further, the British Administration offered public lands as gifts for their resettlement, almost none responded. So much of substance is there to the charge that Jewish Palestine has been erected on the ruin of the Arab peasant.

How is all this possible? Much of the ground now held by Jews was, as we have seen, not only uncultivated but classed as uncultivable. Almost no one lived in the recently drained Huleh swamps or the once malaria-infested valley of Esdraelon. Again, it is now the policy of Jewish land-purchasing agencies, reinforced by law, that a portion of all acquisitions be set aside for tenant farmers who so are freed from the sharecropper's lot.

The over-all effect of Jewish immigration on the economic, social and cultural interests of the Arabs has been indisputably beneficial. Witness the thoroughly objective and responsible judgment of the British Royal Commission of 1937:

"It is difficult to detect any deterioration in the economic position of the Arab upper class. . . . We are also of the opinion that until now the Arab cultivator has benefited on the whole from the work of the British Administration and from the presence of the Jews in the country. Wages have gone up; the standard of living has improved. . . . The large import of Jewish capital into Palestine has had a general fructifying effect on the economic life of the whole country. . . . The reclamation and anti-malaria works undertaken in the Jewish colonies have benefited all the Arabs in the neighborhood. . . . Broadly speaking, the Arabs have shared to a considerable degree in the material benefits which Jewish immigration has brought to Palestine. The obligation of the Mandate in this respect has been observed. The economic position of the Arabs, regarded as a whole, has not so far been prejudiced by the establishment of the National Home. . . . The Arab charge that the Jews have obtained too large a proportion of good land cannot be maintained. Much of the land now carrying orange groves was sand dunes or swamps and uncultivated when it was purchased."

Whence then the antagonism? Its roots are many and diverse. Thus, Arab landowners and urban magnates are almost inevitably hostile to a Jewish immigration that threatens their special interests. To this day Moslem Palestine is very much a feudal society. Wealth and power are highly concentrated. The families in whose hands these rest would now be literally at ease in Zion were it not for the democracy, the economic liberalism, the trade unionism, the expectations of a decent life introduced by Jewish precept and example into the thinking of the Arab masses. This is not to say that Arab leaders are motivated solely by self-interest. Yet Zionism contravenes their economic and political privileges. It would be unnatural if on this count alone they did not set themselves to fight it.

Nor is it to be expected that hundreds of thousands of immigrants shall be introduced into a land without rousing the resentment of its native population. Were the Jews of one background, culture and outlook with the Arabs, some friction between the two peoples would be in the cards. With the social and intellectual climates of the two groups so different, irritation is naturally the sharper. Arabs no more than anyone else enjoy being upset in their wonted living and thinking. This disquiet, however, should tend to fade out with growing mutual familiarity and habituation. Such in fact has been the case. Antagonism to Jewish colonization is highest where the colonies are newest; least where they are oldest.

These natural factors have been strengthened by political forces as well. First among these has been the systematic agitation of Italy and Germany throughout the Arab world. Over a decade ago, the Axis nations set themselves to foment trouble for the Western democracies. British colonies, Palestine included, appeared vulnerable. And so, for years on end, inflammatory anti-British, anti-Jewish propaganda was piped from Bari and Berlin to the Near East; printed literature dripping with anti-Semitism and contempt for

Britain was widely diffused; arms and bribes were distributed among insurrectionists; leading Arabs such as the Grand Mufti of Jerusalem became Hitler's men. That Goebbels did not labor in vain can be seen from Arab conduct during the Second World War. Not until very late in the day did even a single Arab state align itself with the United Nations. On the contrary, Syria resisted the British and French, the revolution in Iraq was pro-Axis, the Mufti of Jerusalem ended up in Berlin.

Nor was Palestine so administered as to abate Arab resistance. We shall, later in this chapter, have occasion to pause over British policy. Right now I am concerned with it only as a contributant to Arab intransigence. That it was to the full. From the very beginning, the British Mandatory Government was conspicuously weak and vacillating. Again and again the Colonial Office and the successive High Commissioners revealed that they were not too firmly committed to the establishment of a Jewish National Home, though this was their confessed obligation. Early in the day, Jews and Arabs drew the inference that that side would have its way which would exert the heavier pressure. So Great Britain virtually invited a contest of strength. Then in 1921 and again in 1929 the Arabs learned a further lesson, that violence was an effective weapon. For when Moslem terrorists took up arms against the government, the upshot was not penalization but concessions.

To make matters worse, British officials in Palestine have not only been weak, they have often been blind. Thus they designated as Grand Mufti of Jerusalem—that is to say, as religious head of the Palestinian Arabs—a man who before his appointment had conspired against Great Britain and the Mandate, and who after it continued on the same course. For years Britain went on honoring, paying the salary of one of its bitterest enemies, a commonly recognized co-conspirator of Axis agents. The import of all this was not lost on the Arabs. Moderates among them, ready to co-operate with the British and Jews, were disheartened; extremists were encouraged to ever wilder extremism.

Yet the largest and most potent factors behind Arab opposition to Zionism remain to be enumerated. The first is the apprehension of the Arabs lest they be engulfed by Jews. It is all too easy for them to read their future unhappily, to envisage the destruction of all their cultural and religious rights, to conceive of themselves as being reduced to serfdom.

With this goes, most potent of all, an understandable aspiration on the part of Palestinian Arabs for political self-determination. Nationalist sentiment in recent decades has been astir everywhere in the Moslem world. The illiterate masses may still be untouched by it, but to thousands of educated Arabs dreams of independence are vivid. Palestinian Arabs of this stamp know that their fellows in other lands—Iraq, Egypt, Saudi Arabia—have realized such hopes. They could count reliantly on similar developments for themselves, were it not for obstructive Jewish claims. But if Zionism were liquidated, the expectations of Palestinan Arabs would be unclouded. Whence, and with the best of motives, an impassioned Arab anti-Zionism.

The causes for Arab resentment are therefore of unequal worth and influence. One, systematic agitation by Axis powers, has disappeared. Another, the desire on the part of the effendi class to protect its vested political and economic privileges, can scarcely be regarded sympathetically by men of good will and democratic commitments. Still a third, irritation arising from the intrusion of an alien group, will evaporate with time and habituation. Those that remain are of greater validity, meriting serious deliberation.

Are they fatal to Jewish purposes, do they make the Arab-Jewish problem insoluble? Or do they still allow for a *modus vivendi* which if not fully satisfactory to either side, is nonetheless just and in the long run conducive to amity?

The fears of the Arabs can certainly be allayed. Zionist authorities have time and again declared that they have no designs on Arab rights or liberties. In 1936, Dr. Chaim Weizmann, President of the World Zionist Organization and of the Jewish Agency for Palestine, wrote: "We consider that Palestine is a country common to both Jews and Arabs; both parts of the population are destined to build up a common Fatherland. It is difficult to think in these terms today, but in spite of the acuteness of the momentary difficulties, there is much more cooperation beneath the surface between Jews and Arabs than people are likely to believe. And I believe that when the Arabs realize that they cannot throw the Jews into the Mediterranean, then they will, just as we are anxious to do, sit around a table and try to work out, on the basis of the actual possibilities of the country, a modus vivendi."

To the same effect the General Federation of Jewish Labor in Palestine has declared in an official statement: "The Jewish Labor Movement consider the Arab people as an integral element of this country. . . . Jewish immigrants who come to this country to live by their own labour regard the Arab working-men as their compatriots and fellow-workers, whose needs are their needs, and whose future is their future. The realization of Zionism is therefore envisaged as the creation of a new economy, not to replace the Arab economy, but to supplement it."

But Jewish declarations obviously have not been enough. British assurances are needed too. Not that Great Britain has been unsparing of guaranties. It has issued them aplenty but always under circumstances suggesting that, if only the Arabs are sufficiently intransigent, Jewish rights will be forgotten. What is required is a clear-cut recommitment on the part of the Mandatory Government to both its obligations, to its duty to facilitate a Jewish National Home and to its pledge that Arab social and cultural rights shall not be breached.

With all this, the Zionist enterprise stands as a barrier to the political independence of the Palestinian Arabs. Have not they the same right to self-determination as others?

No sympathetic person, Jew or non-Jew, can fail to be responsive to this appeal. Let the question be put abstractly and in a vacuum and there can be no doubt as to the answer: every people has a right to autonomy. The question, however, is not up in the empyrean, it is down in the realm of realities. In that domain, moral principle works both ways. The Jews are a people also.

This is the crucial fact—*two* peoples are attached to the land and love it. Both have claims upon it and aspirations concerning it. To one side, the Arabs with their thoroughly legitimate political ambitions, to the other the Jews with all their needs and hopes. Two inherently proper ideals are in headlong collision.

In this moral dilemma, as Professor Reinhold Niebuhr once put it, perfect justice cannot be done to both sides, nor will any solution completely satisfy either. The best to be hoped for is the greater justice, the wiser statecraft, the minimal wrong and, when all things have been considered, the fairer decision.

With this as a goal, let us consider the alternative possibilities. On the one hand, suppose the Arabs have their way. Jewish Palestine is frozen in its present dimensions. Perhaps, if extremists prevail—and among them must be included Moslem personalities as influential as Ibn Saud, King of Saudi Arabia—the Jews now in the country will be expelled. Palestine becomes an autonomous Arab state with at best a tolerated Jewish minority, at the worst none at all.

As against this, suppose the decision is rendered in favor of Zionist claims. Jews continue to immigrate into the land; when they become a majority, a Jewish Commonwealth is established. In this Commonwealth every Arab right—religious, cultural, economic, civic and political, whether individual or group—is assured. Arabs of course vote and hold office, conduct their own school system, develop their own culture and faith. They forego only one prerogative—no triviality to be sure, but still only one—that of coming to constitute another independent Arab state.

Now let us compare these two prospects. How, as to over-all fairness, statesmanship and humanity, do they stack up against each other?

First, as to legality. The civilized world, through the Balfour Declaration and the Mandate, has already committed itself solemnly as to these alternatives. It has given its pledged word to facilitate Jewish immigration into Palestine, and to establish a Jewish National Home there. To the Palestinian Arabs it has made no parallel *political* promises. To them it has given assurances only that in building the Jewish National Home, "nothing shall be done which may prejudice the civil and religious rights of existing non-Jewish communities in Palestine."

Next as to urgency: what are the Arabs of Palestine called on to sacrifice? Injured not a whit, benefited mightily, they are denied at most a political aspiration. Set against this the Jews by the millions to whom entrance into Palestine is literally a matter of life and death, and Judaism to which a Jewish Homeland may be an indispensability for survival.

Again in terms of *Realpolitik*: which is the safer solution, a Jewish minority in an Arab state, or an Arab minority in a Jewish Commonwealth? The fate of the Assyrians suggests that the Moslem world can not always be relied on not to maltreat minorities in its midst. That similar notions anent the Jews are afloat in Arab minds is a matter of public record. But given the Jews as a majority in Palestine, they themselves are secure, but so too are minorities, whether Mohammedan or Christian. Unlike the Arabs, the Jews have readily and often given their word in favor of the equality of all before the future Palestinian state; they have promised to the Arabs an equitable and proportionate share in public affairs. The status of the Arabs will of course be guarded further by international guarantees. And should the vows of Jews and the assurances of the nations fail, a most remote and unlikely contingency, the Arabs of Palestine will still have behind them a vast Arab hinterland.

In the broader view: the Arab world as a unity has broad and largely undeveloped territories on which to realize its desire for political autonomy. The states of North Africa and of Western Asia are either already independent or on their way toward independence. Of this sprawling Arab world, Palestine is by area a mere five percent. Nothing basic or essential to the Arab spirit is at stake in its fate. Arab political and cultural genius will have plenty of elbow room on ninety-five percent of the territory it calls its own. For Israel, where else can it incarnate its peoplehood and root the mainstock of its culture?

The choice is larger than even the Jewish and Arab groups as entities. Implicated in it is the welfare of the entire Near East and, to the perceptive eye, of global mankind. It is of the nature of true statesmanship that it decides issues in terms of the best interests of the largest groups affected. Let such a standard be applied to the Arab-Jewish impasse, and the Zionist case acquires additional, more comprehensive validation.

The Near East in its entirety would be badly served indeed were the Jewish Homeland to be inhibited or liquidated. Jewish Palestine is a lone island of democratic sentiment and practice in a sea of medieval feudalism; the outpost of Western culture in the Orient. It is already a leaven in the Levant, stirring it toward progressive agriculture, industry, hygiene and cultural expression. Should it be permitted to continue its growth, every Moslem land in its environs will be stimulated by it. The march of the whole Mediterranean littoral toward modernity will be quickened.

And how is the world likely to be served better? Let us suppose that every Jew is removed from Palestine, that a purely Arab state arises there, wherein is mankind the richer? To be sure, 1,000,000 human beings have achieved political autonomy. This as a matter of principle is no mean gain. But it is difficult to perceive how one more Arab polity can make any substantial difference to humanity at large.

Now let us assume the second alternative, that the Zionist program is permitted to mature. The gains for the world are large and immediate. The riddle of Jewish homelessness, so troublesome and tragic, is solved instantly and forever. Those Jews who find it impossible or undesirable to live in European lands now have a place to which to turn. Those who elect otherwise are also helped. For, as we have had occasion to point out, pressure against Jews tends to relax as their numbers diminish. So an urgent, explosive matter, one heavy with anguish, is removed from humanity's agenda of unfinished business. At the same time and more positively, a chance is given to the Hebraic genius that in this hour exhibits promises cultural, social and scientific, such as no Arab state rivals. If then the greatest good for the greatest number be an acceptable criterion, Zionism is again vindicated.

None of the foregoing should be taken to deny that the Arabs have a case. It is there, charged with a passion and integrity of its own. But not in painfulness or cogency, not in urgency or import does it begin to equal the Jewish.

THE ROLE OF BRITAIN

We have already had occasion to allude to British policy as contributory to Arab intransigence. As the Mandatory Power, Great Britain has been guilty of two sins. It has indirectly, to some extent inadvertently, given aid and comfort to the forces resisting a Jewish National Home. It has further, itself, held back on the fulfillment of its commitments.

In issuing the Balfour Declaration in 1917, Great Britain declared that it viewed "with favor the establishment in Palestine of a National Home for the Jewish people," and would use its "best endeavors to facilitate the achievement of this object."

The intentions of those who put their hands to the formulation of this document are a matter of public record.

President Wilson interpreted it as an understanding "that in Palestine shall be laid the foundations of a Jewish Commonwealth."

Arthur James Balfour, British Secretary of State for Foreign Affairs, who promulgated the Declaration and gave it its name, construed it to mean that "full facilities would be given to the Jews to work out their own salvation and to build up . . . a real center of national culture and focus of national life. It [*i.e.,* "National Home"] did not necessarily involve the early establishment of an independent Jewish State, which was a matter of gradual development in accordance with the ordinary laws of political evolution."

Winston Churchill, then Secretary of State for War, envisaged that under the Declaration there might be "created in our own life time by the banks of the Jordan a Jewish State under the protection of the British Crown which might comprise three or four million Jews." Such an event, he prophesied, would prove beneficial to the world and the British Empire.

And David Lloyd George, Prime Minister at the time, while denying that the Balfour Declaration implied the immediate setting up of a Jewish National State, asserted: "It was contemplated that when the time arrived for according representative institutions to Palestine, if the Jews had meanwhile responded to the opportunity afforded them by the idea of a National Home and had become a definite majority of the inhabitants, then Palestine would become a Jewish Commonwealth. The notion that Jewish immigration would have to be artificially restricted in order to ensure that the Jews should be a permanent minority never entered into the heads of anyone engaged in framing the policy."

Clearly, the Balfour Declaration committed Britain to the encouragement of mass Jewish immigration into Palestine, contemplated the achievement by Jews of majority status in that land, and projected the eventual establishment of an autonomous Jewish political entity. About these objectives, the Balfour Declaration set only two hedges: first, that "nothing shall be done which may prejudice the civil or religious rights of existing non-Jewish communities in Palestine," and second, that the Declaration shall not be construed as affecting "the rights and political status enjoyed by Jews in any other country."

On April 25, 1920, the Supreme Council of the Allied Nations conferred the Mandate over Palestine on Great Britain. In substance the Mandate (confirmed in 1922 by the Council of the League of Nations, by the United States through a Joint Congressional Resolution signed by President Warren G. Harding) makes explicit the implications of the Declaration. It asserts "the historical connection of the Jewish people with Palestine," reaffirms the objective of a Jewish "national home in that country," binds Great Britain to facilitate Jewish immigration, to encourage close settlement by Jews on the land, including state and wastelands, to accept Hebrew as one of the three official languages of the country, and to recognize the World Zionist Organization (later the Jewish Agency for Palestine) as officially representative of Jewish interests. While the Mandate is solicitous of the religious and civil rights of non-Jewish individuals and communities in Palestine, at no time does it acknowledge political-national obligations to the Arabs, parallel to those assumed vis-à-vis the Jews.

Against this background of covenant and commitment, the record of the British administration of Palestine presents a sorry spectacle. Pledged to

pecific, defined ends, the British Colonial Office for years evaded its re-
ponsibilities and in the end repudiated them altogether.

In May 1921 Arab riots broke out. The British authorities at that time, as
o often later, proved lax in the most elementary duty of government, firm,
dequate policing. Furthermore, they responded to violence by suspending
or a time all Jewish immigration, and, as we have already noted, by desig-
nating Haj Amin AlHusaini, an archterrorist, Grand Mufti of Jerusalem.
Arab extremists would have been stupid indeed not to infer from all this
that crime paid.

Meantime, though duty-bound to put crown and wastelands at the disposal of Jewish settlers, the British released not an acre for this purpose;
instead they distributed tracts to Arabs, many of whom, ironically enough,
promptly proceeded to sell their windfalls to Jews.

In 1922 whittling down of the Balfour Declaration and Mandate began;
the British Government issued the first of its notorious White Papers. This
document averred the intention of the Declaration and Mandate to be not
"that Palestine as a whole should be converted into a Jewish National Home
but that such a home should be founded in Palestine." Most arbitrarily it
withdrew Transjordania, the larger and more sparsely settled eastern portion of Palestine, from the scope of Jewish settlement and interest. Finally,
it set up the rule that Jewish immigration be governed by "the economic
capacity of the country to absorb new arrivals."

In itself, such a principle is reasonable. It would be absurd statesmanship
to admit into a land settlers for whom no employment was in sight. Unfortunately, this apparently unexceptionable regulation became in the hands
of the Palestine Administration a political weapon, a pretext for excluding
Jews even when, demonstrably, jobs and residences awaited them.

The next step in Britain's retreat from its obligations followed in the wake
of the riots of 1929. With the Grand Mufti at their head, Arab agitators
spread the preposterous report that Jews intended to seize and convert the
great Mosque of Jerusalem into a Jewish Temple. Encouraged by inde-
cisiveness and inactivity on the part of the Palestine government which permitted such incitement to go undeterred, Arab extremists succeeded in their
purpose: they precipitated an outbreak of violence. As they had calculated,
terrorism was once more rewarded. Two British investigatory commissions
visited Palestine. The first, the Shaw Commission, cleared both the British
Administration and the Arabs of responsibility, asserting that Jewish im-

migration and land purchase were the root causes of the disturbances. The second, headed by Sir John Hope-Simpson, reported in 1930 that the attempt to establish a Jewish National Home had already created a landless Arab peasantry, that the country could not absorb more than 20,000 additional settlers, that the industries founded by the Jews were unsound and could not endure.

Each of these conclusions has been exploded subsequently. When in 1932 Lewis French, Director of Development in Palestine, set about looking for Arab peasants made landless since 1920, he found only 664 families which might conceivably be so described, and of these most refused to go back to agriculture, even when the government offered them farms as gifts. The country of which Sir John Hope-Simpson asserted in 1930 that it could accommodate only 20,000 additional immigrants has since that date absorbed over 300,000. The industrial economy concerning which dire predictions were made has survived a worldwide depression, a second global war, and is today many times larger and stronger than two decades ago.

Nor was the Permanent Mandates Commission of the League of Nations at all impressed with either the Shaw or Hope-Simpson reports. As a high impartial court of appeals, it refused to accept as valid their interpretations of developments in Palestine. To the contrary, it affirmed in unmistakable terms that responsibility for the disturbances of 1929 lay with the Mandatory Government, its faintheartedness, timidity and, most of all, its reluctance to effect the purposes to which it was pledged.

Nevertheless, the British Government again gave ground. The Passfield White Paper of 1930 declared that "the Jewish National Home is not meant to be the principal feature of the Mandate." It construed the principle of economic absorptive capacity even more narrowly than heretofore. Last of all, it forbade all further sale of land to Jews. This, however, represented so flagrant a breach of faith that it roused a storm of indignant protest on all sides. The British Government, shaken by the tempest, repudiated the Passfield White Paper.

In 1936 Arab disturbances that grew to a near rebellion swept Palestine. Once more an investigatory commission, headed this time by Lord Peel, was sent to survey the scene; once again the British Government made an attempt to throw off its obligations. The old story was repeated but, this time, with unprecedented features. Unlike its predecessors, the Peel Commission substantially vindicated the Zionist case. It affirmed, in contradiction to the

Passfield White Paper, that "the primary purpose of the mandate, as expressed in its Preamble and its articles, is to promote the establishment of the Jewish National Home." It refuted the contention that Jewish immigration had dislocated and expropriated Arabs, pointing out that the contrary was the case. It denied that Palestine had come even within sight of its peak absorptive capacity. It paid tribute to the vision with which Jews had built in agriculture, industry, social services and culture. In sum, it validated every Zionist contention. Yet it concluded that, because of the stubbornness of Arab opposition, the Mandate under its original intentions was unworkable. As a substitute, it recommended the partition of Palestine between the Jews and Arabs with designated areas remaining under British control.

Thereupon a veritable tragicomedy of errors ensued. First, Great Britain announced that it accepted the Peel proposal and would implement it. Then reconsidering, it sent off another commission which reported that the cure was worse than the disease, that partition was less practicable than the Mandate itself. At which Great Britain, abandoning the Peel scheme, convoked a Round Table Conference among Jews, Arabs and Britons to work out an amicable settlement. Unfortunately it selected as representatives of the Arabs some of the most extreme of extremists, who when they came to London refused even to talk to Jews or so much as sit in the same room with them. A monument of futility and mismanagement, the Conference, unlamented, gave up the ghost in March 1939.

The date is of no slight moment. Great Britain, at the time in the toils of appeasement, was in effect very busy sacrificing its friends to its enemies. Debility and fear pervaded governmental circles. What was more, war was in the offing. The Arab world, it was felt, had to be placated. As for the Jews, there was no need to court them. Hitler had already made them inescapably the allies of Britain.

And so, on May 17, 1939, Britain issued the last, the dreariest in its succession of White Papers. In this document it declared that "it is not part of its policy that Palestine should became a Jewish state." It announced the intention of conferring political independence on the land at the end of ten years. To the Jews, who were to be reduced to the status of a permanent minority, it accorded only the vaguest guaranties against oppression by the Arab majority. It surrendered the principle of economic absorptive capacity, proclaiming frankly that thereafter political considerations would control immigration. It fixed the total of all future Jewish immigration at 75,000 persons, and its time span as not to exceed five years. Beyond that number and date, Jewish immigration would require Arab consent. Finally it authorized the High Commissioner of Palestine to prohibit the sale of land to Jews.

Thus it came to pass that a promise to facilitate mass Jewish settlement in Palestine became a course calculated to keep Jews out of the country. And crowning irony, today only Jews are debarred by religion and identity from entering Palestine, or purchasing land within its borders.

The breach of faith was too overt to pass unchallenged. Jews were naturally outraged. But so also were others. Speaking on the White Paper before Commons, Winston Churchill, then not a member of the government, expressed himself as follows:

"I feel bound to vote against the proposals of His Majesty's Government. As one intimately and responsibly concerned in the earlier stages of our Palestine policy, I could not stand by and see solemn engagements into which Britain has entered before the world, set aside for reasons of administrative convenience or—and it will be a vain hope—for the sake of a quiet life. I should feel personally embarrassed in the most acute manner if I lent myself, by silence or inaction, to what I must regard as an act of repudiation. . . . I was from the beginning a sincere advocate of the Balfour Declaration and I have made repeated public statements to that effect. . . .

"There is much in this White Paper which is alien to the spirit of the Balfour Declaration, but I will not trouble about that. I select the one point upon which there is plainly a breach and repudiation of the Balfour Declaration—the provision that Jewish immigration can be stopped in five years' time by the decision of an Arab majority. . . .

"What is that but the destruction of the Balfour Declaration? What is that but a breach of faith? What is it but a one-sided denunciation—what is called in the jargon of the present time, a unilateral denunciation of an engagement? . . .

"Is our condition so parlous and our state so poor that we must, in our weakness, make this sacrifice of our declared purpose?"

Similar sentiments were voiced during the parliamentary debate by Leopold Amery, one time Colonial Secretary and First Lord of the Admiralty; by Henry Snell, Labor member of the House of Lords; by the Archbishop of Canterbury, by Sir Archibald Sinclair, Colonel Josiah Wedgwood and

Herbert Morrison. In the end, only the most strenuous efforts by party whips put the measure through, and then by a slender majority.

If the White Paper was manhandled in Parliament, it was treated even more roughly by the Permanent Mandates Commission of the League of Nations. That body, composed mainly of experts in colonial and mandatory administration, impartial representatives of disinterested countries, heard out the case made by the British Colonial Secretary and rejected it *in toto*. In its official findings it held that "the policy set out in the White Paper is not in accordance with the interpretation which, in agreement with the Mandatory Power and the Council [of the League of Nations], the Commission had always placed upon the Palestine Mandate." *

Some members of the Commission were, as individuals, even more blunt and outspoken.

Thus Professor William Rappard, member for Switzerland, charged Britain with "turning the Mandate upside down." Dr. Daniel F. W. Van Rees, representative of Holland, accused the British of being "the conscious and deliberate fomentors of the trouble in Palestine." Miss Valentine Dannewig, delegate for Norway, characterized the argument advanced by the British as "insulting the intelligence of the members of the Permanent Mandates Commission."

With a resoluteness worthy of a better purpose, the British Government persevered in its course. In the teeth of worldwide protest, in the face of a holocaust of Jewish lives, it has kept the doors of Palestine all but closed. So it made itself an accomplice in Hitler's crimes, refusing refuge to those he hunted. So it took upon itself an immeasurable blood guilt for those who drowned in the harbor of Haifa when the S.S. *Patria* blew up, for those who perished when the S.S. *Struma* went down with all passengers, for the many other thousands who might have been alive today in Palestine had not an arbitrary, legally unjustifiable and morally indefensible document stood between them and redemption.

How shall one account for British policy, both the long-range whittling away of the Mandate and this most recent consequence of it?

Part of the explanation is to be found in circumstances attending the very birth of the Mandate. There can be no question as to the high intentions of

---

* From this conclusion, three members of the Mandates Commission dissented—those representing Great Britain, France and Portugal.

the statesmen who fathered it, nor that the British people endorsed it en-
thusiastically. But from the beginning, powerful elements in the Colonial
Office were unsympathetic to the project of a Jewish National Home in
Palestine. Attempting to oust the French from Syria, eager to bring the
Arab world under British tutelage, these groups, as early as 1917, were op-
posed to the Balfour Declaration and what followed in its wake. To the
misfortune of Jewish Palestine, control of its destiny came to rest with the
Colonial Office, its worst enemy.

Another contributory factor is to be detected in British personnel in Palestine which pretty generally was recruited from older colonies of the Empire. To such persons, whether constables or High Commissioners, Jews
with their education and democratic convictions proved startling people;
Arabs were more to their habits and taste. Besides, to them it must have
appeared that Jews were forever upsetting the apple cart. If only they were
not so insistent on getting into the country, the Arabs would have had no
complaint, all would have been peaceful, and the administrator's lot would
have been a happy one. Between such considerations, with an occasional anti-
Semite thrown in for good measure, Palestine has been run by persons rarely
friendly, often neutral, most frequently hostile to Jewish aspirations.

Meanwhile, at the heart of things in London the Colonial Office was becoming ever more fixed and single-minded in its purposes. It quite clearly
was determined to have, of course under its own auspices, a Pan-Arab Federation in the Near East. In such a scheme, a Jewish Commonwealth could
be only a nuisance.

These factors are responsible for the lax policing of Palestine, for the
vacillations in its administration, for the tenderness shown to Arab terrorism, for the constant propaganda on the unworkability of the Mandate, and
for the decision to nullify it. Having themselves created an impasse in Palestine, in part inadvertently, the anti-Zionists in the Colonial Office now put
forth this impasse as justification for the position they have always maintained.

Is the situation then impossible? Not if Mr. Winston Churchill and other
British statesmen are to be believed. Not if one is prepared to take the word
of the disinterested members of the Mandates Commission. Not indeed if
one is to trust evidences of Arab-Jewish understanding, attained generally
without the intervention of British authorities and sometimes despite it.

From the record one conclusion emerges so forcefully as not to be gainsaid: Great Britain cannot be relied upon for disinterested conduct in Palestine. Not that British officials mean as a rule to traduce their obligations. The point is that, as representatives of an empire, they have their own irons in the fire; their deportment cannot but be affected thereby.

Whatever the final outcome, Palestine is headed for a transition phase. It is to be hoped that for this period at least the land will be entrusted to an impartial authority, preferably an international trusteeship. So, the country, its population and the Jewish people may at last be accorded what they have so sorely missed to the present—a Palestinian administration unbiased by ulterior interests.

THE POLITICAL STRUCTURE OF PALESTINE

Any attempt to draw a precise blueprint for the future political structure of Palestine would be foolhardy. So much is fluid within that land, so much unpredictable as to the postwar world generally, that the most carefully conceived designs now formulated might turn out totally irrelevant. It may even be a consequence of the Second World War that small countries in Europe and Asia may be recast in new, unprecedented forms, perhaps be merged in regional federations.

But to refuse to commit oneself on the future of Palestine is not to desist from thinking about it. Indeed, such speculation is most necessary. For only through public discussion today can proper preparation be made for the morrow and its decisions. There is propriety even in arriving at a conclusion, provided it is held tentatively rather than as an *idée fixe*.

In any event, certain basic principles for the government of Palestine are already clear. It is apparent that the country will have to continue for a length of time as a Mandate, either under British or United Nations authority. The latter, for reasons already indicated, would be the preferable alternative. In the second place, it must be made certain that minorities in Palestine shall be secure in every respect, not only for the present but against any future contingency. To this end guaranties are in order from the United Nations and the international organizations they establish. No matter which people ultimately comes to be the more numerous, there must be no encroachment by one upon the integrity and freedom of the other.

Still again, Palestine must be fostered toward self-reliance. The measure of its democracy should be enlarged at once by reducing the power of feudal overlords and by extending local autonomy. Last of all, and in conformity with our entire argument, no political development can be sanctioned which will prevent land purchase, cultural and religious self-determination on the part of Jews.

Beyond all else, no arrangement can be approved which limits Jewish immigration on *political* scores. Such immigration may and should be regulated to conform to the absorptive capacity of Palestine and the urgency of the Jewish position in Europe. Always, however, the criteria should be what is economically practicable, what is required in terms of human need; never political preferences.

Within these postulates, the field of political forms is wide open. The widest variety of suggestions has already been voiced: that Palestine become a Seventh British Dominion; that it be governed into the indefinite future as a Mandate held either by Great Britain, by some other power less involved in Arab affairs, or by an international commission; that it be declared a Jewish state and endowed with the conventional prerogatives of a State, including sovereignty; that it be constituted as a binational state, either with or without geographical cantonization along the lines of Arab and Jewish concentration, but in any case with political authority divided between the two peoples; that it be partitioned into separate states; that it become a participant in a Near Eastern Federation.

The official Zionist position calls for the ultimate constituting of Palestine as a *Jewish Commonwealth*.

The phrase, coined and given its original currency by Churchill and Wilson, possesses the virtue of being at once positive and pliable. It is positive in that it denotes continued Jewish immigration into Palestine, the right of Jews to become a majority, and the expectation that the Jewish community of the land shall someday achieve some type of political self-determination. It asks, in other words, that to Palestinian Jewry be accorded the same kind and measure of autonomy as the postwar world may confer on other analogous peoples.

Yet *Jewish Commonwealth* is plastic in that it does not specify the exact contours of that autonomy. Note how much more elastic it is than Herzl's slogan, a *Jewish State*. The latter means very precise things by way of sovereignty and its appurtenances. The former is sufficiently comprehensive to embrace many of the possibilities we have just listed. There is then in present-day Zionism, as it deals with the political destiny of the community it has created, firmness on objective and essence, adaptability on method and form.

But why does the Zionist movement press its political purposes right now? Why does it not simply allow immigration to continue and, content with a steadily swelling Jewish population, permit events to take their course?

Such questions have been asked by many sympathizers, Jewish and non-Jewish, with the Zionist ideal. They are asked the more earnestly because the "Commonwealth formula" has proved so much a storm center.

An aura of reasonableness surrounds the suggestion that Zionists concentrate on immediate tasks and forget, for the time at least, all political ultimates. The reasonableness, however, is thoroughly specious. Without the "Commonwealth formula" there will be no further Jewish immigration into Palestine. I have already alluded to the White Paper of 1939 and the dire events it portends by way of closed doors and a finished Jewish Palestine. On what score is the White Paper assailed? As inhumane? That it is forsooth. But then, why should Palestine which has already done so much for homeless Jews be called on for more? Let other countries assume their share of humanitarian duty.

If there is protest concerning Palestine rather than other lands, it is because in this case the Jewish people has rights it does not possess elsewhere, the rights contained in the Balfour Declaration and Mandate. And these boil down to a commitment to a Jewish Commonwealth.

Here is the writ by virtue of which the abrogation of the White Paper may rightfully be demanded, the lease whereby uprooted Jews have a claim on Palestine. Let Jewry surrender it, and it shall have given up its *locus standi* in a crucial cause. At all times then the pledge of a Jewish Commonwealth must be presented in evidence before the bar of humanity's conscience, but especially now when a plot for its abrogation is afoot.

Large and formidable obstacles stand in the way of the fulfillment of the Zionist program. None is insuperable. Meanwhile the urgency is great. Against the barriers press millions of homeless human beings ridden hard by suffering and want; against the walls beat the inner needs of world Jewry, a culture seeking rebirth, a social idealism demanding incarnation.

The impediments are broad and strong. They are not so mighty as the forces pushing against them. As surely as the most resistant object will be dislodged in the end if the weight exerted upon it is great and persistent enough, so surely must the difficulties confronting Zionism yield to a bitter necessity and passionate dynamism. Zion shall yet be rebuilt, a haven for the outcast of the House of Israel, a lamp shining with the light of a rejuvenated Judaism upon the many Jewries and the world, an embodiment of high Jewish vision, a tranquil Jewish community, repeating and restating the timeless message of Judaism; in sum, a free commonwealth in a new and better world order.

16

The Larger Meaning

THAT ZIONISM HAS PERTINENCE for American Jews, the more perceptive
American Zionists are keenly aware. They know full well that their
program reflects self-interest as well as philanthropy. Deep within
them and their group existence are ills that can be remedied, and lacks that
can be supplied only by a Jewish National Home.

Or to put it otherwise, they sense that while Palestine is necessity for the
bodies of other Jews, it is an indispensability for their own souls. With it
they have a better than fair chance of maintaining their religion and culture,
and of bringing both to heightened self-realization. Without it the future is
much less encouraging. Indeed, it is not unlikely that the fate of Judaism
in the New World may be decided, for weal or for woe, by the outcome of
an experiment some six thousand miles removed.

This is not to say that a Jewish Homeland will, of and by itself, resolve
any of the many problems of American Jewry. Jewish theology has never
supported the doctrine of vicarious salvation. No one, rabbis and sages hold,
can be saved by anyone else; in the end each man must redeem his own
soul. Yet in the quest for redemption, one can be helped or hindered, sometimes decisively, by external influences.

So with American Jews in their relation to Palestine. Theirs is the difficult
but inescapable task of disposing creatively of problems, theological, ritual,
ethical, cultural and organizational. Yet in it they can be strengthened or
disheartened by forces from without. Jewish Palestine is already a constructive influence in their lives. It gives promise of playing an even larger role
in the future. It may well prove to be decisive between survival and extinction.

How then is a Jewish Homeland in Palestine likely to make American
Jews the stronger and better as human beings, richer and more resolute in

267

their Judaism? We can best answer this question by reviewing one at a time the crucial issues of American Jewish life, and by asking, in connection with each, how it is further along by virtue of Zionist achievement.

PALESTINE AND ANTI-SEMITISM IN AMERICA

It is not to be expected that Jewish Palestine will have any large or direct influence on the social status of Jews in the United States. The menace of domestic anti-Semitism can be averted only by measures taken at home, by unflagging efforts to preserve and enlarge democracy, to win greater economic competence for the underprivileged, to establish, through education and co-operative enterprises, a deeper mutual understanding among all elements of the American people. Americans are the protagonists, American soil the arena of the drama of Americanism. These are the actors and this the stage on which our way of life is to work itself into either a tragedy of disillusionment or a high climax of triumph. And American Jews, participants in this solemn pageant, are bound by the same conditions. Here and among their fellow citizens they will emerge as freemen or as enslaved, eventualities to which Palestine has no immediate relevance.

Yet, as America itself does not exist in a vacuum, so the position of American Jews is responsive to influences from abroad. The incidence of these may be tangential and oblique. But it will be an element in the situation.

Thus, the success of Jewish Palestine may have a salutary effect on the moral position of Jews. As the world becomes increasingly cognizant of the agricultural, industrial and cultural achievements of the Jewish Homeland, as it witnesses the rise of a new Jewish civilization built with Jewish labor and vision, Jewish prestige everywhere may be sent swinging upward.

A case in point is to be found in a prose poem by Peter Maurin in *The Catholic Worker* (September 1943), a publication sponsored by, and addressed to Christian laboring people:

> "It is said that the Jews
> flock to the cities
> and become
> middlemen,
> and that there are
> too many middlemen
> in America.

> "But in Palestine
> the Jews are building
> both cities and country.
> What the Jews are doing
> in Palestine
> they can do also
> in America." *

On the chance reaction of a lone Christian proletarian to Palestine no generalizations can be based. Yet this sentiment and others akin to it may well be straws in the wind.

Again, the fulfillment of the Zionist program may normalize Jews in the eyes of the world. As matters now stand, Jews are indeed a "peculiar" people. They are in so many respects *sui generis*. They are a religious communion, and yet something more; a culture group, but not that exclusively; a people, but lacking what all other peoples possess—a Homeland. This quality of the abnormal, the idiosyncratic, may have made no slight contribution to the extraordinary position of the Jews in general esteem. Men, as we observed early in this book, tend to be puzzled by and resentful of the unusual and the unprecedented.

Let a Jewish Commonwealth be set up in Palestine, and the aura of the eccentric will be dissipated. Palestine Jewry will certainly constitute a normal sociological and psychological phenomenon, one more of all the peoples rooted in their own soil. Jews in the Diaspora may also take on a new aspect. Like Swedish, Irish or Italian Americans, they may come to be regarded as persons who, though descendants of a people with a land of its own, have elected America for their country and home. Divested of qualities of the bizarre, almost the spectral, they may be accepted more conventionally.

These are possibilities, conjectures as to the impact of Zionism on the social status of American Jewry. Of one other consequence it is possible to speak with greater assurance.

Palestine can help American Jews by mitigating anti-Semitism in those lands that heretofore have been its chief breeding grounds. Prejudice against Jews has for centuries been endemic and fierce in Central Europe. Out of this focal point of infection the virus has seeped again and again to poison the world. Zionism, by draining off a substantial part of the Jews of the diseased areas, will ease long-sustained pressures. The inflammation will

---

* Quoted by permission of *The Catholic Worker*.

subside most immediately at its center, but subsequently throughout the whole organism of society. Baldly stated: let 2,000,000 Jews move from Europe to Palestine, and there will be improvement in the lot of Jews everywhere.

PALESTINE AND ECONOMIC REDISTRIBUTION

An unhappy trait of Jews, we have already had occasion to observe, is their inclination to concentrate in limited fields of economic endeavor. The largest deterrent to correction of that condition is the state of mind of the Jews themselves. Products of a history which has denied them access to a variety of livelihoods, they have made both a habit and a virtue of their disabilities.

But Palestine has broken the mesmerism of the centuries, in fact for its own Jews, in precedent for those of other lands. It has demonstrated that Jews can succeed as farmers, mechanics, sailors and fishermen. It therefore has opened up to the imagination of young Jews everywhere possibilities of which they might otherwise never have dreamed. Under its influence, American Jewish youth is no longer so certain that only the professions and commerce offer acceptable life careers.

The high esteem, almost the religious veneration, in which Jewish Palestine holds physical labor has begun to communicate itself to the Jewries of the world. In Central Europe before the Second World War it had already worked a radical transformation in Jewish psychology; young people increasingly were entering agriculture and the skilled trades. Even in America, omens of a transvaluation of economic values are to be discerned. It is still too early to appraise the present power and future development of this mood. But should American Jewry achieve occupational self-redistribution during the coming generations, no slight share of the motivation will have derived from Jewish Palestine.

PALESTINE AND JEWISH MORALE

Palestine, then, is not without meaning for the social status of American Jewry. Far more significant is its role in internal, spiritual affairs.

Consider, for example, the problem of Jewish morale, that distressing and dangerous tendency of the Jewish personality to slip into self-contempt and self-repudiation. In no respect does Zionism serve the American Jew so signally as in inoculating him against such psychic perils.

In the first place, Zionism represents one of the few Jewish activities that are inherently positive and creative in character. It is difficult for a non-Jew ignorant of the Jewish scene, it is next to impossible for a Jew close to it, to discern how much of what passes for Jewish enterprise is negative and sterile.

In their specifically Jewish self-expression, American Jews expend most of their energy on self-defense and philanthropy. Both of these are necessary; neither is inherently worth while. That is to say, no person of good will would wish for the continuance of anti-Semitism so that Jews may have occasion to go on combating it, or for the persistence of indigence, insanity, orphanhood and senility just in order that Jews may be compelled to maintain charitable institutions. In consequence, the American Jewish community is much like a beseiged hospital. Its denizens are very busy repelling attacks and taking care of the unfortunate, but have much too little to do with sanctuaries and libraries, with the experiences that redeem effort from emptiness and futility.

Men have long known the truth of which James and Lange made a proposition: that, while our actions reflect our feelings, our feelings mirror our behavior. Generally we are first happy and then smile, or first afraid and then run away, but not infrequently the reverse is the case. We run long enough and begin to feel afraid, or force ourselves to smile and end by feeling happy. In other words, what a man *does* about anything has a great deal to do with how he will *feel* about it.

Now, as we have just noted, most of what most American Jews do, *qua* Jews, is negative. A mood is engendered. They begin to feel the way they behave. To be forever repelling attacks by anti-Semites is a weariness of the flesh and vexation of the spirit. To spend one's Jewish existence in the atmosphere of a relief agency or a hospital means that Judaism comes to smell of ether and to suggest the miseries to which the flesh is heir. Neither development favors self-respect or a keen desire to live Jewishly.

Among the handful of Jewish causes that are not woebegone, Palestine is one, perhaps the most conspicuous. It seeks to incarnate an ancient dream, to establish a cultural center for world Jewry, to realize the peoplehood of Israel, all positive objectives, all purposes that would be pursued were there not a single Jew-baiter or baited Jew on earth. To this program, anti-

Semitism has given an extra edge, but as a matter of accident, not essence, as something thrown in for bad measure by the caprice of history.

And because Zionism has worth in its own right, because it is cheerful, it makes a major contribution to the spirit of American Jews. As the Zionist exerts himself for Jewish ends to which his heart can say "Amen," there are distilled in him self-acceptance and confidence in the value of Judaism and the Jewish identity, the prerequisites for psychic health. Not that Zionism is alone in exerting a benign influence on the Jewish personality; Jewish religion, ethic, ritual and culture when properly cultivated have the same effect. But in the catalogue of counteragents to Jewish self-contempt, this item stands very high and looms very large.

Jewish Palestine, moreover, exhibits impressive accomplishments. That circumstance too makes Zionism a stimulant of American Jewish morale. When Professor Lowdermilk asserts that in Palestine he has witnessed a job of soil reclamation unequaled anywhere else in the world; when newspapers report that American soldiers and sailors in the Near East long for furloughs in Tel Aviv so that they may for a time again enjoy the cleanliness and urbanity of a modern city; when it becomes known that 35,000 Palestinian Jews are serving as volunteers with the British Eighth Army and acquitting themselves magnificently; when the story is told of the technical services rendered the Allied armies by the engineers and workshops of Jewish Palestine; when public tribute is paid to the wartime contribution of the hospitals and physicians of the Jewish Homeland; when Arturo Toscanini conducts the Palestine Orchestra, or the Hebrew University announces some new discovery; and when the American Jew realizes that each of these is the achievement of Jews like himself, attained often in the teeth of hazards and obstacles, his evaluation of his people and hence of himself automatically rises. His self-respect, shaken by so many forces, is the firmer.

Louis Adamic in *From Many Lands* relates how American Finns, exhibiting all the insecurities of a minority group, were psychically reassured by the very existence of Sibelius; how American Greeks in a similar pass were made the more self-confident by the heroic resistance put up by other Greeks in their native land. So with the American Jew, Palestine cannot do the whole job for him, but it can and does help.

Towering above all else is the fact that Jewish Palestine has evoked a renaissance of Jewish culture, that the Judaism of every Jew throughout the world is the richer therefor, that his will to be a Jew is thereby enhanced.

Herein consists the greatest contribution of Zionism to American Jewish morale.

Nor can there be any question as to the impact of Zionism on the issue of survival versus assimilation. Root to branch, Zionism is survivalist. In premise and consequence its theme for the Jewish people is that of the Psalmist: "I shall not die, but live." This is the burden of its propaganda, Zionists being, along with religionists, the most passionate opponents of Jewish extinctionism. This is the message of the very existence of the Homeland; this its influence on the Diaspora. By its import and performance, Zionism stimulates Jews everywhere to persevere as Jews.

Indeed, in the eyes of some American Jews, herein consists the unforgivable sin of Zionism: that it is so clearly and vigorously a survivalist force. Those Jews who wish to play down their identities or desire not to live as Jews at all, who want Jewry to melt away so that in the universal dissolution they may make good their own escapes, for such, Zionism is an evil to be resisted to the last breath. There is, as we have seen, an objective, nonassimilationist Jewish anti-Zionism, but much of the current opposition, perhaps most of it, is masked assimilationism. So widely true is this that a generalization can be framed concerning the phenomenon; a law, as it were, of Jewish Reactions. This rule has it: not every Jew who is happy to be a Jew is necessarily a Zionist, but, without exception, every Jewish escapist is an anti-Zionist.

DEFINITIONS AND IDEOLOGIES

Touch whichsoever problem of Judaism you please and, without exception, each will be affected pronouncedly and for the good by Zionism.

Is it the riddle of definitions that bewilders you? Palestine plays a large part in solving it. For, so long as the matter remains in the realm of pure theory, it is possible to contend that modern Jews constitute no more than a religious communion. Zionist achievement has shifted the scene of the controversy. It is no longer being argued on Olympian heights but amid hard mundane realities. Among these, solid and intractable, stands a Jewish National Home in the making. Argue as one will, blink at it as one may, the Homeland is there, not a synagogue nor a synod, but a Homeland for the Jewish people. In its presence, can the least doubt survive of Israel's peoplehood?

This is, indeed, another reason for the frenzy into which the mere mention of Zionism throws some Jews. For there are those within American Jewry who become quite miserable at the very suggestion that the Jews constitute anything other or more than a sectarian denomination. They may regard their notion of Judaism as more genteel than its alternative, or as less subject to misunderstanding by non-Jews. In some instances, no doubt, they consider it to be more conducive to a separation from the Jewish group, for, transparently, membership in a church is more readily surrendered than birth-established fellowship in a people. Be the reason what it will—there are American Jews who insist that their Jewishness is a matter of theology and theology only. Many of them have written elaborate briefs in support of their thesis; others have at times worked themselves into a rage defending it. Then, when the smoke and dust subside, Palestine reappears, and all their ingenuities are revealed as foolishness.

So much from the simple existence of Jewish Palestine. But the Homeland and the Zionist movement have made further contributions to the ideological problem. Over the years, a torrent of books and pamphlets inspired by Zionist conceptions has swept the Jewries of the world. Much of this bibliography has been solid in reason and craftsmanlike in form. Occasionally, moreover, a volume has appeared like *Golah V'Nehar (Exile and Alienhood)*, by the Palestinian, Ezekiel Kaufman, which for erudition and argument constitutes an achievement of the first magnitude. The thinking of American Jews has inevitably been influenced by this literature. In this fashion, too, Zionism is arrayed with the angels against misconceptions and distortions of the true character of Judaism.

PALESTINE AND COMMUNITY ORGANIZATION

Zionism, furthermore, exerts a healthy influence on the reconstruction, now in process, of the American Jewish community. Conflict on this score, as we have already shown, is in no slight measure ideological in origin. In the degree in which Jewish Palestine clarifies the issue of definitions and philosophies, it serves also to determine the structure of the American Jewish community. What is more, the World Zionist Organization and its various constituents are thoroughly democratic in spirit and procedures, expressive of and responsive to a mass popular membership. Jewish Palestine, in its internal structure, is ordered in the same manner. More than theory, therefore, Zionism lends to the problem of the American Jewish community successful precedents. Hence it is no accident that Zionists are among the most fervent and persistent proponents of democratic organization, local and national, for American Jewry.

THE CRISIS IN RITUAL

Or consider the arduous task of reviving and remolding Jewish ritual. Here, too, Palestine has begun to work wonders. For centuries Jewish observance has been frozen in a fixed, unyielding pattern. To compound the injury, Jewry has of late lacked the skill and courage to fashion new designs, whether as substitutes or supplements of the old. But ceremonial is essential to a meaningful Jewish existence. Judaism in consequence is being rent asunder between its own inertia on one side, and on the other the need for venturesomeness.

This tension Palestine has helped to ease. Its Jewish community lives a primarily Jewish life. Wherefore, as Ahad HaAm foretold of it, spontaneously it transforms and invents folkways. In the Diaspora, Jewish ritual practice tends to be either a spastic clutching of the ancestral or a loose-handed and loose-hearted discarding of it. In Palestine it is a natural concomitant of group experience, alive and growing like the community it images forth.

So Palestinian Jews have succeeded in doing what their brethren have not dared attempt. They have recaptured things long lost, such as the all but forgotten yet exquisite celebration of the bringing in of the First Fruits. They have remade into conformity with the spirit of their own epoch ancient customs. To the Passover feast, always consecrated to the cause of liberty, they have given sharper point by relating it to contemporary economic and social realities. Into the Sabbath they worked an interval of group singing and public discussion, the *Oneg Shabbat*. They are calling into being, *ex nihilo,* still other designs, without precedent perhaps, but expressive of their twentieth-century souls.

Not all these developments are adaptable to Jewish living elsewhere, and, of those which are, not all are as yet being exploited. Nevertheless Jews throughout the world are already the richer ritualistically because of Palestine. Some of their wonted forms are being recast; new usages are for the first time in generations being contrived.

PALESTINE AND JEWISH CULTURE IN AMERICA

Large as may be Palestine's helpfulness on other problems, its largest single utility lies in the realm of culture. Here it brings double gifts. It creates and exports music, art, literature; with its precedents it stimulates creativity in the Diaspora.

Most of the stuff of the Hebraic renaissance in Palestine is, in some fashion, whether in whole or in part, transmissible elsewhere. The variety of goods which the Homeland has already shipped to American Judaism is too broad to be catalogued in full; but a partial bill of lading would include the following items:

A revived, reinvigorated, modernized Hebrew language for the enhancement of Jewish religious and cultural life.

A new pedagogy; fresh techniques for imparting to children and adults the content of the Jewish tradition. So potent has been the impact of Palestine in this respect that there is scarcely a Jewish school, no matter what its doctrinal shading, that does not display somewhere its imprint.

A renewed interest and a deepened insight into Scripture.

Literature of all sorts—including poetry, drama, essays, novels—some of which, at least, shows high excellence.

The end products of extensive research in Judaism, conducted by the Hebrew University in particular. In the brief span of one generation the Homeland has become a prime center of scientific scholarship concerning Jewish history, literature, theology, indeed concerning anything relevant to Jews.

Art and the things it fashions. The penetration of this element into American Jewry is far deeper than one would imagine. It is by no means confined to sculpture, painting, to "museum" art. The ritual objects which American Jews use for religious purposes have tended increasingly of late to be Palestinian in origin—not only for sentimental reasons but because Palestinian craftsmen have refashioned ceremonial appurtenances into greater loveliness. In almost every Jewish home in which the commandments are still kept, the touch of Palestine is to be discerned, in the Mezuzah affixed to the doorpost, in the Wine Cup or Candelabrum with which Sabbaths and Festivals are inaugurated.

Music, both formal and folk, but in any case Hebraic in inspiration. In this respect it is interesting to note that Palestinian folk song represents the first fresh element of this character to be introduced into Jewish life since the eighteenth century.

This catalogue is by no means complete. It does not include all the specifically Jewish output of the Homeland, let alone, as it were, non-sectarian commodities such as scientific discoveries. But the list is long enough to establish our thesis, that Palestine has yielded amazing quantities and varieties of grist for the mills of Diaspora Judaism. Indeed, it has been more productive than American Jewry has been receptive.

Once before I paused to deplore the slipshod methods of utilizing Palestine now in vogue. The point is sufficiently important to bear repetition. As a result of a catch-as-catch-can procedure, very much of potential consequence to American Jews is not only unavailable, but unknown to them. The situation is not without mordant irony. It was left to Christians to present in English the two impressive biographies of Jesus and Paul written by Joseph Klausner, Professor at the Hebrew University of Jerusalem. Chaim Nachman Bialik, the greatest Jewish poet since the days of the Golden Age of Spanish Jewry, still awaits translation in full. No community as dependent as is American Jewry on the steady importation of spiritual foods can afford to be so offhanded about its lines of supply. So I say again what cannot be said too often: one of the first and most urgent jobs before American Jews is the cutting of channels for the regular movement of Jewish cultural values from Palestine to the New World.

The Homeland, however, has not only conferred gifts on Diaspora Jewries, it has stimulated them to express themselves. The Hebrew poem that comes to America from the Near East is a piece to be read and translated; it is also a spur to the composition of a poem which, regardless of language, is Hebraic in spirit. The ritual object, made beautiful by Palestinian craftsmen, suggests similar possibilities to American Jewish artists. As great, then, as actual cultural subsidies have been inspiration and example.

In all this retailing of the significances of Palestine for world Jewry, something has been missed, something not to be supplied by extending our catalogue or by filling in its details. The final impetus of Jewish Palestine on American Jews still eludes us. It is to be caught, if it can be captured at all, only in a metaphor. Conceive, if you will, a person bowed beneath burdensome tribulations, but enjoying among them one heart-lifting triumph. This lone happiness will color brightly the whole texture of his being. Or an artist most of whose paintings have been failures, some mediocrities, but one a crowning joy. Is his existence not cheered and vindicated by that one coup? Or, last of all, an animal trapped in a vise which has reduced some of its limbs to bloody pulp; and others, though uninjured, to confinement. If one organ, and that vital such as head or heart, lies outside the clamps, is not the survival prospect of that creature thereby the fairer?

Such is Jewish Palestine in world Jewry. Everywhere Judaism and Jews at best limp along, at the worst are being crushed and mangled horribly. But in one spot, things are not only tolerable, they are radiant with attainment and promise. Here for Jewry is the victory to compensate for failures and half successes.

This is the final gift of Jewish Palestine to American Judaism—a gift larger than all contributions to social status or culture—the gift of *élan*, hopefulness, a conviction of worth, in sum, a confidence in the future of Israel and its way of life.

EPILOGUE

The Game and the Candle

A FINAL QUESTION REMAINS, less an inquiry than a misgiving. Is the game worth the candle? Judaism, we have seen, can be kept alive in the modern world. No impasse hems it in out of which some exit cannot be forced. There is no blighted area in its religion or culture which cannot, if faithfully tended, be made fruitful again. But all this quite obviously will require effort in impressive quantities. Jews can have their Judaism, but only at a cost in thought, toil, devotion and self-sacrifice. Is the price too high?

This question would be less pressing were the only problems *in* Judaism problems *of* Judaism; if, in other words, all that had to be put into this book was the materials of Section III and IV. For though issues concerning the Tradition and Homeland may be hard, bitter and difficult, they represent attempts at self-clarification and self-expression. As such they are to some extent, ends in themselves, pursuits to be followed regardless of success or failure. For what other goals does any man or group exist except that it may understand itself, fulfill its nature, and, as best it can, serve man and God?

But if a Devil's Advocate would find only lean pickings for his argument in the latter half of this volume, with its earlier part he would have a veritable carnival. What a case he could make of it against the whole Jewish enterprise! Is Judaism worth while? Consider what it entails—5,000,000 European Jews butchered, millions more spewed forth naked and homeless to the four corners of the earth, all their achievements, individual and communal, ruthlessly expunged, so that in the countries where they sojourned for generations scarcely a trace of their passage remains.

Compound this with the insecurity of the Jews of democratic lands, who, fortune's favorites among their people, are yet the butts of widely diffused prejudices, hagridden by anxieties over greater ills to come.

Then, to pile Ossa on Pelion, look backward into history, into the bimillennial homelessness of Jews, the weary centuries of political rightlessness, economic suppression, social ignomiy, personal humiliation, seasoned for variety with massacre, expropriation and expulsion.

Now, to cap the climax, after a brief respite the old tragedy is re-enacted once more, save that this time the Powers of Darkness are more fiendish and more skilled. Shall Israel then not cry out with one of its early prophets, "It is enough; now, O Lord, take away my life"?

This is the doubt with which we are now to wrestle. But before we come to grips with it, we must first respond to those who deny that the question is either legitimate or meaningful. Of such, two types exist. There is the Jew who insists that the discussion we propose is out of order. Is it required of other peoples, he asks, that they establish the worth-whileness of their existence? May not everything that breathes say of itself: "I am that I am"? Why then should such an *apologia pro sua vita* be demanded of this one people alone?

True enough. No individual or group needs to justify its being to anyone else. But men do put such questions to *themselves*. Especially when, as for Jews, experience is confusing and effortful, they will refuse to rest until some answer is forthcoming. Besides, though no man may require it of another, all men stand forever in judgment before their own inner values. Before these they must establish the merit of their existence. It is then less impressive than appears at first glance when Jews protest the propriety of our question. For the point is not that the non-Jewish world may deny Judaism the privilege of survival, but that Jews must and will pass judgment on the matter in their own hearts.

The second protestant against our problem is the logician who is likely, if he is no more than a logician, to dismiss it out of hand as artificial and unanswerable. In what scale, he will demand, shall Judaism be weighed, by what ruler shall the disabilities it entails be measured? Can the worth of a religious civilization or of human pain be defined in quantitative terms? But if not, how is one to be compared with the other? Besides, are not all value judgments ultimately subjective? Is not one man's food another's poison? Again, given the inconstancy of moods, objects that in one moment appear as priceless may at the very next, and to the very same person, seem trivial. No, the pure intellect will contend, there is no rhyme nor reason to the investigation here proposed. The human mind is incompetent to handle it. As with the analogous enigma of the worth-whileness of life, it is a futility to ponder it.

So far the logician. And he is argumentatively right on every point. But men are not thought-machines. *La coeur,* as Pascal put it, *a ses raisons.* Perhaps questions of this sort make no sense in strict reason, but men insist on asking them just the same. Is there a human being, no matter how coldly rational, who has not at some time or other hesitated whether he ought to go on living? Is not a Jew a human being? Hath he not eyes? And having them can he look on his own status, can he consider the condition of his less happy fellows (such is the Jewish position that every Jew, no matter what his circumstance, can spot another whose lot is harder than his), can he review the suffering of his fathers without asking himself, whether early or late, For what? To what end? To the service of what good?

It arises, this question of ours, and having arisen will haunt and possess Jews until they have exorcised it. No matter then what the logical difficulties and hazards, the theme of the worth-whileness of Jewish life must be entertained.

Now, it is much easier for men to be objective about the past than the present. Time like space lends perspective. We might do well then to launch our venture by transferring it from the contemporary to the historical. From our question, Is the game worth the candle? let us strike the first word, substituting the aorist verb *was* in its place. Our topic then becomes in effect this: Has the good achieved by Israel throughout the centuries outbalanced the agony it has endured and the discomfort it has occasioned?

So that we may get down to bedrock, I propose that we begin with a radical and arbitrary assumption. Let us suppose that the Jewish people had not created anything in all its history—not a single idea, concept, value, book, artifact or pattern of behavior. Would its life career have been worth-while? I say that even on the terms of this wild and preposterous hypothesis, the answer is in the affirmative.

For two millennia and more, Jews were the universal minority, the dissenters of every land and epoch. When the whole civilized world worshiped Caesar as god, this people alone denied him adoration. When Western society stood as one monolith toward the Christ and Church, Jews, protestants long before Luther, held themselves aloof. When Islam prevailed from the Pyrenees to India, they broke the even texture of its domination. In every country, in every generation to the threshold of the present, they were different. By their very existence, therefore, they made absolute uniformity impossible, marred the *Gleichschaltung* of every authoritarian society, prevented the full self-realization of every co-ordinated order, whether of Imperial Rome, the Mother Church, the Czars or Fascist dictators.

This then was the Jew in history—a precipitate that clouded the homogeneous solution toward which mechanics is forever driving society; a voice singing in private apart from the mass chorus; an irrepressible heckler to the official and respectable thesis of every age.

Wherefore he served mankind beyond all his conceptions of himself. He was, in the first place, an irritant, a goad and gadfly to the sluggish and complacent world, or, after Mommsen's characterization, a "ferment" in a convention-bound society. His role was that of the mutation or sport in biology—to prevent stagnation, in one case of the life stream, in the other of human affairs.

By the same token, he was, in the second place, both an example and guarantee of freedom. There was in the mere fact of his being, a lesson not to be misread. For he not only differed from the norm; he got away with it. Like Ajax, he defied the lightning, except that he came off better than the mythical Greek. No bolt struck him down, no wave engulfed him. Pressures, to be sure, were exerted against him. Somehow he resisted them successfully. Those who stood by and watched could not but be strengthened in their own impulses to rebellion. To them he was a visible and tangible proof that freedom of thought not only could be undertaken but carried off.

Little wonder then that heresies sprang up wherever he walked. By his refusal to deify the Roman Caesar, he all unawares broke a path for the Christian Church. He exerted a strong if unpremeditated influence on the rise of Albigensianism and Protestantism. And it was not entirely a misrepresentation when the charge of Judaizing was hurled by the Catholic Church against Luther, and subsequently by the Protestant sects against one another. Not that the Jew wished to mar the tranquillity of his neighbors. To the contrary, he wanted, in the main, only to be let alone. But even when he hoped to be inert in social affairs, his character made him a catalyst.

With equal inadvertence, the Jew fulfilled still a third function. To each generation he supplied a touchstone on which it might try its tolerance. The periods in which mankind has prided itself on hospitality to divergent opinions have been distressingly few and short-lived. But whenever the claim has been uttered, its sincerity could easily be tested merely by examining the position of minority groups. And since Jews constituted a universal minority, their condition served, so to speak, as an international metric system against which humanitarian professions might be measured.

Last of all, the Jews present perhaps the most vivid demonstration in all history, certainly the most prolonged, of the indomitability of the human spirit. All through the Middle Ages, Christendom resorted now to violence, now to seduction, in the attempt to pry or wheedle loose their hold on their peculiar way of life. The barbarities wherewith they were persecuted are well known; the allurements by which they were tempted less so. Suffice it to say that before potential apostates rewards were dangled, exemptions from discriminatory legislation, life pensions, patents of nobility. Jews refused the bribes as steadfastly as they withstood force. It can be argued that their obduracy was stupid. One point, however, is established by it: drawing on their own souls, they were stronger than the world. They could be killed, but not made to surrender their truth. For those who came after them, even for the societies that persecuted them, they pointed a moral, the truth established at ten thousand pyres; the human spirit can be stronger than any coercion that can be exerted against it.

Q.E.D. therefore may be written after the proposition that, by their very existence, Jews discharged a variety of useful social functions.

The Jews, however, were never poor in spirit. On the contrary, early in their collective career they amassed a rich spiritual endowment from which they made frequent and varied gifts to the world at large. At their hands humanity received its classic religious faith, its conception of reality as the manifestation of an infinite Spirit fulfilling a cosmic design. By their prophets mankind first was instructed in the infinite worth of the individual, the unity and brotherhood of men, the pre-eminence of the co-operative over the competitive way, the superiority of persuasion over coercion, and the supremacy over all else of justice and compassion. From Judaism and Jews stem the great religious systems of the Western world, doctrines and moral values, sacred writings, patterns for worship and piety, designs for ritual, schemes of ecclesiastical organization. One of the great monuments of literature, perhaps the greatest, was quarried, carved and polished by Jewish hands after dreams dreamed in Jewish hearts. Through themselves, the members of this people strained much of the spiritual yield of all the nations of the Occident, sifting out the chaff, processing the edifying elements, sending them forth into general circulation. During one period of half a thousand years Jewry was the only bridge between Christendom and Islam, two titanic but self-contained and mutually hostile civilizations.

Nor did Israel's historic role exhaust itself in the Middle Ages. As Heine put it, there is not a battlefield of thought on which Jews have not fought and bled. In all the campaigns of the modern spirit they have participated, in considerable numbers among the rank and file, but occasionally also as generals and chiefs of staff. From their loins sprang some of the great heroes of the human mind and social scene: Spinoza and Bergson, Marx, Lassalle, Brandeis, Einstein and Heine, let alone fractional Jews like Montaigne, Felix Mendelssohn and Proust. This impressive record takes on heightened impressiveness when one considers that the total number of Jews in the age of Spinoza was less than 1,000,000, in the time of Heine only 4,500,000, and in the days just before Hitler, under 16,000,000. Or to put it in percentages, in 1648 the Jews were two-tenths of one percent of the world's population; in 1848, six-tenths; and in 1936, eight-tenths.* Is not this amazing creativity for a people which never achieved the dimensions of even one percent of the human mass?

But might not equal results have been obtained from the Jews as individuals had the group entity been dissolved? This question does not bear on the distant reaches of Jewish history, the Biblical, Talmudic and medieval eras when Jews led a distinctive existence, the output of which carried unmistakably the hallmarks of a unique craftsmanship. It is to the great Jews of modern times that our inquiry pertains especially. Is it so certain that their Jewishness had anything to do with their greatness? Might not Spinoza have still been Spinoza had his Marrano ancestors earnestly forsworn Judaism? Would Heine have been other than he turned out had his remote ancestors adopted Christianity? Or Marx? Or Lassalle? Or Trotsky? Or Einstein?

This "iffy" question cannot be answered in either direction with assurance. But one consideration looms out of the welter of all possible argument: Jews have been intellectually and socially productive beyond their numbers. Race, let it be said categorically, does not explain the disproportion. The differential traits Jews exhibit are the consequences not of heredity but environment, and that in turn is the resultant of two forces—the adverse social

---

* *A Social and Religious History of the Jews,* by Salo Baron. Vol. II, pp. 165-166.

position of Jews and their traditional culture. The former operates to make Jews extend themselves. It spurs them on to attainments after which otherwise they might not so much as have aspired. No less potent is the second influence, the momentum of the Jewish tradition with all its entropy toward things of the mind and of the good life. What is more, the intellectual and ethical impetus of Judaism may continue even after formal Jewish allegiances have been surrendered. Social values are hardy plants; often they survive the breakup of the containers which nurtured and housed them initially. So, many a de-Judaized Jew exhibits in himself, all unawares, the undimmed imprint of Jewish ideals, whether of the mind, the heart or human relations.

Between these two differential elements, a differential social situation and a differential cultural heritage, the mystery of disproportionate Jewish creativity is lifted. It may be ghastly unpleasant at times, this business of being a Jew, but it is pretty constantly stimulating. Witness the record that has just passed before us.

And now returning to our original problem, what price shall we put upon that record from its beginning to its end, from the first words of Genesis to the last lines of the latest scientific paper by Einstein? And at the same time, at what value shall we estimate the suffering and anguish of all Jewish generations? Clearly we are now dealing with matters qualitative, not quantitative, with objects that can neither be weighed nor measured, at least not in the same system of weights and measures, with, in a word, incommensurables. The logician whom we silenced for the nonce begins to stir restlessly. Let me then say straightaway that the inapplicability of arithmetic to our problem does not mean that we are altogether resourceless. On the contrary, a very simple standard of comparative judgment is at our disposal.

Succinctly put, it is this: the career of Jewry will be adjudged as one cherishes ideas and ideals, or alternatively contemns them. The Jews, to be sure, have suffered mightily, but they have achieved mightily as well. Now if insights, outlooks, aspirations and dreams are held of slight account, then Jews throughout the centuries have been making a bad bargain. But if the adventures of the intellect and the questings of the heart are taken for the chiefest glories of human existence, then, in the words of an ancient epigram, losses are swallowed up in gains. Or to state the point more concretely: if it was worth while that Jeremiah sit in stocks at the Temple gates, so that out of humiliation he might come to comprehend what it is over which a man might properly vaunt himself; if it was good that Socrates play the gadfly to the sluggish steed of the Athenian city-state though in the end it meant the bitterness on his tongue of hemlock and of death; if the Sermon on the Mount outbalances Golgotha; if the child compensates for birth pangs, and all of life's thinking, hoping and striving for its pain—then Judaism outweighs its cost. Suffused with tears as its history may have been, what came out of it was such stuff as vindicates human existence.

Even Jewish suffering and sacrifice cannot be written off as dead loss. They too fulfilled creative functions. Pain, men have long known, can fructify as well as blast. Sometimes growth is not otherwise possible. That is why Isaiah, calling Israel to be God's servant, summons him also to endurance. That perhaps is the Psalmist's meaning in his saying concerning those who must first sow in tears before they can reap in joy.

Consider the warp and woof of the fabric of Judaism, the threads that run through the whole, binding its parts into a unity, unfolding its dominant design. Of these strands one is reverence for the intellect and its integrity, a second a high esteem of the human personality, a third ideals of justice and mercy, a fourth the dream of the Kingdom of God on earth. All weave together to make up humaneness, the basic texture and clearest pattern of the Jewish tradition. Not, to be sure, that only Judaism exhibits these values or is impelled by them. In the spirit there is neither patent nor monopoly. Yet no communion, culture or people was spun earlier of these fibers, or is more persistently held together by them.

Whence came these motifs? That they do not stem from an idiosyncratic bloodstream or a freakish but favorable heredity we have already argued. They can derive then only from experience. And in the experience of Jews suffering was a prime element. Had the ancient Israelites been conquerors, prophets might never have arisen in their midst or, having risen, might not have been heeded by a nation drunk and fat with spoils. But this was a people despoiled and acquainted with sorrow. Unable to subdue the world, it learned to tame its own spirit. Knowing defeat, humiliation, rapine and exile, it thought more upon, and responded more fervently to preachments of justice and loving-kindness, to visions of an end of days when swords would be beaten into plowshares and men should have ceased to hurt or harm.

As with the fathers, so with the sons. Had medieval Jews enjoyed free entrance into the council chambers, armies and castles of feudal society, they might well have spent themselves there. The world shut them out, wherefore they had no recourse except to stake out intellectual kingdoms within the four ells of their minds. Victims of injustice, they developed a heightened passion for righteousness; butts of innumerable cruelties, exquisite and crude, they became the more avid for mercy. The process in essence was this: as they made virtues of necessities, necessity confirmed them in virtues. A codicil must therefore be appended to our judgment of the worth-whileness of Judaism in the past, namely, that the worth-whileness was not despite but because of suffering.

Souffrir passe, said a mystic, *avoir suffert ne passe jamais.* The truth of this epigram is often for evil. In the case of Judaism it was for blessing and not for curse.

All this is water over the dam. The place of Judaism in history may be an interesting theme for exploration; it may, since the past is forever invading the present, be even an item of some contemporary relevance. The crux of our problem, however, is the present. Is the game worth the candle *now,* in our own day and generation, for Jews alive in this very hour? Is there in the Jewish tradition and identity, both battered of late, anything so vital and significant as to offset the disadvantages and hazards of a Jewish existence?

The matter is no sooner broached than it becomes clear that Judaism has taken on rather than lost in pertinence of late. For what is the crux of the global struggle now in process? Democracy versus totalitarianism, the conventional response would have it. But are these and their connotations anything other than universals of which Jewry and Judaism are particulars? Or to rephrase the answer more specifically: what is involved in the present conflict is just the ideals taught by traditional Judaism, just the values always incarnated by Jewish group existence.

At stake are the following:

Whether society shall be variegated as among individuals and groups, or made homogeneous through force.

Whether the right and possibility of dissent shall continue.

Whether minorities of political opinion, religious conviction, economic outlook, culture or race, shall be permitted, as long as they do not infringe on others, to live out their destinies in conformity with their own characters.

Whether the human spirit can be coerced.

But these are just the themes on which Jewry has always meant very much, to which even today its existence is relevant. Far from being played out, the old role is still central to the drama. There may have been occasions in recent decades when the Jew might have made a graceful exit from the stage. The present, when an assault is in progress on everything he represents, is scarcely such a moment.

The world today requires as urgently as in the past those values which the Jew incarnated unconsciously and in the mere fact of his being. It needs even more fiercely his convictions and ideals. The present global struggle is ideological in the deepest and most radical sense. That is to say, not only social forces and national states are in conflict but, moving behind and through them, philosophies of life and systems of value. The human situation ought not to be oversimplified. It does not divide neatly into light and darkness or good and evil. But for all its obscurity, it cannot be misconstrued as to its ultimate significance.

A conspiracy is afoot against the Judaeo-Christian world outlook, and in consequence against the Judaeo-Christian ethic, the concept of the infinite worth of every human being, the thesis of the brotherly unity of mankind, the doctrine of the objective validity of moral law, the norms of justice and mercy as regulative of individual and social relations. The attack has been long in the making; the forces behind it are many and diverse, deriving from virtually every area of human interest. The defense is equally composite. All sorts and conditions of men have for all sorts of reasons rallied to its banners. Quite fortunately, this is everybody's fight. Anyone—white or black, Gentile or Jew, believer or denier—is welcome to enlist in it.

One does not have to be anybody in particular or accept any special dogma to be in on this, the climactic episode of modern history. Yet he will fight better who knows what he is fighting for. He will fight better still who fights out of both necessity and conviction, whose conscience and circumstance unite to permit him no alternative.

This is exactly the condition of the Jews. Whether they like it or not, they are in this business up to the neck. It is for their hearts that the enemy has sharpened his long knife; it is their souls he has vowed to obliterate. Between him and them there can be no armistice. They have no choice except battle to the death.

Whips and scorpions drive Jews to the right side. So also does inner aspiration. A Jew, if the least spark of Judaism glows in him, is incapable of even considering a truce with the adversary. Everything he has been taught since infancy, everything he believes, everything he implies in the liturgy of the Synagogue and professes in domestic rites, everything that his ancestors were, that he is and that he hopes of his children, is totally incompatible with totalitarianism in any form, no matter what the proper name under which brutality, inequality, tyranny and obscurantism may dignify themselves. No, quite obviously, one does not have to be a Jew to stand for democracy and progress; but it helps, the Jew being the one person who is precluded both by conviction and iron necessity from a negotiated peace.

All of which is to say that if ever there was a wrong time for him to quit, it is the present; that the role of his fathers has devolved on him; that their destiny is his also. Or, to put it more accurately, their role and destiny can be his if he is willing to assume them.

His is a choice between alternatives. He can, on the one hand, protest that he would prefer not to be an element of differentiation, a precedent of dissent, a touchstone of tolerance, a proof of the spirit's intractability and a bearer of a uniquely humane tradition. He can, when the usefulness of his existence is indicated, respond that he is disinclined toward heroic destinies, that he desires neither their sting nor honey. In which case he will most likely have the destiny anyway, but without heroism; the sting but no honey.

Or he can consciously make a purpose of his lot. With premeditation and deliberateness, he can so handle his tradition that it shall afford him an occasion for asserting the right and value of difference; so dispose of his cultural heritage that it shall yield abundantly to his pleasure and to the sustenance of mankind; so exploit the ethical principles of Judaism as to make them the rule of his life and a regenerating power in the world at large. Because he is a Jew, he can stand forth more boldly for freedom, justice, truth and mercy among men. In a word, he can by his deportment guarantee that the game shall be worth the candle.

To this end considerable courage will be required of him—more indeed than he has been wont to display in latter years. It has become almost a fixed practice for Jews to play down and suppress the elements of difference in their creed, ritual, culture and outlook, to gloss over especially the moral commitments to which their Jewishness binds them. A bolder temper than this will be needed if Jews are to measure up to their opportunities. Regardless of applause or disapproval, they must go about the business dictated by their consciences, doing their duty as they see it, as best they can, prepared to take the consequences.

That there will be consequences, and generally of an adverse character, they may be sure. A firm allegiance to Jewish moral values will often be tantamount to enlistment in mankind's most unpopular causes. The Jew, if he is meaningfully a Jew, must be a thorough and militant democrat, one who believes in and is ready to fight for universal freedom and equality. His will be a deep restlessness in the presence of economic affairs as they are, and a passion to remake them into what they ought to be. Without any diminution of patriotism, his outlook will be global. He will "pray for the welfare of his land." Yet above all peoples he will set mankind; above the enactments of the state, the moral law; above all human authority, that of God.

When then charges beat upon him as they no doubt will, when fascists call him author and chief protagonist of democracy, when reactionaries denounce him for disturbing the peace of entrenched wrong, when chauvinists attack him as an internationalist, and when brutalitarians accuse him of fostering a "slave morality of compassion," there must be no cowering or seeking for a crevice to hide in until the storm shall have passed. Beyond all else, let there be none of the whining expostulation in which many a Jew has indulged of late, the tearful complaint that false witness has been brought against him, that in actuality he is no more fervently democratic or liberal or internationalist or compassionate than the next. Let his concern rather be whether he has been true to his purpose, whether it is indeed because of his devotion to the good that evil men are roused against him.

Is this a fantastic prospectus for the Jewish group? Does it ask too much from people who are no more than normal human beings; who, if their enemies are to be believed, are considerably less; who, to boot, are ensnared in a close-knit and clinging web of circumstance; who, in any case, are as diversely individualistic as any other? Can a sword of the spirit be forged out of separate molecules, or a monolith of conviction from unfusible grains?

Never, of course, with complete success. In this sense our proposal is visionary. And yet time and again a community, even a whole nation, has attained a consensus as to objectives which if not total was sufficiently general to be preponderant. In every domain of human interest, masses of men have at some time or other reached shared commitments. Such a *Stimmung* —for evil in this case—was achieved by the bulk of the German nation in our own day. If one people can consecrate itself to Satan, Baal, Moloch or Wotan, another should be capable of dedicating itself to the God who commands justice and righteousness.

Our prospectus takes on greater realism when it is recalled that there is nothing at all novel or untried about it. The dream here outlined is as old as the Jewish spirit.

"Be thou a blessing." "In thee shall all the families of the earth be blessed," says God to Abraham.

"And ye shall be unto Me a kingdom of priests, and a holy nation"—so Moses charges Israel at the foot of Sinai.

And during the Babylonian captivity when as now the question of game and candle cried peremptorily for determination, the prophet intoned in the name of his God:

> "But thou, Israel, My servant,
> Jacob whom I have chosen,
> The seed of Abraham My friend;
> Thou whom I have taken hold of from the ends of the earth, . . .
> Behold My servant, whom I uphold;
> Mine elect, in whom My soul delighteth;
> I have put My spirit upon him,
> He shall make the right to go forth to the nations.
> He shall not cry, nor lift up,
> Nor cause his voice to be heard in the street.
> A bruised reed shall he not break,
> And the dimly burning wick shall he not quench;
> He shall make the right to go forth according to the truth. . . .
> I the Lord have called thee in righteousness,
> And have taken hold of thy hand,
> And kept thee, and set thee for a covenant of the people,
> For a light of the nations;
> To open the blind eyes,
> To bring out the prisoners from the dungeon,
> And them that sit in darkness out of the prison-house."

The dream, moreover, is not merely ancient; it has always possessed extraordinary potency. On all generations it has worked its spell. In all centuries it has inspired Jews to tend the light more faithfully, to minister more devotedly to man. It has been nothing less than the seed corn and germ plasm of whatever humaneness in thought and deed the Jewish people may have manifested throughout its history.

Nor need the vision die in our time. Within Jewry today there glows even now a spark, as it were a smoldering ember, of the great flame kindled on high altars in distant days. The Jewish religion, ethic and culture still open up opportunities to Jews for more exalted self-realization, for broader service to mankind. What is required is the imagination, courage and will to keep again an old rendezvous with destiny.

To this then does the issue of the game and the candle resolve itself. Jewish life has in the past been eminently worth its price. Its value in the present and future depends on the use which modern Jews make of it. If they are so minded, they can neglect its content and potentialities and so render it undeserving of the least exertion. Or they can, if they will it, make the game so meaningful to themselves and all the world as to compensate, and more, for all the candles that have been consumed and shall yet be kindled in its playing.

When John Milton pleaded in his *Areopagitica* for freedom of the press, he invited the imagination of his readers to a consideration of what libertarianism might mean for England. The sober men of his time knew the perils of untrammeled public discussion. They could discern only dimly the glories for which these dangers might wisely be endured. Wherefore to hammer home his case, Milton described, as though it were present before him, the future to which his course would lead. In a passage which has gone ringing down the years, he envisions the people which freedom might fashion. "Methinks I see in my mind a noble and puissant nation rousing herself like a strong man after sleep, and shaking her invincible locks . . ."

The device was not original with Milton. Scripture had long anticipated it, as had the Apocrypha. The prophets spurring a reluctant people to moral heights, resorted often to visions of the heights attained. And the Apocalyptist, heartening a people beset by hardships and threatened by greater woes to come, sought to give them courage by speaking of "the end of days" when, after history had come to its denouement, all evil would be uprooted.

I, the writer of these lines, make no claim to the majesty in utterance and thought of Milton, the inspiration of the prophet or the vivid imagination of the Apocalyptist. But insofar as, amid present difficulties, I seek to project a course aimed at distant and problematical ends, my situation is akin to theirs. The reader, I hope, will indulge me if, following their example, I too portray as though it were actualized the future as I hope it, as I am confident it can be made:

I see in Palestine a Jewish Commonwealth where the homeless Jews of the world have found rest, where the Jewish spirit has been reborn, whence flow to the dispersion inspiration and the stuffs on which it feeds.

I see the Jewries of the world, each at ease and firmly rooted in the land of its residence, each unswervingly devoted to the polity and culture of that land and at the same time the bearer and transmitter of a living Hebraism, significant to itself, its environment and the world.

Most specifically, I see an American Jewry, emancipated along with all other Americans from the restraints of prejudice, secure against violence, free to fulfill itself without hindrance.

An American Jewry alight with a religious faith hallowed by antiquity and responsive to the mystery of all things, yet sanctioned by the best in modern thought and clean with reasonableness.

An American Jewry standing four square by Judaism's great moral ideals, sharpening them into the keenest contemporaneousness, applying them boldly, imaginatively—so that the name Jew is a synonym for the practice and advocacy of justice, compassion, freedom and peace.

An American Jewry literate in both its heritages, the American and Hebraic, creative in both, cross-blending and fertilizing the two until all devotion to one shall connote blessing for the other as well.

An American Jewry that in its observances is both reverential of the tradition and awake to current needs, so that the precious freightage of the past is enriched by new gifts in each generation.

An American Jewry whose household is set in order.

An American Jewry which, having labored that Zion be rebuilt, now draws waters in joy from the fountainhead of the Jewish spirit.

I see in sum a Jewry which in its inner life has made of Judaism what it is intended to be, what it is now in some measure, and what it can become in infinitely greater degree—that is to say, a source of blessing.

And I see all this set in a new, brave and free world which Jews, together with all men of good will, have helped to set free, laboring as individuals but also as Jews, as members of a fellowship consecrated from the womb to the ideal of a new, brave and free world.

Should that day arrive, should a better ordering of human affairs be won, and from its elevation a backward glance be cast over mankind's long, weary pilgrimage, what answer then will be appropriate to our question as to the game and candle?

Shall not Jewish dreams and ideals, hands and hearts, blood and anguish have contributed to this end so long desired and prayed for? Will it then be a little thing—will it not rather be accounted a very great thing—to have played a part, not the largest perhaps but not the meanest either, in the building of the Kingdom of God on earth?

BIBLIOGRAPHY AND INDEX

SELECTED BIBLIOGRAPHY

Historical Background

Baron, Salo. *Social and Religious History of the Jews*. Columbia University Press, 1937.

Elbogen, Ismar. *A Century of Jewish Life*. Jewish Publication Society, 1944.

Janowsky, Oscar, Ed. "Historical Background," *The American Jew—A Composite Portrait*. Harper and Brothers, 1942.

Kastein, Joseph. *History and Destiny of the Jews*. Viking Press, Inc., 1933.

Lebeson, Anita L. *Jewish Pioneers in America*. Brentano's, 1931.

Levinger, Lee J. *A History of Jews in the United States*. Union of American Hebrew Congregations, 1930.

Marx and Margolis. *History of the Jewish People*. Jewish Publication Society, 1927.

Roth, Cecil. *Bird's Eye View of Jewish History*. Union of American Hebrew Congregations, 1935.

———. *Jewish Contribution to Civilization*. Harper and Brothers, 1940.

Sachar, Abram L. *A History of the Jews*. Alfred A. Knopf, Inc., 1930.

———. *Sufferance Is The Badge*. Alfred A. Knopf, Inc., 1939.

Steinberg, Milton. *The Making of the Modern Jew*. The Bobbs-Merrill Co., 1933.

Waxman, Meyer. *A History of Jewish Literature*. Bloch Publishing Co., 1938.

PROBLEMS OF STATUS

Rehabilitation of European Jewry

American Jewish Conference. *Survey of Facts and Opinions on Problems of Post War Jewry in Europe and Palestine*. 1943.

American Jewish Committee, Research Institute on Peace & Postwar Problems. Publications.

Bernstein, Philip S. *Jews of Europe*. Nation Associates.

Gottschalk & Duker. *Jews in the Post War World*. The Dryden Press, Inc., 1945.

Institute of Jewish Affairs of The American & World Jewish Congress. Publications.

Interallied Information Committee, No. 6. *Conditions in Occupied Territories*.

Janowsky, Oscar. *Jews and Minority Rights*. Columbia University Press, 1933.

Jewish Labor Committee, Research Institute. Publications.

Anti-Semitism

Fineberg, Solomon. *Overcoming Anti-Semitism*. Harper and Brothers, 1943.

Graeber & Britt. *Jews in a Gentile World*. The Macmillan Co., 1942.

Levinger, Lee J. *Anti-Semitism in the United States.* The Macmillan Co., 1936.

Pinson, K. S., Ed. *Essays on Anti-Semitism.* Conference on Jewish Relations, 1942.

Samuel, Maurice. *The Great Hatred.* Alfred A. Knopf, Inc., 1940.

Strong, Donald. *Organized Anti-Semitism in America.* American Council on Public Affairs, 1943.

Valentin, Hugo. *Anti-Semitism.* Viking Press, Inc., 1936.

Weinstein, Jacob J. "Anti-Semitism," *The American Jew—A Composite Portrait.* Harper and Brothers, 1942.

Economic Redistribution

Engelman, Uriah Z. *The Rise of the Jew in the Western World.* Behrman's Jewish Book House, 1944.

Koenig, Samuel. Chapter VIII, *Jews in a Gentile World.* Graeber & Britt, The Macmillan Co., 1942.

Lestchinsky, Jacob. Chapter XV, *Jews in a Gentile World.* Graeber & Britt, The Macmillan Co., 1942.

Reich, Nathan. "Economic Trends," *The American Jew—A Composite Portrait.* Harper and Brothers, 1942.

Ruppin, Arthur. *The Jews In The Modern World,* The Macmillan Co., 1940.

PROBLEMS OF SELF-ACCEPTANCE

Lessing, Theodor. *Jüdischer Selbst-Hass,* Berlin. 1930.

Lewisohn, Ludwig. *Upstream,* Boni & Liveright, 1922.

Liptzin, Solomon. *Germany's Step Children,* Jewish Publication Society, 1944.

PROBLEMS OF THE TRADITION

The Ideological Problem

Agus, Jacob. *Modern Philosophies of Judaism.* Behrman's Jewish Book House, 1941.

Dinin, Samuel. *Judaism in a Changing Civilization.* Columbia University, Teachers College, 1933.

Eisenstein, Ira. *Creative Judaism.* Behrman's Jewish Book House, 1936.

Goldman, Solomon. *Crisis and Decision.* Harper and Brothers, 1939.

Gordis, Robert. *Jew Faces the New World.* Behrman's Jewish Book House, 1941.

Hirsch, S. R. *The Nineteen Letters of Ben Uziel.* Funk & Wagnalls Co., 1899.

Jung, Leo. The Jewish Library Series: I. The Macmillan Co., 1928. II. Bloch Publishing Co., 1930. III. Jewish Library Publishing Co., 1934.

————. *Judaism in a Changing World.* Oxford University Press, 1939.

Kaplan, Mordecai M. *Judaism As A Civilization.* The Macmillan Co., 1934.

————. *Judaism in Transition.* Covici, Freide, Inc., 1936.

Kohn, Eugene. *Future of Judaism in America.* Liberal Press, 1934.

Levinthal, Israel H. *Judaism, An Analysis and an Interpretation*. Funk & Wagnalls Co., 1935.

Levy, Beryl. *Reform Judaism In America*. Bloch Publishing Co., 1933.

Steinberg, Milton. "Current Philosophies of Jewish Life," *The American Jew— A Composite Portrait*. Harper and Brothers, 1942.

Problems of Religion

Goldman, Solomon. *The Jew and the Universe*. Harper and Brothers, 1937.

Goldstein, M. *Thus Religion Grows*. Longmans, Green & Co., 1936.

Kaplan, Mordecai M. *Meaning of God in Modern Jewish Religion*. Behrman's Jewish Book House, 1937.

Pool, David de Sola. "Judaism and the Synagogue," *The American Jew—A Composite Portrait*. Harper and Brothers, 1942.

Reconstructionist Foundation. *Toward A Guide for Jewish Ritual Usage*. Reconstructionist Foundation, 1942.

Schauss, Hayyim. *Jewish Festivals*. Union of American Hebrew Congregations, 1938.

Problems of Culture

Halkin, Abraham S. "Hebrew in Jewish Culture," *The American Jew—A Composite Portrait*. Harper and Brothers, 1942.

Spiegel, Shalom. *Hebrew Reborn*. The Macmillan Co., 1930.

Syrkin, Marie. "The Cultural Scene: Literary Expression," *The American Jew— A Composite Portrait*. Harper and Brothers, 1942.

Communal Organization

Baron, Salo. *The Jewish Community*. Jewish Publication Society, 1942.

Duker, Abraham G. "Structure of the Jewish Community," *The American Jew— A Composite Portrait*. Harper and Brothers, 1942.

Karpf, Maurice J. *Jewish Community Organization in the United States*. Bloch Publishing Co., 1938.

PROBLEMS OF THE HOMELAND

Ahad HaAm. *Selected Essays*. Jewish Publication Society, 1912.

Bardin, Shlomo. *Pioneer Youth in Palestine*. Bloch Publishing Co., 1932.

Bein, Alex. *Theodore Herzl*. Jewish Publication Society, 1940.

Goldman, Solomon. *Undefeated*. Zionist Organization of America, 1940.

Gordon, A. D. *Selected Essays*. League for Labor, Palestine, 1938.

Lewisohn, Ludwig. *Israel*. Boni & Liveright, 1925.

———, Ed. *Rebirth*. Harper and Brothers, 1935.

Lowdermilk, Walter. *Palestine, Land of Promise*. Harper and Brothers, 1944.

Samuel, Maurice. *Harvest in the Desert*. Jewish Publication Society, 1944.

INDEX

Abraham, 146, 291

Adamic, Dr. Louis, 116, 272

Ahad HaAm, 226, 228-229, 232, 233, 243, 275

Ahad HaAmist Motif, 224, 228-229

Aide-Memoire on Post-war Emigration Needs of European Jewry and Resettlement Possibilities in Palestine, 247

Ajax, 282

Akiba, 140

Albigensianism, 282

Algiers, 26, 27, 41

Alice in Wonderland, Carroll, 200

American Council for Judaism, 235, 236, 237

American Council of Voluntary Agencies for Foreign Service, 34

Americanism, 30, 139, 141, 159, 169, 180, 268

American Jew—A Composite Portrait, The, 104

American Jewish Committee, 72, 208, 209, 210, 211, 212n., 215

American Jewish Conference, 210, 211, 215, 216

American Jewish Congress, 72, 208, 209, 210

American Jewish Joint Distribution Committee, 22, 25, 34, 206

American Jewry, proposed program of relief, 25; organization of, 65, 72, 200-203, 206, 208, 210, 211, 214-216; economic status, 92, 105-106, 112; social stratification, 121; population, 135; as a "nation," 149ff.; and "Mr. Z," 171; creativity, 192-193, 195; represented at United Nations Conference, 212n.; how Jewish National Home affects, 267, 269-278; hope for future, 293. *See also* American Jews

American Jews, Judaism, 129, 183, 186; allegiance, 130, 131, 181; as a "nation," 149-150, 152; social identity, 182; creativity, 193, 195; big problems, 206; occupational redistribution, 207; anti-Zionism, 238; meaning of Zionism to, 267-278. *See also* American Jewry

American Judaism, 204, 207, 276

Amery, Leopold, 260

Amin AlHusaini, Haj, 257

Amsterdam, 37

Andes, 41

Anti-Defamation League of the B'nai B'rith, 72, 207, 208, 209, 215

Anti-Semitism, outlawry of, 32; in Central Europe, 28, 29, 31, 36; in South America, 41; explanation, 44-45; product of indoctrination, 45-48; of economics, 48-49; psychological factors, 50-52; Maurice Samuel on, 53-54; manipulation, 55; paradoxes, 56-57; recent history, 58-61; third paradox, 61-64; defense against, 65-66; self-suppression, 66-69; self-correction, 66, 69-70; self-Gentilization, 66, 70-72; education, 72; normal association, 73-74; and law, 75-76; in Russia, 78-81; and democracy, 81; constructive defense, 82-84; in the United States, 85-88; danger to non-Jews, 88-90; attitude of Jews, 91; four principles, 92-99; and economic distribution of Jews, 108-112; most urgent problem, 115; effect on Jews, 117-119, 124, 125, 127, 128, 129, 138-139; and "Mr. X," 168; not related to knowledge, 198; lack of organized defense, 207, 208, 209, 212, 214; and Herzl, 224, 225; and the Jewish Homeland, 238, 268, 269, 271, 272; Axis propaganda, 249; mentioned, 22, 26, 37, 39, 161, 193, 200, 203

Anti-Zionism, 123, 169, 233, 235, 236, 237, 238, 273

Apocrypha, 292

Apostles' Creed, 147

Arabs, opposition to Jews in Palestine, 26, 226, 245, 247-255; rise in population, 240; advanced by Jews, 242; and Mandate, 256; riots, 257, 258; proposed partition of Palestine, 259; British Colonial Office, 262

Archbishop of Canterbury, 260

Areopagitica, Milton, 292

Assyrians, 253

Augsburg Confession, 147

Australia, 38, 39, 40, 221

Austro-Hungarian Empire, 30, 157

Auto Emancipation, Pinsker, 226

Babylonian captivity, 291

Bahai, 30

301